THE SHAF

Other books by Margaret Laing

ROBERT KENNEDY
EDWARD HEATH: PRIME MINISTER
JOSEPHINE AND NAPOLEON
WOMAN ON WOMAN (ed.)

PTC

THE SHAH

MARGARET LAING

SIDGWICK & JACKSON
LONDON

First published in Great Britain in 1977
by Sidgwick and Jackson Limited

Copyright © 1977 by Margaret Laing
Reprinted February 1977

ISBN 0 283 98336 1

Printed in Great Britain by
The Anchor Press Ltd
for Sidgwick and Jackson Limited
1 Tavistock Chambers, Bloomsbury Way
London WC1A 2SG

Author's Note

AMONG those I should like to thank for their help and kindness to me when I was researching and writing this book are Their Imperial Majesties the Shah and Shahbanou of Iran, Mr Assadollah Alam, Mr Amir Khosrow Afshar, Mr Ali Shapurian, Miss Shusha Guppy, Mr John Ardagh, Sir Martin Gilliat, Mr and Mrs Robert Graham, Mr Robert Mauthner, Sir Anthony Parsons, Le Rosey School, *The Times* and *The Sunday Times* libraries, and many others in Tehran, Paris, England and Scotland who have generously given assistance and advice.

November 1976   MARGARET LAING

'Gentlemen, you cannot expect me to be shot at every week to keep you on your toes!'

The Shah to his Cabinet, 1949

'Finally I became so exasperated that I decided we would have to dispense with democracy and operate by decree.'

The Shah in 1969, after his White Revolution

'The Security Service in this country [England] is not established by Statute, nor is it recognized by Common Law. Even the Official Secrets Acts do not acknowledge its existence.'

Lord Denning, after the Profumo Affair in 1963

'The Shah, indeed, may be regarded at this moment as perhaps the best existing specimen of a modern despot.'

Lord Curzon on Nasr ed-Din Shah, 1848–1896

'To foreign culture open both the windows of thy home. Let foreign culture seep in through one window and leave from the other. Do not let foreign culture remain in thy house.'

Persian proverb

Contents

List of Illustrations

THE SHAH

Part I

1 The Shah soon after his accession at the age of twenty-one

anything could, Iran's curious position at the crossroads of East
and West. And as I sat I thought about the man I was about to
meet, and what I knew of him.

He is one of the most, if not the most, powerful political
figures in the world: the gathering of the reins of power increasingly into his own hands for nearly twenty-five years means that
he is no longer impeded by an executive, like the premier of
the USSR or the President of the United States. He also has the
power of SAVAK behind him. Yet he is a man who hates the
sight of pain and grief so much that he almost invariably sacks
people at secondhand, by asking one of his other ministers to
advise the unwanted man to resign.

He is also possibly one of the richest men in the world. He
takes great care to point out frequently in public that he is not
the richest man in Iran. Unlike Reza Shah, who had no foreign
investments, he has invested in two houses in Europe, one in St
Moritz, Switzerland, and one in Avignon, France.

His investment portfolio used to be spread over a vast variety
of fields, from petrol tankers to real estate, and land was once
one of his greatest possessions in his own country. But he is
probably speaking accurately in terms of property and money
inherited in Persia itself when he says: 'I have given my personal
fortune away, or at least 90 per cent of it.'[1] The personal assets
he gave to the Pahlavi Foundation in 1961 were valued at 135
million dollars, and included oil tankers, hotels, a toll bridge,
banks, factories and even orphanages.

From the Iranian Civil List he has an unspecified income. He
also has a budget of up to 15 million dollars to run a court of
1,500 people. His whole life-style, now that he is older, is far
from opulent or self-indulgent, though it is much more comfortable and luxurious than that of his father. The importance
to him of money is shown not merely by his political acts and
dealings in oil, but by the extreme care he takes of his own
personal means. This care is shown by the fact that though he
loves playing poker and was a remarkable player (as he still is at
the poker of politics) he gave the game up after losing an estimated 10 million rials – about £700,000 – and now sticks to
bridge. A rich man who gives up his favourite card game to save

money shows that the gambler in him is controlled by the caution in him; and that he has both self-control and a puritanical streak.

This seems to be borne out by his life-style and habits in general. He has given most of his palaces to the state. The highly decorative Golestan Palace, named after the rose gardens in which it is set, houses most heads of state when they visit the Shah: at other times it is a museum, open to the public. The former winter palace has been turned into a museum of the Pahlavi dynasty; their present palace, the Niavaran, set in north-east Tehran, like France's Elysée, belongs to the state. Built in the early 1960s, it was based on plans prepared by the Empress Farah herself.

The Ekhtessassi villa, whose forlorn appearance first shocked the young Soraya, was entirely revamped as Iran grew richer; but the Shah has now given it to the Prime Minister, Mr Hoveyda, as his personal residence. The former palace of the Dowager Empress, Tadj-ol-Molouk, has become the home of the famous collection of Qajar paintings based on the Amery Collection and brought back to Iran at the Empress Farah's wish: she herself contributed the most expensive painting, and suggested the elegant design of the interior.

The Saadabad Palace in which I now sat waiting is the only palace still belonging personally to the Shah; in smaller palaces in the grounds most other members of his family have their principal residences although most of them also own luxurious palaces and mansions elsewhere.

One remembers the fact that nepotism is a family *duty* in Iran. 'Nepotism, where possible under modern conditions, is a strict family obligation.'[2] The Shah is said to be exceedingly generous to his relations, although some have incurred his displeasure by being greedy (as in the case of his nephew Shahram, forbidden to continue in his business deals), or by flouting his wishes, like his daughter Shahnaz (by his first marriage to Princess Fawzia). Shahnaz, after divorcing her first husband, eloped with a musician deemed 'a hippy' by the family and lived in virtual exile in Switzerland for two years. She returned as a prodigal to forgiveness but it later transpired that her husband had also been smuggled into the country. On hearing this the Shah was furious. But in the end he relented and he is now said to be on good terms with them both.

This reconciliation is typical both of Iranian family feeling and, it seems, of the Shah's own nature, which tends to be generous with others. Like the ancient Emperor Darius, many believe he could claim 'I was a friend to my friends'. But he is demanding of all his subjects, particularly of those in responsibility and of his ministers, and he is also very demanding of himself. His timetable is strict, his régime simple.

He gets up at about 7.30 each morning, does some exercises and, while he bathes and shaves, usually meditates a little. He breakfasts alone on fruit juice, one slice of toast, and a cup of black coffee. Breakfast takes three minutes; but he sits at the table for forty-five minutes reading the Iranian newspapers and those from the US, Britain and France in the original, and translations of German and Italian newspapers. By 9 a.m. (often earlier) he is at his office desk. His first appointment every morning is with Mr Alam, the Minister of the Imperial Court, who may stay for about an hour and a half reviewing the day ahead and making plans for any state visitors or foreign travel. The next two or three hours consist of giving audiences to people usually connected with the apparatus of state. He sees the Prime Minister at least once a week, chiefs of the military establishment usually twice a week.

Rank is no guarantee of anything. 'Often I order minor officials to tell their superiors what I want done,' the Shah declares.[3] Sometimes this is merely from convenience, because the minor is present when the Shah has the idea, but often it is to undercut pompous and lazy officials, in an abbreviated form of the way in which Nasr ed-Din Shah used Mirza Taqi Khan, a cook's son, first to undercut the aristocracy by having him as Prime Minister, and then reversed the procedure by allowing courtiers to undermine the Prime Minister with him, and so cause his death. Thus there is a considerable, and very reasonable, sense of insecurity at any level below the Shah's own.

For this reason, and also to encourage the telling of truth (no easy thing, from the historical point of view, to nurture in the

Middle East), the Shah often sees people, particularly informers, alone; but even so one doubts whether he is really very much more in touch with his people than his father, of whom he himself says: 'One of the few mistakes my father made was to rely upon a narrowing circle of advisers.'[4] One senses that most people would deem it wise in Iran to tell the Shah what he hopes to hear; one of the very few reliable links between him and his subjects must be the Empress, who still moves round the country more freely.

His first meeting with the Empress each day is usually at lunchtime (as it was with the former Empress Soraya). Luncheon is usually at 1.30 and, while not as spartan and monotonous as Reza Shah's boiled-rice-and-chicken-twice-daily menu, is usually a light meal: sometimes Persian, sometimes European, sometimes a mixture of the two. The Crown Prince Reza now often joins his parents for lunch; and occasionally a minister or friend joins them as well. But the conversation tends to revolve round work, and the Shah does not drink at lunchtime – nor, for that matter, does he drink very much at other times, though he is not a strict teetotaller as the head of a Muslim society might be expected to be.

More reading of the newspapers follows lunch, and sometimes, if there is time, a nap of some forty-five minutes. By this time most other Persians have usually finished their day's work (Tehran offices tend to work from 7 a.m. to 2 p.m.; some of them, and the Ministries, open again for a couple of hours in the late afternoon). But from 3.30 p.m. or so until at least 8 p.m., often later, the Shah is hard at work meeting visitors or his own officials, travelling the country to examine progress on his various plans, or, quite often, abroad, usually on state visits.

Very often when the weather is more temperate, in spring and autumn, there are official dinners and receptions for the floods of foreign dignitaries who inundate Iran in search of fuel, funds, friendship. The Shah is extremely alert at all these functions; it is not for him to be found, as a recent British Prime Minister was, asleep between two of his guests.

When there are no public or state occasions in the evening, the Shah and Empress – who usually dined alone in the early days of their marriage[5] – keep to a fairly strict rota of family visits:

on Wednesdays and Saturdays they dine at the home of Tadj-ol-Molouk, the Dowager Empress, on Thursdays and Sundays at Princess Ashraf's palace, and on Mondays at Princess Fatemah's palace. However, since all these palaces are set in gardens within the same outer walls as their own palace, it is not far to go. The Empress's mother, Mrs Diba, is frequently included in all these invitations, as she is also of course on Tuesdays and Fridays when the couple dine at home. Family life is still the basic structure of Persian society: at one dinner party I went to in Tehran, I met nearly all the forty grown-up children, ranging in age from early twenties to late seventies, of one man (now dead) and his three former wives.

Entertainment takes place principally at home for the Shah, as it does for his subjects, and apart from the advent of television and cinema has not changed greatly; though the atmosphere at court is very much more relaxed than it was in the time of Reza Shah. Film shows, card games, chess and some of the more childish games which the Shah still enjoys – he is quite likely to make a courtier jump fully dressed into a swimming pool, in a fashion reminiscent of Nasr ed-Din's sense of fun – take up the rest of the evening. 'I also take a rather child-like delight in electric trains, and every so often I operate a set I bought in Switzerland,' he admits. He bought them when he was about fifty.[6]

Though the Empress no longer has time to practise playing the piano she still loves to listen to music: the Shah's own tastes are for Strauss waltzes and the Romantic classics – Chopin, Tchaikovsky, Rimsky-Korsakov – as well as Beethoven.

Reading, other than endless official documents and letters, is a memory rather than a relaxation nowadays: the days of being able to bask leisurely in a book for pleasure are so long past. Fortunately he speaks the truth when he says, 'My life, destiny and happiness are those of my country. I really love my work.'[7]

The pace slackens only on Fridays, the Persian day of rest, when the Shah tries to spend at least part of the day enjoying some sport. This may be volley-ball, at which the Empress excelled, when they are joined by some friends. It may be riding, probably with Mr Alam, particularly if he is feeling at all 'down'. Intense physical activity, if possible involving some measure of

risk, seems to be the antidote to any difficulties. Not only
the most difficult horse, but the fastest car or plane or speed-
boat, the steepest ski run, are deliberately sought after: it seems
as if the challenge of work and of political strain can only be
alleviated by an equal risk in sport. He even occasionally dives
out of a hovering helicopter for fun, and the Empress admits a
problem faced by many wives the world over when she says:
'Danger seems to excite him.' But the risk is measured: the Shah
is not reckless with his life, and even gave up his 1976 skiing
holiday in Switzerland, leaving the Empress and children to go
without him, when it was rumoured that the hired killer Carlos
had taken out a contract to kidnap him.

The innate sense of superiority that seems a heritage from the
past is seen in the instinctive behaviour of many Persians. In the
Shah it is cultivated as another useful weapon with which to
berate the West. Even the Israelis have been called 'almost
masochistic' by him, as have the English; his sneers at Western
countries have usually been based on allegations of permissiveness and laziness, but he has also demanded why they have
developed no alternative sources of energy to oil.

The clue to his fundamental attitude to the West is seen in his
education of his son. Some forty-five years ago Reza Shah made
an unselfish decision to educate Mohammed Reza in Europe:
the Shah would have done the same for Prince Reza had he
believed this necessary. Instead, the Crown Prince attends a
special school convoked at the palace where his classmates come
from other Iranian families. 'We can have the same training
here, if not better,' he says, adding, 'but I think that for his job
he must certainly concentrate on two things. One, he should
absolutely have a military education and then also in economics,
because his position will require him knowing not only a little,
but quite a lot.'[8]

In allowing his son to live in his own small house in the palace
grounds the Shah has also shown that he thinks it necessary for
the Crown Prince to develop as soon as possible a sense of personal self-reliance and self-preservation. In effect, the Shah's
encouragement of the separate household says that he must
learn to live alone, to depend primarily on himself, and to accept
that a degree of isolation is part of his heritage, though he can

always count on the immediate and full support of his family. The aim of giving an impression of self-sufficiency, emotional detachment, and even severity is cultivated quite deliberately. The image is protective: but now it reflects part of the truth.

Just as the Empress is at pains to demonstrate the kindness and idealism she finds in her husband and which she knows will appeal to other women, male members of his entourage hope to give the impression that he is a being above all others, impervious to mere mortal emotions, a Shah not to be challenged by men.

When I asked Mr Alam if he thought the Shah modelled himself at all on the closest nationalistic figure I could think of, General de Gaulle, the Minister of Court replied: 'He is very, very independent. You know, a man who is missioned by the gods, how can he choose a model for himself?'[9] The Shah himself is careful not to overstep the mark when he claims divine protection: 'That does not mean that I consider myself an indispensable instrument of God or anything of that sort. I want to make it perfectly clear that I do not.'[10] This balance is carefully held and it is important both from the political and religious points of view. The Shi'a sect of the Muslim faith which predominates in Iran has a strong attachment to the family of the prophet: Shi'ites believe that the twelfth heir did not die but disappeared to make an awaited return. Interim rulers are accepted 'on suffrance'.[11] Therefore the Shah claims divine protection, but not divinity.

His position is also strengthened in religious eyes by his marriage: the Empress Farah is descended on her mother's side from a branch of the Safavid dynasty which included Shah Abbas the Great in the sixteenth century,[12] and retains a right of accession to the throne.

The Shah tries to maintain a dignified distance even from those of whom he is most fond (outside his immediate family); and this effort is if anything exaggerated by those who feel it and understand the motive behind it.

Mr Alam has known him for more than a quarter of a century but says, 'He talks to me about what it is necessary that I should know: no more. Even if I try I am not successful to find out about other things.

'He is very calm, you never see him worried. If something is not necessary to be mentioned to me, he never mentions it. He is not a man to sit and talk to you just for the sake of talking. I have never seen him emotional in my life – never – only once, and that was during our celebrations [at Persepolis] when he was addressing the tomb of Cyrus. He was so emotional that he had to stop for a second.

'The old history of Persia has taught us how to face difficulties and problems – we are less emotional than the Arabs.'

Intelligence and sensitivity were two other principal Persian characteristics, said Mr Alam, describing an abstract Persian. 'Are there any faults at all in this Noble Persian Character?' I asked. With the instant reflex that is itself one of the hallmarks of the national character, Mr Alam laughed, genuinely, and said, 'Every quality has some default, shortcomings – too much flexibility – result of so many invasions.'[13]

With such contradictions and complexities in even the ordinary Persian personality (as time passed I agreed with Mr Alam more and more that he had covered the principal qualities) what would the Shah himself be like? I sat and checked that my tape recorder was working properly.

My ignorance of Iran had so far been a help as much as a hindrance. On my first day in Tehran one of the Shah's advisers had suggested that among those I should interview about him was 'a very old schoolfriend of the Shah's, Hossein Fardoust'. I thanked him happily and put the name down on my list: afterwards I found out that he was referring to General Fardoust, the head of the Imperial Inspectorate that is above SAVAK. No doubt my innocent reaction was an advantage: a well briefed spy (for example) would have known the given name, as well as the fairly common surname, at once. Nevertheless, once warned, I decided to ask to see General Fardoust, and then was told: 'He is a military man. Like your high-ranking generals, he prefers to remain in the background. I am sure you understand.' Indeed I did.

It was perhaps because of this that I had not been searched as I entered the palace: nobody had even bothered on this occasion to look inside my handbag or bulging briefcase, or to inspect my ominous-looking tape recorder. As I looked once more round the waiting room (to me the scarlet walls were not the right background for all the beautiful objects it held) I realized that I felt excited, and extremely interested in the man I was about to meet, yet at the same time strangely detached. A French diplomat had described the Shah as 'the most formal head of state I have ever met'. I wondered: would I be able to get through to him, to establish some rapport? A challenge lay ahead for both of us.

After only about ten minutes a footman entered and motioned with a white-gloved hand for me to follow him. The Shah is noticeably more punctual and prompt than many less busy statesmen (though in the course of the day there had been about a dozen phone calls to change the time for the interview, sometimes by two hours, sometimes by only half an hour). As I came out into the vast main hall, silence rang around me.

With a sweep of his arm the footman indicated the course I should steer across the immense, watery-green marble floor, looking like translucent onyx, which was only partly covered by a series of some of the most immense and magnificent Persian carpets I have seen or ever will see. Feeling like a new skater thrust suddenly on to the immense set of *Swan Lake*, I started in that direction, hoping that my very high heels would not slither away from beneath me on that reflectingly polished floor.

Suddenly a small white figure appeared and observed me: a Skye terrier, who stood still and silently watched my progress across the vast space. At last I reached the far side and another footman waved another white-gloved hand to indicate a door. Inside was a small study, again with French antiques, but this time largely in subtle olive green: and there stood the Shah, waiting to shake hands.

Serious-looking, but with a smile: he looked intently into my eyes. Neat. Dignified. Dressed in a dark suit and striped tie. Prematurely grey, as he has said? – less so than I expected. He is careful of his appearance, has had one of the bullet scars removed from his upper lip by plastic surgery. Nothing to be afraid of.

I went in.

Visions of all the heads of state and ministers, including that very week Denis Healey, whom I had seen photographed in the *Kayhan* and the *Tehran Journal*, bowing as they shook hands with him flashed before my inward eye, and as he took my hand I gave a small and very un-Persian curtsey. In any case, I thought, he probably believes, like the Persian proverb that (apart from the Empress) 'women have more hair than brains'.

He motioned me to a sofa as he took a wing armchair and we sat down. As I took out the tape recorder and explained how I hoped to research my book I noticed almost simultaneously, and with surprise, that my voice was shaking slightly and that the Shah was, almost imperceptibly, trembling. Snap.

I discovered afterwards that it is quite unusual for him to be interviewed without an aide present, and no doubt memories of his extraordinary interview two years before by Signora Fallaci had left a scar: but it is typical of him to meet difficulties head-on, to overcome his own fears. Thus he is inwardly a courageous man, as well as being, it seemed to me, the one man in Iran who was not usually afraid of anyone else. Interviews and assassination attempts come into a special category; but in general the Shah fears no man, whereas every other Iranian has some apprehensions about the superconstellation that shines above him.

But he does not gamble unnecessarily with his own life. Since the Marble Palace plot against his life in 1966, when he found himself unarmed in his office while bullets flew through the door, he has always kept a revolver within reach. There was no sign of it, of course; nor of *his* tape recorder (several perhaps), which I was sure must also be recording our conversation: an impression partly borne out (though it may also have been the result of Tehran gossip) when someone asked me several days later, 'I hear you asked His Majesty about torture . . .?'

He no longer seemed at all nervous, but to picture him as a hard or unimaginative man is plainly wrong. I remembered how hard he had fought for his marriage to the former Empress Soraya, a loyal and loving as well as a brave act in a Muslim society where barrenness is regarded as a curse; how it was rumoured that he had to take sleeping pills after his divorce and after the coup and countercoup in 1953, when he regained possession of his own throne; how he had told Annigoni that he had given up smoking, not only because it was bad for his health, but because it made him nervous.

He is no man of iron like his father but, as two of his wives have said, sensitive, rather shy, gentle, often kind; as well as tough, ruthlessly decisive, increasingly capable of rages such as palace officials dreaded in the reign of Reza Shah, but usually, and in public always, very controlled: a product not only of his past but of his will also – a self-made Shah.

Chapter 2

Corruption and Resentment

THE vaunted 'immortality' of the Persian Empire seemed to be succumbing to a fatal weakness as this century opened. Most of the top posts in Government and the provinces were filled by the Qajar princes, relatives of the Shah; and most of *them* were illiterate.[1] Government offices were *ad hoc* affairs, set up in ante-rooms and coffee houses. Those who could write, the secretaries, were often described contemptuously as 'the sweet-eaters'.

The collapse of the world silver market had left Persia in a crucially vulnerable position,[2] desperately trying to keep afloat on 'concessions' sold to the British and Russians. Much of this money found its way into the privy purse, which was indistinctly divided from the Treasury. And the British and Russians used their power to dissuade Persia from building a major railway, the key to industrialization and modernization.

Yet Persia's wealth was literally weeping from the ground. Arthur Arnold, who journeyed through the immense country in the 1870s, wrote: 'There seems to be no doubt about the quality or quantity of the petroleum. All the streams around us were covered and coloured with the outflow. But no one attempts to make use of it . . . doubtless Englishmen would be found ready to sink wells . . . if it were safe to deal with the Persian government.'[3]

It was to be nearly another hundred years – to 1973 – before Iran gained complete control of her greatest asset, her chief source of revenue, and her most powerful political tool.

One hundred years ago, Nasr ed-Din Shah was on the throne. He was in many respects an innovator: he experimented with many forms of government, but corruption, malpractice, extortion and simple inefficiency were everywhere. It was, in Curzon's words, 'an administration in which every actor is, in different aspects, both the briber and the bribed'. And he asked, 'In every rank below the sovereign, the initiative is utterly wanting to start a rebellion against the tyranny of immemorial custom; and if a strong man like the present king can only tentatively undertake it, where is he who shall preach the crusade?'[4]

The boy who was to become this crusader, and the father of the present Shah, was born in or about 1878. He came from an illiterate but military family in Elasht, a village near the Caspian Sea. At this time Persia was a feudal and nomadic society, less advanced in many respects than medieval Europe. Yet more than 2,000 years ago it had been renowned as an empire, and (with Egypt, China, and its neighbour Mesopotamia, now Iraq) as one of the world's oldest civilizations. The coming of Islam with the Arab invasion in AD 651 had meant the repression of women, and the further fragmenting of an already heterogeneous society.

The Persians had first settled and formed the small kingdom of Parsumah at the foot of the Bakhtiari mountains. From these compact origins they had developed, under Achaemenes and his descendants, first unity and purpose, and then size, organization and communications. When Cyrus the Great conquered the Medes he united his nation with a people who knew how to write, who possessed wheeled vehicles, who kept cattle and horses. But division accompanied unity. As Shahs have done till the present day, Darius encouraged some of the differences between his dominions.

The vast empire could be crossed by couriers in fifteen days, using horses from closely spaced posts; then it shrank, until with the loss to Russia in 1813 of Georgia and eight other provinces it was reduced almost to its present size, which is still the size of all the Common Market countries put together, and twice the size of Texas. The country's basic living unit was, for safety's sake, not the isolated farmstead but the village, and 'there grew up also a consciousness of a common heritage . . . there was not only variety but also unity. The Persian peasant, as well as the townsman, was the heir to this civilization. He often lived, and sometimes still lives, in primitive conditions, but in general he is not primitive.'[5]

In 1890 Nasr ed-Din Shah granted a tobacco monopoly to a British company. This meant that not only a vast national resource but a national *habit* which permeated all classes and regions was being given into foreign hands: and an immediate call for resistance came from the clergy, who were at once supported by the merchants. Two years later the outcry had reached such proportions that the concession had to be cancelled. Britain naturally wanted power in Persia for its own sake, but she felt even more in need of it to protect her interests in India. 'If we lose control in the Gulf, we shall not rule long in India,'[6] said Lovat Frazer, one of Lord Curzon's most devoted admirers.

In 1878 Nasr ed-Din Shah visited Russia, then Britain's chief rival and potential enemy in many fields. He asked the Tsar to lend him a few Cossacks to form a 'Persian Cossack Brigade', originally also to be his bodyguard, with Persian soldiers serving under Russian senior officers. At first the Cossack Brigade seems to have been rather ineffective: the Shah was assassinated in 1896. But Qajar policy, or rather lack of positive policy, continued. The British and Russians both had banks in Tehran and the power to issue notes, which gave them immense leverage. 'Your British bank was guilty of pure exploitation,' Mr Alam, the Minister of Court, told me bitterly. 'The notes were only valid in Tehran, and if you spent them in another city an extra tax was chargeable.'[7] In 1901 the still unrecognized wealth of rights in oil were given to the British in the form of a sixty-year concession to William D'Arcy Knox, an Englishman who had been prospecting for gold in Australia. This included oil throughout Persia except the northern provinces bordering Russia.

In 1906 (the year of the first Russian Duma, or Parliament) demands for more democratic government spread quickly through the country, and especially the major cities, with a rising of 'Constitutionalists'. The Shah was forced to agree to the election of a national assembly or *Majlis*. But over 90 per cent of the population was illiterate, and the members elected

2 Reza Shah the Great, father of the present Shah, shortly before his death in 1944

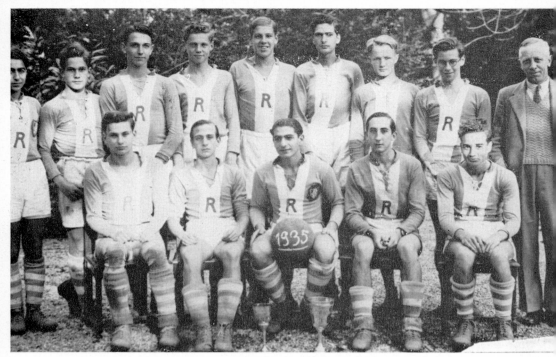

3 *Above*: Mohammad Reza excelled at sport and at his school in Switzerland he captained Le Rosey football team

4 *Below*: The Shah's full brother Ali Reza (*left*) and (*left to right*) Gholam Reza, Abdul Reza, and Hamid Reza, three of his five half-brothers

were either *mullahs* (the Muslim clergy) or members of the famous top 'Thousand Families' (the rich landowners) or both. Humiliated, the Shah died within months. The Qajar throne was tottering, but the turn of political events in far-off Europe stopped it falling. A newly unified Germany posed a serious threat to both Russia and Britain, and they signed the Anglo-Russian convention of 1907; this, indirectly, guaranteed the Qajar throne a longer life.

The convention, which claimed to protect the 'independence and integrity of Iran', apparently virtually sliced the country into two spheres of influence for the Great Powers with a national strip between them. Britain's area of influence was the south-east corner of the country: but in the south-west D'Arcy had the right to build pipelines to the Persian Gulf, so this was an area of the greatest importance should oil be mined. In 1908, oil was struck, and afterwards the D'Arcy concession was taken over, with the blessing of the British Government, by the Anglo-Persian Oil Company.

In 1909 the Constitutionalists rose again. This time the Shah fled to Russia, leaving his eleven-year-old son, Ahmad, to succeed to the throne with a Regent to help him. With the former Shah at last trounced, his Russian backers defeated, and a boy of thirteen on the throne, Iran's position was both extremely vulnerable and essentially hopeful. Now, if ever, was the time for new policies. But constitutional government had broken down completely. There was no longer even a glimmer of administrative hope: only a miracle, it seemed, could achieve any progress in the chaos that was Persia now. Such a miracle was in the making.

The Shah says:

> My father had been born in 1878 in the province of Mazanderan near the Caspian Sea. Unlike the Qajars, who as I have mentioned were of Turkish origin, my father was of genuine Persian stock. Both his father and grandfather had been officers in the old Persian army . . . when Reza Khan, as my father was called in his early days, was only forty days old, his father died. His mother decided to bring her infants on to Tehran, but on the way the baby almost perished in the intense cold of the mountain roads in winter.[8]

General Hassan Arfa says that on the death of Reza Khan's

C

father a family quarrel broke out about the succession, and 'the young Reza's mother had to leave the family property and came with her son to Tehran'.[9] Presumably this was her dead husband's property.

When he was 'only *about* fourteen' [my italics], he enlisted in the Persian Cossack Brigade. At that time he was completely illiterate, for education remained a monopoly of the clergy and the very wealthy. But the young Reza had a mind very much of his own: at the end of each day's army duties he sat down in the barracks and with the help of those who had at least some education he learned to read and to write sufficiently for his needs.

If the boy was going to get anywhere he had first to make the jump from private to the officer ranks. The Shah says: 'Although normally that didn't happen in the Persian army, in my father's case his personality could not be ignored. Broad-shouldered and tall, he had prominent and rugged features, but it was his piercing eyes that arrested anybody who met him. Those eyes could make a strong man shrivel up inside.'[10]

Mr Alam, the Minister of Court, bears out the impression that he made in later years. He told me, 'It was impossible to be natural with him. Nobody could be natural with him, because besides being a powerful military man he was, I think, a *super-man*, and it was difficult just to face him. I remember quite well that for all of us it was difficult to face him. He was immensely tall with an extraordinary power in his eyes and a very powerful face and structure.

'I remember once he came to congratulate Princess Ashraf on the birth of Prince Shahram. It happened that as he was coming all alone by himself I was going out of the Palace all alone by myself, and I was just *faced* with him. I couldn't escape and for a few moments I was with him.'

Reza Shah's eyes have been described variously as grey-green, or golden; perhaps they changed colour in different lights and moods. But according to General Arfa, penetrating they certainly were: 'His complexion was rather dark and his eyes of a strange golden hue were large with a searching look which it took courage to meet.'[11] One can imagine him staring at his fellow men like a bird of prey.

Soldiers did not receive regular payment in those days, because the Government was so weak that it was unable to collect taxes. One day when the Foreign Secretary was to give a dinner for a distinguished foreign visitor, it found it had no funds: so the shops in the bazaar lent the Ministry money for the banquet.[12]

In 1914 the young Shah came of age and was crowned but fears about another Qajar reign were justified. No elections were held after 1915, and 'many parts of Persia were in a condition of chaos'.[13] Even in Tehran itself people would not venture out of doors at night for fear of cut-throats, unless in some emergency such as trying to find a doctor. The once famed roads had deteriorated to the point where now to go from Tehran to Meshed one had to travel via Russia, and to travel from Tehran to Khuzistan in the south-west one had to go via Turkey and Iraq.[14] The only carriage road still existing in Iran was the road from Rasht to Qazvin and Hamadan.[15]

Outside the capital it was still worse. The Shah says:

> Much of Persia was in the grip of local chieftains paying nominal allegiance to the King . . . actually they were doing whatever they pleased in their own regions . . . there was no modern army, and none that owed true allegiance to Persia; there was no law and order; there were no Persian courts save those of the clergy and the tribes. In most of the country it was the law of the stronger that prevailed. The pillagers pillaged, and the common people suffered.[16]

Against this background there was something to be said for any strong man, even for a half-brigand, half-leftist leader such as Kuchik Khan. His followers investigated the people's complaints in their area in the north, took control of water for irrigation, and in some cases kidnapped the landlords and held them up to ransom in the cause of getting them to pay something to the peasants. And often it was against such intrepid leaders as this that Reza Khan found himself fighting, as a member of the Cossack Brigade. For a Persian, it was an unenviable position. But his strong sense of national identity combined with opportunism and instinct for timing to bring him rewards: by the end of the 1914–18 war he was known as a colonel who 'had risen from the ranks, and was renowned for his strong personality, iron will and extraordinary capacity for leadership, and who was clever and ambitious'.[17] Even the man's height was prodigious – he was some six feet four inches.

With the young Shah Ahmad on the throne the Regent was listened to no longer, and the war added to Persia's difficulties. Though she had declared herself neutral, the fact that Russians occupied her northern territory, the British her southern parts, and the Turks also invaded, made this claim farcical. General Arfa says:

> Except for a few Paris-educated Francophiles in the upper classes and fewer genuine Russophiles – the majority of these being so only by opportunism – the great majority of Iranians of all classes were pro-German, not for Germany's sake, but from hostility to Russia, and were rejoicing, thinking that with the defeat of Russia, that country's intolerable pressure on Iran would be removed.[18]

In 1918 Azerbaijan declared itself a Republic. Savouring their victorious revolution, the new Russian Government denounced all Tsarist privileges together with the Anglo-Russian convention in a Note sent to Tehran; in June 1919 a further Note cancelled all Iranian debts to the (now non-existent) Tsarist Government: then, early in 1920, Bolshevik troops landed on the Caspian coast of Persia, allegedly in pursuit of a few hundred White Russians (who had already fled the area), and pushed on to the south, where they met and supported Mirza Kuchik Khan's rebel forces. Kuchik Khan formed a 'Soviet Republic of Gilan' with Bolshevik backing.

The Bolsheviks in the north formed one side of a pair of pincers: the other side remained the British. When the terms of the proposed Anglo-Persian Treaty of August 1919 were made public it became evident that Britain was planning to turn Persia into a protectorate. As the *Majlis* was not sitting the agreement was not ratified, but it was signed by the Central Government and some of its terms were put into effect.

On *Nowruz*, the Iranian New Year (21 March), of the following year (1920) the depth of revulsion against the treaty felt by many Iranians became clear. Lt-Col. Fazlollah Khan, a member of the joint Anglo-Iranian military commission appointed under the treaty, was found shot in his room. In a letter he explained that rather than agree to the subordination of the Iranian Army to British Command he had chosen to die. This was an omen.

In 1917 a liberal-minded Russian officer, Colonel Clergé, had been appointed to command the Persian Cossacks. Before long he had begun telling the Iranians that the only job of the Russians was to train them and then return home. Naturally enough the Russian officers in the Brigade took a poor view of this propaganda, and planned Clergé's exit for him – without his knowledge. When the second-in-command of the Brigade, a Russian called Colonel Staroselsky, approached him and asked if he would be willing to undertake a special mission, Reza Khan accepted. One evening soon afterwards when Clergé was having his tea at home, his house was surrounded by Iranian Cossacks. Then Reza Khan entered his room and 'quite politely'[19] invited him to come and sit in a carriage which was waiting by the gates. This took him under escort to Enzeli, from where he embarked for Russia.

The simple success of this operation apparently made a deep impression on Reza Khan and 'made him think how easy it would be to change the Iranian Army by transferring power from the hands of a few foreign visitors to those of a strong and enterprising Iranian',[20] especially as the Russian officers were now needed back home. Within a short time the seventy or so Russian officers in the 3,000 strong Brigade had been replaced by Iranians. Colonel Reza Khan now had a clear idea of where his future might lie, and, as usual, was doing something to help fate on its way.

Chapter 3

From Colonel to Shah

BY the end of 1920 Persia was a plum ripe for the picking by
whoever was strong enough to seize her, full of smouldering
resentment. 'The Iranians are a politically-minded people, and
always very suspicious and critical of their Government, and it
must be recognized that public opinion was against [the Anglo-
Persian] treaty,' says General Arfa.

The British had much more opposition to face than this
internal reaction. Many of the great foreign powers were also
deeply opposed to Britain's plans for turning Iran into a protectorate. This plan was based on fear as well as the desire for
expansion. General Arfa summed up Britain's attitude:

> It was obvious that if Iran was abandoned to its own devices,
> without money or military force and with a weak central govern-
> ment, it would become the prey of anarchic forces represented by
> well-armed predatory tribes and leftist revolutionary elements, and
> would drift towards Bolshevism, and eventually would become
> engulfed in the wave of the Communist advance towards India
> and the Middle East.[1]

Thus, what seemed to be needed was a new, strong Central
Government which would be well-disposed towards Britain.
Meanwhile Britain was morally supporting the anti-Bolshevik
Governments in Russian Azerbaijan, Georgia and Armenia.

Azerbaijan, particularly, was in a precarious position. Just how much so was illustrated one evening when the Azerbaijan Government invited some members of the newly arrived Iranian delegation to a gala performance at the municipal theatre in Baku, the capital. Arfa and his father were also invited. To their utter astonishment, a good proportion of the audience came in carrying daggers, swords and guns, and took their seats with their weapons between their knees. In the interval a quarrel broke out between two men, and then 'every spectator armed with rifle or pistol began to shoot in every direction. . . . Half a dozen dead or wounded were taken out on stretchers, and the manager came on stage to announce that "the direction regrets the little disturbance, but it is now over and the play will continue"' – which it did!

The Iranian delegation had arrived with a notable young man, of about thirty-three, at its head. His name was Seyid Zia ed-Din Tabatabai. Arfa knew him already: he was 'a former prominent journalist, whom I had met five years before in Tehran in a *mullah*'s garb, but who was now wearing a frock-coat'. He was the son of a *mullah* and editor as well as owner of a crusading newspaper, *Ra'd*, or 'Thunder'. He was also, it was widely and correctly believed, equipped with pro-British sympathies.

Seyid Zia ed-Din was a crusader, with revolutionary ideas which he expressed forcefully in his newspaper. But his middle-class *mullah*'s background (like most Iranians he belonged to the Shi'a sect) meant that he was in touch with many of Iran's most famous families, and this lent weight to his writing. For the British he seemed an ideal tool. With his influential background, his dynamic writing, and his personality, which had already brought success to some minor political missions, he could lead a new Government sympathetic to Britain.

The scene was set. A British military mission had been in Tehran for some time, originally to discuss the organization of a new Iranian Army. There could be no doubt as to who was the dominant and most promising military figure among the Iranians – it was Colonel Reza Khan. The combination of Zia ed-Din and Reza Khan sounded virtually unbeatable, and so indeed it turned out to be, though with different results from those expected by the British.

Reza Khan was by now a formidable and experienced figure.

At forty-two he had been twice married: his first wife, a cousin whom he had married when he was seventeen, had died in childbirth nine years later leaving him a daughter. She was looked after by his second wife, Tadj-ol-Molouk ('Crown of the King'), who had produced a daughter of her own, called Shams, in 1917.

Whereas his first wife had been sweet-natured and docile, Reza Khan had found in his second bride a fiery spirit. Tadj-ol-Molouk today, at about eighty, is still a formidable but much mellowed Dowager Empress. 'Her Majesty has an extraordinary character,' says Mr Alam, 'She has always kept her personality vis-à-vis Reza Shah: she is the only person that Reza Shah couldn't impose himself on. She sticks to her ideas and to her friends and to her principles: she is very fascinating, independent.'[2] The Dowager Empress herself says, 'I come from a military background. My father was a Brigadier and before our marriage my elder brother was a close friend of Reza Shah the Great. In fact it was he who was responsible for our marriage.' Mr Alam explains: 'In those days if two officers were friends, one officer was marrying the daughter of the other: it was very customary in this country.'

'I believe he was eighteen years my senior. Now I am seventy-plus,' the Dowager Empress says. 'I think I could stand up to him, but I do not think I could ever change his mind.' She believes her husband's patriotism was inspired by 'the way in which Russian Cossack officers and instructors looked down on Iranian people and rudely treated the Iranian officers and soldiers. . . . He was working all the time. He dedicated almost all his time to the affairs of state. His sole aspiration was that Iran should achieve greatness.'[3]

It was with Esmat (Chastity), his fourth wife, described to me as the true 'love of his life', that he really seems finally to have relaxed; with her he used to love to walk and talk in the palace gardens. But for the present all remained to be achieved: and Tadj-ol-Molouk was a wife who must surely produce sons with great character.

Like the vast majority of Iranians, particularly the military-minded, Reza Khan longed for a son whom he could bring up as tough, a fighter, a man. On 26 October 1919 his wife gave birth

to twins – a girl, Ashraf (his third daughter), and a boy, Mohammed Reza, his first son. Reza Khan at last had an heir. But for the
moment he had very little to pass on to him. The family lived in
a modest house in the southern part of Tehran (since destroyed).
He acquired two more wives, though even as a successful soldier
he had a struggle to support his family. But with Zia ed-Din he
saw a way to greater power and prosperity, not only for himself
but for the country as a whole. This was the background to the
events of February 1921.

On 20 February the Cossack Brigade, now a purely Persian
body, was stationed at Qazvin, north of Tehran. Four days later,
in spite of the appalling condition of the roads, the Brigade
reached Tehran. Reza Khan had picked his date carefully. On 18
February General Ironside, in charge of British forces in Iran,
left for a conference in Cairo. His plane crashed halfway: but
even if it had not, he would have known nothing of the coup
until it was a *fait accompli*.

On 20 February people in Tehran were told that some 1,000
Cossacks had rebelled at Qazvin as they had not received any pay
for several months and were marching on the capital. This was
taken as the whole truth. Towards midnight Lieutenant Arfa,
who was defending the western approaches of Tehran from the
Qazvin Gate to the Bagh-e-Shah Gate against the rebels, heard
the sound of gunfire from the centre of the town, and telephoned
his commanding officer to ask what was happening. He was told
that some 1,500 Cossacks had entered through the Gomrok
Gate. The Central Brigade which had been assigned to defend
this had surrendered. The Cossacks then marched on to the police
headquarters in Topkhane Square (now Sepah Square). The
police, unlike the soldiers, had refused to surrender. The
Cossacks had opened fire and killed three of them: and this was
the only blood shed in this revolution. The next day Reza Khan
issued a proclamation explaining that they were saving the
country from traitors and wanted an independent, strong and
prosperous Persia. And he invited the inhabitants of Tehran to
'obey and keep quiet'.

The British were taken aback. The men they had intended to
back had taken charge of the situation themselves, had shown
themselves independent. Even the Dowager Empress says: 'On

the night of the coup d'état I was in Tehran and unaware of it.
Even after the success of the coup I did not know immediately
that my husband was Commander-in-Chief.'[4]

In the four weeks before the coup, four different governments
had been formed, and each had resigned.[5] The last did so as soon
as the capital fell, and Seyid Zia ed-Din Tabatabai was at once
appointed Prime Minister. As for Reza Khan, without whose
Cossacks the coup could never have succeeded, he was given the
title of Sardar Sepah – General of the Army – became Minister
of War, and received a jewel-studded golden sword, a symbol of
the future.

The British decided to let the new men prove themselves. A
period of some confusion could normally be expected to follow
a coup d'état. When the Young Turks had risen in arms against
Sultan Abdul-Hamid, ruler of the Ottoman Empire, in 1908, their
victory was nearly lost within a year when the loyalists had
launched a counter-attack. The eventual success of the revolu-
tionaries owed much to Mustapha Kemal, the future Ataturk. It
was perhaps partly his example that had added the power of
action to Reza Khan's inspiration.

Mr Alam explains why Reza Khan was not at once chosen to
be Prime Minister: 'In those days it was not so digestible for the
Tehran Government to digest a military man. Reza Shah was the
real power, but somebody else had to be chosen, among the
lower class – although I must say that he [Zin ed-Din] was not
so low!'[6] According to Arfa, when Reza Khan had first been
approached by Seyid Zia ed-Din he 'knew very little about [him]
and cared less about his aims'. Years later the present Shah used
him as an adviser. 'I think my father disagreed with him more as
to tactics and timing than the substance of his political and
economic ideas,' says the Shah.[7]

In May 1921 Reza Shah became Minister of War. He at once
united the various separate brigades and regiments into a regular
army and introduced conscription. Seyid Zia ed-Din felt in the
same month of May, after only three months at the head of a
promising new Government, that he no longer had a future in
Iran. 'Even the British were less partial to him, and the necessary
pressure was exercised to induce him to resign,'[8] General Arfa
remembers. Resignation alone was not enough: Zia ed-Din did

not feel safe until he had left the country. He fled to Baghdad and did not return to Iran for two decades. He was welcomed by the present Shah. He died at home in his eighties.[9]

The tone of the new administration had, however, already been set. Five days after the coup d'état, in February, the Anglo-Persian Treaty had been denounced; on the same day, 26 February 1921, the Irano-Soviet Treaty was signed, by which the USSR relinquished almost all the rights and concessions that had been acquired in Iran by the Tsarist Government. These two acts allowed the world, and particularly the two great former friendly oppressors, Britain and Russia, to see that the new Iran meant it when she said that she stood for independence.

The internal problems were far more complex. In the summer of 1921 the fourth *Majlis* was elected, and in the next two years, before he was twenty-three, Ahmad Shah appointed two more Prime Ministers. Reza Khan continued to serve in each cabinet as Minister of War and Commander-in-Chief of the Armed Forces. The Shah sums up the problem his father had to solve: 'Throughout our history, whenever the Central Government has been weak, tribesmen have pillaged, robbed and raped as they chose. But when the Central Government has been strong and could control them, the tribes have played a constructive role in our society.'[10]

Apart from the Minister of War himself, the Central Government was still not strong enough, so Reza Khan set out on a series of campaigns that took him all over the vast country. Iran is a land of many contrasts: of desert and tropical vegetation, of soaring mountains and deep ravines, of temperature which may rise in summer to over 120°F in Sistan, and in the north-west in winter fall far below freezing, of rainfall that usually tops fifty inches a year near the Caspian while the average in Baluchistan is three to four inches, of pasture and wasteland, of forests and bare rock. In each region not only the climate and vegetation were vastly different, but the people too.

The nomadic tribes, particularly, were a law unto themselves. Arthur Arnold quotes a friend of his who had met the Bakhtiari and found them 'hospitable, obliging and free from caste prejudices', as well as happy, but had told him 'I was in more than one place asked whether the Emperor of Russia was not the Shahanshah'.[11]

In his campaigns Reza Khan gradually defeated all the major antagonists of central rule. In October 1921 he defeated the new Government in Gilan. Kuchik Khan had retired to the forest with his followers; he then tried to escape to the Khalkhal region, but while trying to cross the high, snow-covered mountain pass of Masuleh he froze to death.[12] Reza Khan's strategy was to disarm the chiefs and break both their power and influence. Having subdued Gilan, he went on to defeat the separatists in Azerbaijan, Luristan, Kurdistan, Fars and Khorassan, and brought all these provinces under control. 'Before long,' adds the Shah, laconically, 'the vacillating Ahmad Shah departed for an indefinite stay in Europe.'[13]

The very next day Mustapha Kemal (later Ataturk), the man so admired by Reza Khan, engineered the voting of the Turkish National Assembly to depose the Caliph, and to elect himself, unanimously, President of the Republic. This was on 29 October 1923. Six months later, in April 1924, having convinced a submissive *Majlis* in Tehran that Iran, too, should become a republic, Reza Khan put this suggestion to a meeting he had convoked of the Shi'ite clergy.[14] They, fearing that this would be the quickest way to lose their power, came armed with legal and religious objections to the proposed republic. Not even Reza Khan could cut through their opposition, and he returned to Tehran determined to gain sufficient power to implement his own ideas by whatever means should prove necessary.

From this confrontation with the clergy, and the recognition that they alone had the strength and resources to resist him, and his aims, sprang Reza Khan's deep feud with the *mullahs*. The Shah says, 'Deep in his heart he was [religious] but acting just the opposite, because he knew that the old religious people were the root of our backwardness. He had to crush it and I had to do the same.'[15] Arnold had noted that 'unless stirred to unwonted effort the Shah's Government is far less powerful than the chief priests of Islam'.[16]

According to Mr Alam, when Reza Khan began to pacify the country, some of the feudal barons and tribal leaders who had previously been under the sway of foreign powers responded to his call for unity with fundamental pleasure. 'I remember my father's little army, but I must say my father was still suffering from your influence in that part of the country [north-east]; and he was one of the first who hailed Reza Shah and joined him and stayed till the last moment with him.'[17]

The *mullahs* were one of the chief groups of landlords and the Islamic laws of inheritance protected their interests. Yet they were nearly always absentee landlords,[18] wielding power without responsibility. But the ecclesiastical enemy was intangible, elusive, equipped with more than physical powers.

Another very powerful element was Sheikh Khazal, the chief of Khuzistan. He was known as a British protégé and it was believed that they had promised to support him in the event of an attack on Khuzistan by the forces of the Central Government,[19] because he kept order round their oilfields in the south. Thus, when Reza Khan defeated Khazal in December 1924, this was interpreted not only as an internal triumph but as a victory over the British.

Ahmad Shah, who was now about twenty-seven and had spent the past four years or so wandering the casinos and watering places of Europe, realized what dangers he would face if he ever dared set foot again in Iran. At last he sent word that he definitely refused to return. On 31 October the final vestiges of the Qajar claim to rule was ended after 131 years. On that day the *Majlis* voted his deposition and the end of the dynasty, by a majority of 117.[20] There were only five abstentions: but among them was a name that was going to be a longlived thorn in the life not only of Reza Khan but of his son: Dr Mohammed Mossadeq.

A new *Majlis* voted to revise the Constitution. Reza Khan was invited to assume the title and power of the Shahanshah (King of Kings) of Iran. It made little difference to his powers whether he became the head of republic, as Kemal Ataturk had done, or the first Emperor in a new dynasty. 'I am sure that my father for a time preferred the concept of a republic,' says the Shah. 'But the tide of public opinion now shifted back towards the idea of continuing the monarchical system which after all had for thousands of years been our tradition. Most of the Constitutionalists all over the country had always been firm supporters of the monarchical principle.'[21] But by complying with the deep feelings of his fellow-countrymen, Reza Khan had strengthened his position. In this country traditional means could be used to ensure the quickest progress.

On 25 April 1926, only five years after he had been number two in the coup d'état, Reza Khan was crowned in the Golestan Palace, the fabulous building whose throne room, alive with lights reflected from a million slivers of mirror which made up its walls and ceiling, had witnessed so many similar ceremonies: but this was not merely the beginning of a new dynasty, it was the beginning of a new era.

The new Shahanshah was given the title of Reza Shah Pahlavi. His son, Mohammed Reza, was exactly six and a half years old. He received the title of *Valiahd*, Crown Prince. The little boy who, dressed in a miniature version of parade uniform, that day watched his father crown himself – as Napoleon had done – must have been awed and thrilled by the spectacle around him. The new prince could not know that in assuming the throne his father was taking the first step towards his own exile, and that, as a result of this day, Mohammed Reza himself would come face to face with the threat of violent death as well as glory.

Chapter 4

Crown Prince

THE Coronation ceremony, full of pomp and circumstance, probably set the seal on the boy's belief that his father, the King of Kings, was the greatest man in the world. 'You can imagine the awe it inspired in a six-year-old like me,' he confesses, 'In my case my father influenced me more by far than anyone else.' Since the new Shahanshah was held in trembling respect by strong, mature and clever men alike, this was hardly surprising. His investiture as Crown Prince marked the end of Mohammed Reza's childhood proper. Reza Shah decreed that he should be separated from his mother and receive a special education, emphasizing that he was a boy who would one day have to rule one of the most physically primitive and socially complex countries now emerging as a modern power.

The Shah's memories of his life before this time are vague: the beauty of the Elburz mountains, behind Tehran, which they had been able to see from their modest house in the south of the city; the look of consternation on his mentor's face when he, the precious heir, slipped and hit his head in the bath; and, above all, the imposing figure of his father coming and going in his carriage to his duties as Minister of War – when he was not out in the provinces campaigning in the saddle. Till now he had taken family life for granted. Later he would react against its pattern.

'Your own children, your Majesty, are you bringing them up

in a very different way from the way you were brought
up?'

'Absolutely. Absolutely. Again it's the change of time. And
so far I can even say that – except their nurses and governesses –
we are not even trying to bring them up: we let them grow!'

'Your father was very, *very* strict with you, wasn't he?'

'Umm – Hmmpph.'

'All of you, and particularly yourself?'

'Er – I don't know; well he loved me more than his eyes. But
still the whole set-up was so rigid and so disciplinary that you
could not *imagine* that it could be different. That was the atmosphere reigning everywhere. An atmosphere of *absolute* discipline
and almost rigidness.'

'That was as soon as you left the harem, because when you
were born you were with your mother and your father's later
wives and the other children . . .?'

'No – no – no. There was no question of harem.¹ My mother
was living in another place. My father had another wife, while
my mother was his wife, but they were separate.'

'Oh I see, not in the same house. So you didn't have the companionship of the other children? You had your brother Ali
Reza, I suppose – he was how much younger than you?'

'Two years.'

'And Ashraf of course was the same, and Princess Shams was
three years older?'

'Again, two years.'

'So you really were a nice little group together but you had
to be very good.'

'Er – er – *Yes*, I think so. I think so, but fighting all the time
obviously.'

'But you feel that your own children are brought up in an
atmosphere of much more give-and-take and much more understanding, much more psychologically balanced?'

'Totally, totally, and they are at least less [divided] – except
one but she is so much older and she lives separately and she has
her own children² – it's *one father and one mother*. It's not a split
marriage or things like that that sometimes could create . . .'

'And do you feel that your daughters will have a very much
happier life than say a woman of your mother's generation?'

separate the Crown Prince for his special education very hard on
her too? 'Of course, separation from my beloved son was indeed
very hard on me,' replied the Dowager Empress, 'but separation
came when he was sent to Europe to continue his studies at the
age of twelve and not at the age of six.'

When I asked how much time the Crown Prince actually spent
in his father's company, the Dowager Empress said it was
'mostly at meal times'. Were there ever, I wondered, any open
disagreements between father and son, particularly as he grew
older? 'This question could best be answered by His Imperial
Majesty,' said the Dowager Empress. Her own attitude to life is
shown not only in these remarks but in her belief that the position of Shahanshah is not inevitably lonely 'because the al-
mighty God is always with him'; and, asked whether she herself
would have preferred to have been born later, when women
could enjoy more freedom: 'I am satisfied with my past.'

Reza Shah founded an elementary military school especially
for his son. His brother and half-brothers eventually joined him
here. In his own class were twenty-one other pupils, carefully
selected from the children of army officers and Government
officials who had '*actively* worked with Reza Shah during or after
the revolution of 1921' (my italics).[7] One is reminded of the
similar rewards system favoured by the Kennedys: those who
had supported them in their early political days received special
treatment later on.

'Proverbially, to get things done in Persia one must both
reward and punish,' the Shah admits. 'My father relied more on
punishment than he did on reward or even encouragement.'[8] Yet
there were a few fixed points. Mohammed Reza 'always managed
to be first in his class at school'.[9] Anything else would have been
lèse-majesté.

There was a good deal of military drilling. A photograph of
the Crown Prince at the age of seven, shows him standing
proudly in his uniform as a Colonel of the Iranian Army. As well
as formal studies, there was considerable emphasis on the
physical, with riding, and later boxing and football. But the real
education of the boy came from his father. From the age of six,
he spent an hour a day with him. As he grew older, the affairs
of state were gradually introduced to him. From the age of nine

he lunched daily with his father. This was probably far more of an ordeal than a delight.

The former Empress Soraya has given her impressions of the Shah's childhood as rather unhappy, and remembers him telling her, 'We were all frightened of him. He needed only to fix his piercing eyes upon us and we went rigid with fear and respect. At the family table we never dared express our own views. Indeed, we were only allowed to speak when asked a question.'[10]

The Shah himself remembers:

'He could be one of the pleasantest men in the world, yet he could be one of the most frightening.'[11]

Very rarely he would show his affection to his son. 'When we were alone together, he would sing me little songs,' he says. But this was all. The Empress Farah ascribes her husband's slowness to hug and kiss his own children to the fact that his parents did not do this to him. Yet in time he learned that the sternness sprang partly *from* love; and today the Shah remains too loyal to the memory of his father to criticize him publicly.

Reza Shah was suspicious of everyone until their behaviour proved that they were loyal. Knowing well the flattery that is second nature to the aspiring Persian, he distrusted all compliments. He himself was a man of few words, and often violent actions. The Shah himself has given a mild example of his father's ruthlessness: 'On one occasion Reza Shah arrived at our Ministry of Finance just after opening time and ordered all the doors closed. A number of sleepy officials, including the Minister, found themselves locked out; they were all promptly sacked.'[12] 'He had no personal charm, and did not seek popularity,' says General Arfa bluntly. 'He never promised anything in his rare speeches. He merely said that this, this and this must be done.'[13]

Often he took the law into his own hands, quite literally; or, as the Shah puts it, 'To inspire his people to ever greater efforts, my father relied upon his own force of character.'[14] This consisted partly of enormous brute force.

When a jockey failed to do well in a race that Reza Shah had set his heart on winning, the terrified man sat paralysed afterwards in his saddle in the paddock as the giant Shah strode up to him. He plucked the loser from the saddle, threw him to the ground, and in front of the crowd kicked the man in the stomach, according to *Time Magazine*.[15] Today Iranian officials deny this story.

Not surprisingly, Reza Shah was known as a man of violent temper. His son disagrees: 'He was often angry when he thought it necessary, but he never lost control.' It is still more unnerving to think of a twentieth-century ruler deliberately committing such acts, although those familiar with Iran will recognize the temptation for anyone determined to get things done to resort to desperate methods.

Yet Reza Shah did have enormous self-discipline. He rose at 5 a.m., breakfasted on tea, arrived at his office at 7.30 a.m., worked until 11.30 a.m. when he lunched on rice and boiled chicken. His afternoon's work began at 2 p.m. and lasted until 6 p.m., after which he spent two hours studying the reports received during the day. At 8 p.m. he had a supper of rice and boiled chicken. At 10 p.m. he went to bed, as he did even when visiting Ataturk, when only the first course of a banquet had been served! His main outdoor exercise was riding, and twice a year or so he went hunting. Otherwise his exercise was chiefly indoors: walking while he thought. 'In my memory it seems as if he were *always* walking, either pacing up and down in his office or inspecting troops or projects on foot, or, in the late afternoon, taking long walks in the garden,' says the Shah.[16]

He wore home-made stockings and liked well-worn short boots. He always slept on a mattress which was on the floor itself: this again was typical of his generation, and even of many younger Iranians, who still entertain on the floor sitting on rugs, or, occasionally, cushions, unless they live in a town or belong to the upper or, now, the new middle classes.

Such an ascetic example was impressive and the Crown Prince gradually came to realize what Reza Shah was trying to do for his country. However, he did not always set about things in the most sensible way. Later his son wrote: 'Without benefit of any overall plan or system of priorities, he would plunge enthusiastically into one new project after another.'[17] One example of a plan that began well but was never completed was the updating of the land taxation system. This was begun in 1926, but never covered the whole of the country.[18] In his first priority, on the other hand, Reza Shah never faltered. This was to establish Iran as an

unshakeably independent power, a country to be respected as he
himself was feared. 'He was patriotic almost to excess,' his son
commented later. Since the Shah himself today, and still more
some of those who work for him, tend to give the same impression on some counts, this gives some idea of the gigantic proportions of Reza Shah's patriotism. Evidently Reza Shah's feelings
for his country were on the same huge scale as everything else
about him, including his ambition.

He made this very clear in a typically dramatic incident when
he was Minister of War, while Ahmad Shah was still nominally
on the throne. A march past of all units, including foreign units
serving in the country, was being held at the Golestan Palace.
When Reza Khan came face to face with General Westdahl, the
Swedish Chief of Police, the Swede deliberately saluted without
allowing his fingers to touch his sheepskin cap. Furiously, Reza
Khan seized Westdahl's hand and completed the salute for him,
shoving his hand upwards with such force that the cap was
toppled to the ground. 'You are a General but you do not know
how to salute,' he snarled. News of the incident swiftly passed
from mouth to mouth. According to General Arfa it brought
home to everybody, Iranians and foreigners alike, that foreigners
were about to lose their privileged positions, and this 'changed
overnight their behaviour towards their Iranian subordinates and
collaborators'.[19]

It was Reza Shah who insisted that the country be called Iran,
by foreigners as well, to emphasize how much bigger it was than
the kingdom originally settled by the Persians. And, as Shah, he
continued to push out foreign influences.

The construction of a trans-Iranian railway had been one of
his greatest dreams since as a young soldier he had campaigned,
footsore and exhausted, after travelling the appalling roads. Work
began on the track in 1927, and took until 1939 to complete,
entailing 900 miles of miraculous engineering over the most
difficult terrain imaginable, and the cost was stupendous. Reza
Shah did not deign to accept a foreign loan for this. Instead, a
special tax was levied on sugar and tea, the two favourites of the
Persian palate. The taxes were terribly hard for the peasants,
who spend much of their tiny income on sugar and tea;[20] but
such hardship was in Reza Shah's eyes the price of national pride.

He sought friends on his own frontiers, and treaties were concluded with former enemies, notably Afghanistan (which had seceded from the Empire 200 years before), Iraq, and Turkey. Ataturk continued to influence Reza Shah: Turkey had not only railways, but also had ports, factories, an industrialized society, the importance of all of which Reza Shah had fully recognized for years. There were also social changes, which appeared subtler but were in fact a pervasive and fundamental influence in introducing a modern climate into the Middle East.

Following the example of Ataturk, Reza Shah commanded that there should be a penal code and a civil code based on French and Belgian models. The Ministry of Justice was closed for three months (which probably made little difference) while a new Ministry was organized on more modern lines. Previously the courts had been essentially ecclesiastical courts: under the new laws, judges would be laymen. In the late 1920s the Turkish dictator passed laws which obliged male Turks to cut off their beards and to wear European dress, and Turkish women to abandon the sacred protection, the veil, without which a Muslim woman felt as naked as a European woman without a blouse.

One day Reza Shah ordered Tadj-ol-Molouk, his second wife, and their daughter Princess Shams, to prepare to go with him to the opening of a new college in Iran. They were to wear formal dresses: and no veils. As the mother of his eldest son, Tadj-ol-Molouk had retained her position as senior wife and Empress in spite of his two subsequent marriages. Describing their agitation, Mr Alam merely said: 'They were very excited. In the car, Reza Shah said "You know for my personal feelings I wish I had *died today*: but for the country I take you there like this".'

The Empress says simply, 'I did not mind it at all to appear unveiled in public, because there was no other way. I remember while I was for the first time unveiled and driving together with Reza Shah to the ceremony which was being held at the teachers' college, he told me that he would have rather preferred the world ruined upon his head than to see his wife appear in public without her veil, but in the interests of state it was necessary that it should be done.'[21]

Nothing could have been more of an audacious slap in the collective face of the clergy than the appearance of the Empress in this way, and the order which then went out to all Iranian women to do likewise. But, as so often with Reza Shah, there were personal scores to be settled. He heard shortly afterwards that the mujtahid (officiating priest) at Qum, one of the chief religious centres in the country, had publicly denounced the Empress for appearing unveiled. Enraged, Reza Shah drove straight to the mosque. There he strode from his armoured car into the mosque and beat the Imam with his iron cane so hard, he later told his son, that the metal was bent.

While preserving the Shi'ite law in questions of inheritance, births and marriage in deference to the strongly traditional inclinations of the people, Reza Shah also introduced some laws to the very poor lot of women in Iran. It became possible to insert in marriage contracts such clauses as the obligation of the husband not to take another wife (four are permitted according to Muslim law), the right of a wife to divorce as easily as a man, and the right of the wife to choose where to live. Little by little, the Central Government was asserting itself and extending its power; and the power of the landowners and official classes was waning. This decline would gather speed until towards the end of his reign there would be a marked reduction in the political and social status of the landowners.[22]

Mohammed Reza was introduced to these facts in his daily luncheons with his father. This was his real elementary education. It began when he was six and ended when he was twelve.

Chapter 5

Seeds of Independence

REZA SHAH could and did control his son's environment and education, but he could not see his son's thoughts, and from the age of six Mohammed Reza's inner life began to develop. This was to progress on surprising lines, for the boy possessed a temperament and fundamental outlook very different from both parents. Comparisons would always be made. They were 'basically different in character', the Empress Soraya was to comment later. 'Reza Shah was known for his violent temper. By contrast I never saw his son really lose his. He was a gentle, even a shy man.' Reserve was a means of self-defence against his almost omnipotent father. Shyness, in so far as it stemmed partly from lack of confidence, made him vulnerable. It was a safety-valve when, within a few months of leaving the protection of the nursery, he found another supremely powerful being to protect him.

He had never been a robust child, and now he contracted one of Iran's most dreaded diseases – typhoid fever. For weeks he lay in bed, hovering between life and death, while his father agonized over him, his mother walked to and fro holding a Koran above her head and praying, and the doctors doubtless trembled to think of the fate they would suffer if their patient died. On the night of the fever's crisis, little Mohammed Reza had a dream. He saw Ali, who was the son-in-law of the Prophet Mohammed, hand him a bowl, and he drank some liquid from it. The next day he seemed much better, and from then on his recovery was rapid.[1]

The following summer the family went to a cool and beautiful place high in the mountains above Tehran. The journey was on horseback, along a very steep and winding trail. Suddenly the boy's horse stumbled: he fell head first on to a jagged rock and fainted. When he came round, he found everyone looking at him in amazement: he was not even scratched. He told them he had seen and felt Abbas, one of the Muslim saints, catch him as he fell. When Reza Shah heard of this he scoffed. 'Knowing my father to be a very strong-willed man I did not argue with him,' the Shah said later, 'but I never doubted that I had seen Saint Abbas.'

Later, he was walking with his guardian along a cobbled street near the palace when he saw a man with a halo round his head and recognized him as the Imam, the descendant of Mohammed expected to come again as a saviour. Evidently Reza Shah's attitude had made him a little wary of talking about his supernatural experiences, for he merely asked his guardian, who was walking beside him, 'Did you see him?' He seems to have half-expected the answer he got, which was No.

This only increased his faith. He could argue in himself that it was clear that he, and no one else, had been chosen to see these saints, therefore that he was someone special. This conviction must have given him his first independent feeling of strength. It was the first time he had disagreed with his father, and though he dared not continue to argue openly, he refused to be laughed out of his beliefs. His undoubtedly sincere, near-fanatical, sense of mission later in life, and his subsequent coolness in the face of danger and even of assassination attempts, bear out his story: he is not only a fatalist, but a fatalist who feels he has divine protection. Even so he has always possessed a strong practical streak as well, and he has certainly always done everything possible to help the gods help him. In adult life the story of the visions has been of great practical use, to quell the superstitious and add to his political aura.

After these three experiences, which he calls 'dreams, visions, apparitions', he had no more. Nor, he says, did he hope for more, 'because I knew that I had some links after those visions and then apparitions . . . then I *knew* that there was a contact'.

'So you felt safe?' I asked. 'Yes – I think so, I think so,' he replied calmly and happily.[2]

Perhaps still more significantly, he received a very different reaction when he told his mother about the visions. A devout Muslim, she says simply, 'Yes, he told me about them and I was very happy to hear them.'

I asked the Shah if his father had perhaps been slightly afraid that he might turn into a religious fanatic. There was a considerable pause and then he said, 'Eventually, I think so.'[3]

His sense of independence and individuality was also fostered by a decision of his father's. Reza Shah decided that his son needed a governess to take charge of his domestic life: and that he must be able to converse easily with Europeans. So he took what would otherwise have been the extraordinary step of engaging an English governess, Mrs Arfa. She spoke excellent French and Russian and before marrying a Persian had been a ballet dancer. She was a woman of skill and tact.[4] She organized his rooms, his home timetable, his meals (introducing him to French food – although he would never become a gourmet) and his cultural life. It was, in fact, mainly thanks to her that the latter existed at all.

When he was twelve and a half he left the elementary military school. Reza Shah now faced a crucial dilemma about the Crown Prince. He wanted to see him cast in the same hard mould as himself, yet he recognized that the boy needed to understand and absorb the attitudes and working ways of the West. The Prince's future was decided by the needs of his country. Mohammed Reza would be sent to finish his education in Europe and would not be allowed to return to Iran for five years.

Because it had no history of territorial conflict with Iran, and had a healthy climate, he would go to Switzerland. With him, to soften the separation and isolation, went his eleven-year-old brother Prince Ali Reza, and two friends carefully chosen by Reza Shah. Some of the tracks on which his son's life would always run were being firmly laid down. More than half a century later one of these friends, Hossein Fardoust, would rank among the most powerful and feared men in Iran, while within months the other friend would be called home in disgrace.

After the ship had sailed, General Arfa went to Reza Shah and found him in the palace garden, 'the persons of his suite standing respectfully in a circle round him'. As usual, he was pacing up and down. He looked very sad. 'It is very hard for me to part with my beloved son,' he said, 'but one must think of the country. Iran needs educated and enlightened rulers. We, the old and ignorant, must go.'[5]

Chapter 6

A European Education

NONE of the four young Iranians had been abroad before. Even their Shah had not yet crossed his own frontiers. So it was with intense excitement that they stared out of the train windows as they travelled through Poland and Germany, into Switzerland. It hardly looked real to them: so neat, so sweet, so lush compared with the savage splendours, the bald mountains, the immense untouched deserts, of Asia. The Crown Prince's high spirits disturbed Dr Nafici, his guardian and physician. Realizing that his own future depended on the wellbeing of his precious charge, he tried to impose on Mohammed a régime as strict as the one he had left behind; and he did so pompously. 'The physician could not perhaps get over the importance of his position as guardian.'[1]

The first few months that the two young princes spent in Switzerland were probably the happiest, especially for Mohammed himself. Reza Shah had still not finally decided which school should be entrusted with the main education of his heir, and meanwhile the boys were sent to a private school in Lausanne, the Ecole Nouvelle de Chailly. Their two friends were boarders but the princes were not. They lodged with M. and Mme Mercier, who had three sons and two daughters of their own. Although they liked it, it must also have been a shock to adapt to such a very different way of life. Somewhat stiltedly the Shah would later write 'I enjoyed my informal relationship with M. Mercier and his wife and children.'

In 1932 Reza Shah decided to move them to boarding school, Le Rosey, between Lausanne and Geneva. Le Rosey had fewer than one hundred pupils, and there were no girls as there had been at the first school. His brother and two friends studied with him, but while the others were free sometimes to go outside the school grounds and into the town, he was not allowed to go with them. The worst time was perhaps during the Christmas holidays, when the others were invited to parties and dances but Dr Nafici insisted that the Crown Prince should stay behind alone in his room.

M. C. Vuilleumier, who taught at Le Rosey for fifty years and had the Shah among his pupils, remembers the arrival of the Crown Prince on 7 September 1932.

'His father had agreed that at school he should be called simply Pahlavi, like all the other boys who were known simply by their family name, and that he should be given no special privileges. And, in fact, he was treated and considered like any other boy. I must say that he played the game perfectly, although possibly the régime demanded, on his side, at least at first, quite a bit of adaptation.

'There was one exception, however, and an important exception: Pahlavi, in addition to his complete academic programme, saw his professor of Persian Mr Mostapha and his guardian, Dr Nafici, who was responsible to the Shah for the Crown Prince and who was instructing his charge in the history and institutions of his country and preparing him for his future task.

'As a result, his hours of leisure and sport were very limited. I should add that Pahlavi, on orders from his father, was not authorized to leave the school by himself, and that all his excursions were made in the company of one of these gentlemen who came to fetch him from school in a big Lincoln car driven by an imposing Iranian chauffeur.

'At first Pahlavi showed a certain timidity, which was perhaps reserve in the face of what was, for him, a totally new milieu. But he soon got over that. He adapted very well to the demands of school discipline and the practice of sports – tennis, rowing, athletics, football – where he excelled to such an extent that he became captain of his team, not through any favouritism, but because of his qualities of leadership, his will to succeed, the seriousness which he brought to everything he did, and also a certain natural air of authority.

'He had a studious adolescence, a little on the austere and rigid side, and very soon became aware of his responsibilities as a future sovereign and the tasks that awaited him, very devoted as he was to the Persian people of whom he was proud and to whose destiny he swore to devote himself.

'This did not preclude moments of relaxation and pure gaiety among his fellow-pupils or the joys of outings in school holidays in the Jura Mountains, where they cooked sausages and potatoes in ashes. He showed himself most active in lighting campfires, and as with everything else he made sure it was perfectly done.'

Mlle Helen Schaub also saw the Crown Prince daily during his four years at Le Rosey. She remembers forthrightly: 'Lessons come first at Rosey and did in his time. Fortunately the Crown Prince had already spent a year at a school in Lausanne in order to learn French and therefore did not have any difficulty in following his programme.

'As far as I can remember he was an average student, not outstanding but eager to learn and making steady progress. He was well disciplined and already had a great sense of responsibility. He also became a leader and had no fear of directors or masters though treating them with respect.

'I remember one instance when he came to Mr Carnal, the Headmaster and owner of the school at that time, with a small delegation to plead for a boy who was about to be expelled, saying that he and his fellow-students would take the responsibility for the behaviour of this boy if Mr Carnal would accept to have him stay on – and so saved the boy from disgrace.

'As he was always very keen on sports, he was quick in making a place for himself at Rosey and became the captain of our very successful football team. He also played a good game of tennis and would certainly have been a good skier if his father had allowed him to practise that sport. However, he made up for it by playing ice-hockey which, in those days, was one of Rosey's main sports.'[2]

So was skiing, and the Crown Prince longed to ski with the rest of the school. But this was strictly forbidden. The Empress Farah believes that it was Reza Shah who imposed the veto. The

Shah has allowed himself a rare complaint about this period in his life: 'I had a radio and gramophone to keep me company, but what fun were they compared with the festivities my friends enjoyed? I think it was quite wrong.'[3] Years later he told the Empress Soraya that the teachers had instructions to be even firmer with him than with their other pupils. When I pressed him about his feeling of being burdened and isolated in his position as Crown Prince he replied, 'When I was at school in Switzerland, yes, yes; terrible. [Feeling] different, and feeling as you said in a straitjacket, like a prisoner. And maybe this is a lot of the reason that I give so much freedom to my children, just to make up for myself.'[4]

He had learned what was doubtless the most valuable lesson of his adolescence: that friendship was worth more than any amount of traditional Iranian foot-kissing. If his claim that 'my room became a meeting place for the boys, who often filled it to capacity', is an understandable exaggeration from one who had so often had to cope on his own, he was certainly well liked by his contemporaries. And he showed a great streak of kindness which led to a surprising and close friendship.

Living at Le Rosey was a young man called Ernest Perron, some ten years older than Mohammed. He was not a pupil but the son of the school's odd-job man. He helped his father in the garden, and one day as he was pushing a heavy wheelbarrow along a group of the boys ran up and overturned it. The Crown Prince instantly went to help the victim – and from this moment sprang an understanding which was to last for many years. Perron was one of the very few Europeans for whom Reza Shah would later lift his ban on Europeans at the Imperial Court of Iran. That he made such a close friendship not with one of his social peers, or someone close to the same position, but with the son of servants, does suggest that the Crown Prince was homesick in a particular way: he was, perhaps, missing the natural obeisances that he would have had in his daily contacts in Iran, and establishing a relationship with a social inferior was one way of creating a social echo of Iran. It also suggests that he may not have felt wholly at ease, or indeed in some ways even equal, to the boys of good social standing who came from countries so much more advanced in most ways than Iran.

One thing he could not avoid: for the first time he had to compete on equal terms with others boys intellectually. Naïvely he remarks, 'My marks in Tehran had been excellent. Even now I don't really know whether this was due to my own merits or to my position.' At Le Rosey, though he won occasional prizes, he was on the whole only an average pupil. He enjoyed history and showed great interest in science, but was poor at plane geometry. And of course his workload was heavier than that of most other boys, with his extra subjects to master.

He wrote home to his father each week, and occasionally corresponded with other members of his family. In September 1934 his four younger half-brothers, the Princes Gholam Reza (aged eleven), Abdul Reza (ten), Ahmad Reza (nine) and Mahmoud Reza (eight) joined him at Le Rosey. But the Dowager Empress recalls that she saw him only once, when she visited Europe.

But his father's iron hand made itself felt even here. One day young Mehrpour Teymurtash, the third son of Reza Shah's Minister of Court, packed his bags and left. His father had fallen from favour and been dismissed, and in true Persian tradition the sins of the father were visited on the son.

In 1936, three weeks before he would have sat for the Swiss equivalent of his 'O' level examinations, the Shah summoned his son home. If there were doubts that he might not shine in a public examination, better that he should not take it. But he had excelled in sport at Le Rosey.

He had matured both physically and mentally. He was still only of medium height, a good head shorter than his six-foot-four father, but a photograph of him playing football soon after his return to Iran, wearing shorter shorts than his team-mates, shows how the delicate, even puny, little boy had grown into a muscular young man.

There were many deeper changes. Though he said his Muslim prayers regularly, any fears his father may have entertained that he might develop into a religious fanatic were obviously groundless. Religion would be his tool and not his master.

And if it was not true that he had become a democrat, the benevolent side of his nature, which was something his father did not possess outside family affairs, had developed. Dreaming

E

of future power he longed to create an individual aura as ruler, not merely continue as an extension of Reza Shah. He hoped to 'let each peasant family amass a little fortune which it could use to build a house or buy new cattle or do other things', by declaring a moratorium on tithes from peasants working the royal estates – millions of acres of land which had been annexed or confiscated by Reza Shah, or simply impounded from the vast areas of land where no one lived. Remembering the example of the great Emperor Naushirwan, who had a bell hung outside his palace so that anyone with a complaint could ring it and speak to him, he planned to have a public complaints box.

The mind of the young man of sixteen and a half who returned to Iran in the spring of 1936 had been opened more than a little, but he had been insulated both by his Persian companions and the régime imposed by his guardian from entering completely into the spirit of what he instinctively termed '*Western* democracy' (my italics).

His own nature and what he had seen of relationships between Americans, Swiss, French, Germans, English and the boys of other nationalities at Le Rosey encouraged him to think that régimes could be built on foundations other than pure fear: on the other hand he despised the thought of a weak ruler, with a loose society. 'Gradually,' he says, 'I realized that discipline without democracy is authoritarianism, and that democracy without discipline is anarchy.'[5]

But for the present it was back to authoritarianism, to the rigid rule of Reza Shah, for him. Nearly five years had changed nothing about his father, nor about their relationship. Crown Prince Mohammed still dared voice none of the criticisms he felt, make none of the suggestions he had considered. The heir to the throne had returned from a Swiss education, but the final honing of his character was to take place against the harsh conditions and hard traditions of his homeland. Only a deep-dyed Persian could possibly rule Persia.

Chapter 7

A Marriage is Arranged

WHEN the Crown Prince returned to Iran the feat of constructing the Trans-Iranian Railway was three-quarters completed. Ports and factories were opening and operating. The drift from countryside to town had begun. Women who still wore the *chodor* – the veil to which the working classes still clung, especially in remote and strictly religious areas – had it literally torn off them if they passed a policeman: the law that they should go barefaced was pitilessly enforced. Both country and heir were still subject to the absolute will and whim of Reza Shah. Deep within both the urge for change and independence stirred, but both country and Prince were bred with the Persian political instinct that urges flexibility, apparent compliance, caution, while any other plans mature within.

Overt resistance to the régime had been almost stamped out, but Iran still felt herself underprivileged. The Anglo-Persian Oil Company had sold the majority of its shares to the British Government in 1914; during the First World War huge amounts of oil had fuelled the British Navy but no accounts returned to the Iranian Government. In 1920 the sum of £1 million was given for the previous six years' consumption. Over the next ten years Iran continued to do very badly out of her most precious resource, which had become increasingly important with the changeover of many steamers from coal furnaces to oil, with the motor car, and the invention of the aeroplane.

In November 1932 Reza Shah decided to cancel the concession
and negotiate a new contract on terms more favourable to Iran.
In 1933 a new contract provided more for the Iranian Treasury
but deprived the leaders of the Bakhtiari tribe, in whose region
the richest deposits lay, of the 3 per cent royalty they had
enjoyed until now. Reza Shah offered to buy their holdings for a
peppercorn price.

Princess Soraya, a member of the Bakhtiari tribe on her
father's side, has described what happened next. One of her
uncles, the leader, refused the Shah's offer on behalf of them all.
Immediately, 'the Shah ordered his guards to take my uncle
away, and he then set about a methodical roundup of the
Bakhtiari. All my uncles were arrested.' Her father's eldest
brother, the leader, was condemned to death and shot. A message
was delivered to the rest of the family: 'It is a matter of the
deepest regret to His Majesty that he has been compelled to make
an example of your brother. Here is a deed of sale, drawn up in
legal form. Are you prepared to sign it?'[1] They were indeed.
And the sum they received was still lower than the previous
offer.

At Court the prevalent atmosphere was the same as it had
been when the Crown Prince left for Europe. Son obeyed
father in everything. But his thoughts were more independent
now. 'Luckily I discovered in Switzerland what the word freedom means,' Princess Soraya remembered him telling her later.
'I saw with my own eyes the advantages of a democratic education. From then on I was inwardly in revolt against my father,
and I took an oath to myself that as soon as I came to power I
would do everything quite differently from the way he did
it.'[2]

After a summer holiday the Crown Prince plunged into his
new work. It was two-tier. He was to spend two years at the
Military Academy in Tehran – he now says 'I am professionally
a soldier' – a copy of the famous French academy St Cyr, with
French military advisers. Still more important, he was to under-
study his father as Emperor: he had to present himself half an
hour before lunch for a 'discussion' which went on throughout
the meal; and was continued for an hour later. Reza Shah plied
his heir with questions, demanded solutions to real and hypo-

thetical problems, posed teasers and traps for him, pressed him
to produce plans for exigencies, exhorted, demanded, pressed,
pressed, pressed . . .

'The word "discussion" is really a misnomer,' he admitted
later. 'I, and all the officials of my father's Government, had such
respect for him and were so much in awe of him that "discussion" with him had none of the give-and-take the word implies.
I advanced my views and made hints and suggestions, but discussion in any usual sense was out of the question.'

It must have been a relief to escape back to the rigours of
military drill. In addition to the standard military course, he took
special advanced courses in strategy and tactics. In the spring of
1938, aged eighteen and a half, he graduated as second lieutenant:
a second lieutenant who had of course been a colonel for eleven
years.

Very occasionally now he dared to put forward a timid proposal or suggestion of his own. Still more occasionally, his father
listened. This was such a *volte-face* that he recorded a note of 'how
seldom he rejected my proposals'.

One such occasion, which he would later have cause bitterly
to regret, concerned Dr Mohammed Mossadeq, the most voci-
ferous critic of Reza Shah's assumption of power. As a very rich
landowner he saw the power of himself and his like being whittled
away by Reza Shah's steady policy of erosion of the influential
classes. Like Reza Shah himself Mossadeq was now nearly sixty;
and he was in poor health. But he had not ceased to agitate
against the upstart régime, and to do so with a loquacity and
style that attracted much attention and support. Along with
many others whose crime had been simply to oppose or criticize
his régime, Reza Shah took him as a political prisoner and
despatched him to one of Iran's most primitive and isolated
prisons.

Mohammed Reza, now nineteen, showed fresh signs of the
soft heart his father had feared in him as a child and had tried so
hard to harden. He suggested that his father should free Mossadeq. Incredibly, Reza Shah agreed.

Incredibly, that is, until one considers that there was another
result that could be expected from the Crown Prince's suggestion. In him idealism was closely twinned with practicality, even

expediency. He knew his father and his country better than to argue that Mossadeq should be released on humanitarian grounds *alone*. He knew the power of martyrdom, especially in a Muslim country. If Mossadeq should perish in his isolation and privation his enmity would be immortal. If he were released he might drop his vendetta against the Pahlavis, at least when the Crown Prince came to the throne. Reza Shah listened. And, in spite of the misgivings of Tadj-ol-Molouk, Mossadeq was released from what the Shah himself has called his 'unsavoury prison' a few months later.[3]

Reza Shah was perhaps still worried about his son's 'softness'; the Crown Prince, on the other hand, was beginning to appreciate that his father's demands and the strict régime that he had imposed on him had sprung from his father's desire to make him not only powerful but indeed *invulnerable* as a monarch.

Obviously he respected and instinctively loved his father. I asked: 'Would you say you liked him as well?' There was a considerable pause. Then he replied, briskly, 'Yes, I can say that as well.'[4]

But he was still inhibited by his reserve, the defence he had thrown up round himself in the family to protect himself against the overbearing personalities of both parents. This, if anything, had been deepened by his comparative isolation at school in Switzerland. While others had skiied and gone to parties, he had sat and thought. As a result, he felt that he had become perhaps *too* serious. Now the greatest reason for his reserve was to avoid arguments with Reza Shah. He also lacked confidence with strangers.

'When you were young did you feel perhaps that you were too shy and gentle?' I asked. 'I was; that I was,' he replied. 'I was shy: very, very.'

There was a considerable group of people, some half of the total, with whom he did not feel shy but, because of an instinctive sense of superiority to them, totally at ease: In feminine company the Crown Prince found that he could relax and feel confident. He was extremely interested in those around him – genuine unprying curiosity can be very appealing. He had great charm. He seemed sure of himself without being overbearing in the company of women. They found him attractive in himself:

and he was the Crown Prince, a fact of still greater importance in a country like Iran.

Reza Shah noted his son's movements, both for reasons of security and because he felt he should guide every aspect of the young man's life. He became perturbed as news of his latest interests piled up in reports on his desk. The Crown Prince loved adventure and speed, and was busily buying a string of the world's fastest sports cars. He loved night clubs, where he savoured an atmosphere so different from the spartan régime of the palace and the ascetic example and life of his father.

Reza Shah was concerned. Might Mohammed Reza turn out to be little better than some of the Qajar Shahs? Had his own early struggles to learn to read and write in his army tent at night, had the coup d'état of 1921, the hard separation from his son while the Crown Prince was in Switzerland, the endless hours of planning and drilling, had all this come to nothing? He considered his own life at the same age of nineteen. He had been married for two years. It was surely time for the Crown Prince too to marry, to make plans for the third layer of the Pahlavi dynasty.

Reza Shah did not mention any of these thoughts to his son. But he determined to scour the Middle East for a suitable bride for him. There were certain standard requirements: she should be a Muslim, pliant enough to be obedient, attractive enough to hold his son's attention, and combining the certainty of virginity with the probability of fertility. According to one of his contemporaries, Reza Shah was 'methodical and secretive'. This was an accurate assessment of everything in his political and public life, and now it became plain that that was also true in his personal affairs.

Arranged marriages were, and indeed still are, the norm in Iran as in other Middle Eastern countries. In spite of this, however, the couple concerned are usually aware of the arrangements as these are being made, and since cousins often marry, or the bride is the daughter of a colleague, there has usually been some chance for the couple to become acquainted. But as a patriarch who believed that he could judge all issues better than anyone else, Reza Shah had not the slightest intention or interest in ascertaining what his son's preferences about a bride might be.

The marriage must be a business contract, with international and political advantages.

'My father had evidently seen pictures of the lovely Princess Fawzia of Egypt. With his characteristic forthrightness – perhaps better adapted to engineering projects than affairs of the heart – he started his investigations. First he had the girl's pedigree checked.'[5]

Pedigree: the giveaway – to some Muslims a wife is only a chattel, sometimes a little more, sometimes a little less, valuable than one of his sheep; or she is a mare to breed from. Fawzia evidently passed the necessary quality-control tests. 'The first thing I knew I was betrothed,' the astonished Crown Prince said later. 'Up to that point I had never laid eyes on the girl.'

Cecil Beaton rhapsodized: 'If ever Boticelli were reincarnated and wished to paint an Asiatic Venus or Primavera here is his subject. He would delight in the Queen's features contained in a perfect heart-shaped face: strangely pale but piercing blue eyes; crimson-coloured lips curling like wrought-iron volutes; and the way in which the dark chestnut hair grows beautifully from the forehead.'[6]

At the quiet ceremony on 15 March 1939 they were married. For the first year of their marriage it was said that the young couple were rarely apart when the Prince was not working. Like her bridegroom Fawzia had been educated in Switzerland; and she was a comparatively modern girl who had never worn the veil. The couple had the same sporting interests. They enjoyed their home-made pursuits in the palace, dances with Paul Jones to mix the guests, amateur theatricals, riding, and, usually some four nights a week, a film show. But they had little real privacy. Princess Fawzia was expected to fit into her new family as if it were her own, and to obey her father-in-law, the Shah, and the Empress Tadj-ol-Molouk who, like the mother-in-law in many Iranian families, was the real ruler in home and personal affairs.

Fawzia was used to the luxury of the Egyptian court, one of the oldest and most sumptuous in the world, to the modern facilities of Cairo, and, as the eldest and most beautiful of the King's sisters, to having her own way in most things. Before long she felt homesick, isolated and thwarted in her new home. Iran was still at this time an extremely poor country and even at

Court there was no luxury, certainly no pampering, for the Princess.

Before long there were rumours that all was not as well as it might be in the household of the young royals. Soon the rumours became more specific: it was said that she refused to share the burdens of state, hated the climate, and felt that her young husband had a cruel streak.[7] There was doubtless some truth in the first two reports, but positive and deliberate cruelty in his private life would not seem in keeping with the character reports on Mohammed Reza which were given by his two later wives. But he was certainly self-centred.

It was some time before there was a complete break, which Mr Alam thinks came because 'she was under the influence of her brother later on'. But after the first year of their marriage the couple began to lead more separate lives in their separate apartments. Princess Fawzia had a trump card which neither of her successors held: she was a Princess in her own right, with a powerful King, family, and country to take her part if need be. Undoubtedly they had enjoyed some happy times together before the marriage soured. But in retrospect, the Shah today remembers the happiest part of his marriage as being the birth of his daughter, Princess Shahnaz, in 1940.

It was at this time that Mr Alam, whose father had been one of Reza Shah's first and firmest supporters, began to gain an intimate footing in the palace. He remembers that: 'The first time I met him personally was the day he summoned me to take pictures of the Princess Shahnaz, who was just born. I was very young. In those days photographers were not allowed to come to the Court so easily because Reza Shah the Great, he was a very strict soldier and didn't like people to wander round his palace – but as I had relations with Princess Ashraf through her marriage with my brother-in-law – just through that . . . [I had an entrée]. Princess Shahnaz was only five or six days old. He [the Crown Prince] was very excited.'

Was he disappointed that she was a girl, I wondered?

'Not at that time because they were hoping that a boy will come. In Persia we have a saying that if a girl comes she comes to clean the way for a boy.

'Afterwards he [the Crown Prince] used to summon me to

Court and little by little we started to become friendly, especially because his great father expressed his wish that people like me and his sort of people should be allowed to have the honour to be presented to His Royal Highness. The atmosphere with Reza Shah was very different. Reza Shah was a very tough soldier and was very careful about his children being mixed with other people – not because he didn't want them to be mixed, he was particular about mixing them with *good* people, those people who were known to him or his administration. And the Court atmosphere was very, very strict atmosphere – *very* strict atmosphere. For us it was impossible to be natural with him. Nobody could be natural with him because besides being a powerful military man he was also a *superman*. . . . In those days we were so *proud* of our country, that generation, and about what Reza Shah did that I think the whole youth had this in mind – that we have anyhow a supremacy *over the whole world* – it's a remarkable feeling, but all of us we had it.'[8]

By 1938 the majority of Iran's trade was with Germany, who supplied most of Iran's industrial machinery, railway materials and similar equipment. The Germans had also supplied a large number of pro-Nazi books, among others, to Iran's national library, and there was a large educational and cultural exchange between the two countries.

Reza Shah had formulated a plan to retire from the throne early in the 1940s and act only as a background counsellor to the new young Shah.[9] This explains the background to a conversation which took place when the Crown Prince was nineteen, and led to a minor crisis of anxiety.

'My father said that he wanted to improve the Government's administrative machinery to such a degree that, if he should die, the day-to-day process of administration would operate almost automatically without the need of continuous supervision from the top.

'I was still rather young and perhaps not very mature; and I took his remark as an insult. "What does he mean?" I thought. "Does he think that if he were gone I couldn't take over and continue his work?" Although naturally I didn't say anything, his remark nettled me.'

Personal feelings were overtaken by external events. On 1 September 1939 Hitler invaded Poland and set in motion a train of events that would lead to the abdication of Reza Shah. 'Maybe this is one of the reasons why I give so much freedom to my children, just to make up for myself,' the Shah says. 'When I was older there was not much time for anything because I got married very quickly; and then the war came. And during the war *who* expects to have any kind of pleasure? We were just remaining in the palace, that's all.'[10]

THE SHAH

Part II

Chapter 8

World War and Succession

REZA SHAH immediately stated that Iran would remain neutral.

To the Allies this must have seemed a suspect statement. Iran continued to import goods from Germany after the outbreak of war, and was used to the same authoritarian system of government. 'On the other hand,' the Shah claimed later, 'my father had little use for Hitler. . . . As a leader who himself had authoritarian tendencies, my father resented another dictator such as Hitler.'[1]

After Hitler's attack on Russia on 22 June 1941 Iran for the second time declared her neutrality. Churchill and Roosevelt promised to help Russia with armaments, food and raw materials. But how were they to reach Russia? The safest route lay through Iran. The recently completed Trans-Iranian Railway, which had previously seemed to run from nowhere to nowhere, suddenly made geographical sense. What irony! Reza Shah's greatest internal achievement was once more to help Iran's traditional exploiters, Britain and Russia.

In July 1941 a joint Anglo-Soviet Note demanded the expulsion of the Germans. Reza Shah hesitated, and was lost. He did not accede to the demands, nor did he throw in his hand with the Axis. Instead, he stalled, and tried to talk. 'Forgetting his dignity as a Sovereign, he went so far as to request his Minister in London to ask the Allies if they would explain their real needs and wants.'[2]

Iran was invaded simultaneously by Britain from the south-west and south, and by Russia from the north. The Russian and British troops met, and newsreel pictures showed them laughing together. It was announced that an allied front had now been formed 'from the arctic to Libya'.[3]

Three weeks passed – an enormously long time in the life of a man of action such as Reza Shah, now aged over sixty, who for forty-five years had been used to making decisions within seconds and demanding similar promptness from others. These three weeks must have been a time of great agony of mind. Finally, on 16 September 1941, he summoned the Crown Prince to his presence and without prior warning told him that he had decided to abdicate. He explained to his son: 'I cannot be the nominal head of an occupied land, to be dictated to by a minor English or Russian officer.'[4]

'I felt as if the ground on which I stood had been taken from under me. The world was foundering about us,' wrote General Arfa. And his wife remonstrated with a taxi-driver who took her the wrong way down a one-way street and received the sullen and despairing reply, 'Oh! It does not matter, now that Reza Shah has gone.'[5]

Ministers, officers, courtiers, were all now summoned to the palace to take the oath of allegiance to the twenty-one-year-old new Shah, Mohammed Reza Pahlavi. He knew, of course, that he faced an extraordinarily difficult situation. Reza Shah's pride had been well earned.

Sir Clarmont Skrine, who in 1942 was working at the British Consulate in Meshed, later described the difference between the Persia of 1918 and the Iran of 1942. The Armistice celebrations at the end of the First World War had included a public feeding of the poor by the Allies. A repeat performance was planned in 1942, but 'word had also got round that any Persian going to either of the Consulates-General and asking for food would get into trouble. . . . No Persian unconnected with the arrangements came near the place.' Why? The answer was very simple. 'National pride was hurt by the implication that Persians were so backward, so lacking in public spirit, so incapable of managing their own affairs, as to let foreigners publicly feed their poorer fellow citizens on a large scale.'⁶ What a lesson in the proud and independent attitude of the new Iran.

Reza Shah had abdicated not only his pride, his power and responsibilities, but also his difficulties, to an heir three weeks short of his twenty-second birthday. Eleven days later, on 27 September, Reza Shah, no longer a fit man, was taken by packet boat from Bandar Abbas to the British steamer *Bandra*.

The *Bandra* had been due to sail for Bombay. The former Shah hoped to go from there to Canada to settle, but he was not even allowed to choose his place of exile: when the *Bandra* was only six miles from Bombay he was transferred to another vessel, the *Burmah*, and taken to Mauritius. The climate, so different from the high and very dry climate of Tehran, did not suit him and eventually he was taken to South Africa.

Into exile with Reza Shah went his favourite and fourth wife, Esmat (Chastity), the new Shah's only full-blood brother Prince Ali Reza, his older sister Princess Shams, a docile and compliant daughter, Princess Fatemah (Esmat's daughter), and all Mohammed Reza's half-brothers – Prince Gholam Reza, and Esmat's sons, the Princes Abdul Reza, Mahmoud Reza, Ahmad Reza, and Hamid Reza.

Left behind in Tehran with the new Shah were his mother, Tadj-ol-Molouk, as determined as ever, his fiery twin sister Ashraf, and Princess Fawzia herself, in whose company Mohammed Reza found increasingly less pleasure and consolation.

Reza Shah had sent his son and sovereign a telegram as he was leaving Iran. It read simply: 'Your Majesty, never be afraid of anything.' But though the young Shah might not be afraid at the moment, he was, by nature of the extraordinary forces surrounding him, thwarted, powerless, and, as would later become apparent, furious. Not for nothing was he a Persian, bred with a fine feeling for intrigue, and hardened to withstand political heat and pressure.

He behaved magnanimously with many about whom his true feelings must have been at least ambivalent. But externally his attitude was extremely cool and lucid, and while his feelings about the reoccupation of his country could doubtless have filled a library with invective he has nearly always restrained himself.

F

His true feelings were shown most clearly years later, when he publicly regretted that he had not adopted a scorched earth policy to stop the Allies gaining a foothold on pure Iranian soil. 'We could have mined all the bridges, railroads and major highways so that Iran could not be considered a communication link for the invading armies. We should have taken measures aimed at denying our vital oil resources to the invader.'[7]

Shah Mohammed Reza's passions have always been muted by the toning power of reason. In modern political terms this is a strength, not a weakness. The young Shah who burned to see the invaders fall into a bottomless pit of their own or of his making behaved affably with them and conscientiously sought to win the best for his country through diplomacy. His main and immediate internal task was to reunite and boost the morale of his people, and to give them confidence in his ability to lead them, albeit under the pall of the Allies. So he must create a new foreign policy.

After he had been on the throne for only four and a half months Iran signed a tripartite agreement with Britain and Russia. This insisted that the Allied occupation of Iran did not constitute a 'military occupation', and that foreign troops would be withdrawn from Iranian soil within six months of the end of the war. He also made sure of his witnesses.

On 31 January 1942, two days after the signing of the Treaty, the Shah sent a telegram to President Roosevelt, drawing his attention to the Treaty.

Roosevelt's reply, dated 6 February 1942, included the statement: 'I have taken note of this treaty and am gratified to observe among its provisions an undertaking by the Allied Powers to respect the territorial integrity, the sovereignty and the political independence of Iran.'[8] If Germany was *non grata* as a third power now, the US was enlisted as an arbiter in advance.

This was no small achievement for someone who, until September 1941, had lived in the shadow of a super-Shah. Admittedly in the very last years of his rule Reza Shah had not shown the dynamic thrust that he had shown immediately after the coup d'état but the Crown Prince's own power had been purely theoretical. It is no wonder that he admitted later he had felt (with the slightest of misquotations) that he had been plunged in a 'sea of trouble': in real life, as for Hamlet, the troubles were many. But one British observer realized that the Shah was 'bound to lose some of his popularity now that his position of a strongly defended neutrality has failed'.[9]

He was in a doubly difficult position at home. No one has captured better than General Arfa the air of outrage, frustration and smouldering resentment that prevailed among the Iranians, and particularly the young army officers, when they saw their country once more brought to heel by Russia and Britain:

> They were obliged, by special order, to salute foreign soldiers of a superior rank, although foreign soldiers, NCOs and officers did not bother to salute the Iranians, in spite of the order they had received to do so. . . . They were unanimously pro-German . . .
> Foreigners walking and talking with Iranian girls drove the Iranians to acts of disrespect towards the Allied officers and caused brawls with them and noisy demonstrations of loyalty to the young Sovereign, who had become the symbol of Iranian independence and was *supposed* to share their feelings and ideas [my italics].[10]

Supposed: how deeply in fact he did so, and how hard it was to let his people know this. It was just one more layer of irony in the emotionally deep and desperate situation in which he was determined that the new Iran, built by his father, should not drown.

Politically, the situation threatened to become still more humiliating, as well as internally unstable. In 1942 there was a grain shortage, followed by the worst bread-riots in Tehran for many years. 'On 12th December 1942 a mob attacked and tried to burn down the house of the Prime Minister, Ahmed Qavam, and another demonstrated outside the *Majlis*. Persian troops put down the rioting with machine guns and some loss of life, and the Prime Minister ordered the suspension of all newspapers; later, he resigned.'[11] At the same moment the British, without consulting the Shah *at all*, arrested one of his most senior officers, General Zahedi, in Isfahan. If they could do this, the Shah thought, they would 'do anything'.[12] American observers were deeply concerned at the tremendous cutting edge felt in the relationship between the Iranians and the British at this time.

In spite of these difficulties, the Allies, who were paying their forces in Iranian money, demanded that more currency should be circulated: Qavam had refused the request, explaining that the *Majlis* would never ratify such a decision. 'So one day the British Ambassador came to see me,' the Shah said later. 'He then asked me to dissolve Parliament. What a proposal by the representative of a foreign power!' The Shah refused the request, but when British troops later entered the capital to quell some of the disturbances which originated from the people's hunger and unhappiness he claimed that 'they intimidated Parliament into meeting their demands'.[13]

Morale in the country was low. There was a black market in sugar;[14] and the result of speculation and hoarding was that the rich grew richer and the poor grew poorer. Such soil provided ideal conditions for the growth of a political party which had been formed about the time of Reza Shah's abdication. The party had originated among fifty-two Communists who had been political prisoners under Reza Shah but had been released under a political amnesty following the Allied invasion. It introduced itself in the autumn of 1941 as the Tudeh (masses) Party, 'in order not to frighten the public by the term Communist'.[15] It says much for the local loyalties which had always been so strong in the feudal structure of Iran, that in spite of the low standard of living and morale that had followed the occupation, the Tudeh Party did not sweep the country.

Less than three months after it was formed, a pro-German party was formed.[16] But the only party in opposition to the Establishment that had any real popular following was the Tudeh Party. Strangely, the British as well as the Russians received some blame in the Shah's thoughts for the party's influence. Sir Clarmont Skrine commented: 'Truly, the myth that the British are behind everything dies hard. It was a standing joke among our friends at Meshed. "If a Persian divorces his wife", they used to say, "it was the British who made him do it."'[17]

The Iranian way of settling things and making decisions was very clearly shown by two events in the autumn of 1943. The first was the Shah's declaration of war on Nazi Germany, which came on 9 September. The date is important. As an official biographer, Ramesh Sangvi, has pointed out: 'By the summer of 1943 he had little doubt as to the ultimate outcome of war.'[18]

His declaration of war was no gamble but a simple throwing-in of his hand with the side he was now certain would win. If, in fact, the Germans had broken through the Russian line of defence at the Caucasus, they would have had access to the communications and oil that the Allies were using: and the Shah himself has pointed out in his memoirs that 'in all honesty' he cannot claim all the credit for the fact that there were no acts of sabotage in Iran during this period: he thought the Germans had postponed any such action in the hope of utilizing the supplies and supply lines themselves.[19]

The other illuminating event in the autumn of 1943 was the election of the fourteenth *Majlis*. At Meshed much comment was aroused by the fact that the Tudeh candidate, who according to all objective calculations should have won, lost to a local grandee. It was rumoured that the Soviet Commandant had complained about the result, and the Tudeh candidate was returned for another constituency. 'It became obvious to everyone that the Administration had to let him in,' commented Sir Clarmont Skrine, 'but drew the line at returning him for the provincial capital.'[20] Such substitution was possible because the custom in Reza Shah's time was still instinctively followed. Under Reza, provincial elections to the *Majlis* were conducted by an Election Committee appointed by the Tehran Government. 'Sometimes there was trouble, but the Tehran Government usually got their way in the end.' Eight Tudeh Deputies were returned in 1943, all from the northern provinces close to Russian backing. 'What none of us realized at the time was that Moscow aimed at quality rather than quantity in the Communist block they needed in the *Majlis*.'[21]

Small wonder that at this time particularly the Shah's words ring true: 'During the occupation I was full of sorrow and had many sleepless nights. . . . I was revolted by the way in which some wealthy Persians became yet more bloated, in utter disregard of the welfare of their country.'[22] Both the Shah and the Allies wondered whether it was possible to reverse this trend in time to save the country from total corruption which would almost inevitably lead in turn to a Tudeh-led revolution.

This was the background that led to the rather surprising venue of the Tehran Conference between the Three Big Powers,

Russia, Britain, and the United States, in the autumn of 1943. It was plainly something of a *quid pro quo*. There was much to be grateful for: the Western Allies sent over five million tons of goods to the Soviet Union via Iran during the war, and Iran's oil was continuing to fuel all types of Allied armaments.

Sir Clarmont Skrine thought that the Persians were 'secretly flattered' by the choice of Tehran for the conference of those rightly termed by an Indian filing clerk the 'Three Bigs'. It was known that the idea had been put forward of establishing a more rigorous and active occupation of Iran, complete with a puppet Government.[23] But the United States, now ultra-conscious of Russia's ambitions in this part of the world, was determined to support democracy.

If anything, the Shah felt still more nervous about Russian intentions. Here again, he believed, the Americans could prove not merely valuable allies but an actual fulcrum round which the balance of tripartite power could be tipped to Iran's advantage. From this moment on, the young Shah began to feel that he was at last beginning to impress the Allies with some of the depth and weight he intended in future to wield as the Shah of Iran.

At the Tehran Conference the fate of Poland was sealed: the Allies had saved it from Germany only now to abandon it to Russia. The Shah was determined this should not happen to Iran. His fears were well based. General Arfa wrote that he was

> informed by a usually trustworthy source that in the entourage of Stalin the formation of independent entities in Iranian Azerbaijan, Gilan, Mazanderan and Gorgan had been envisaged, which would after a time secede from Iran and join the Soviet Republics of Soviet Azerbaijan and Turkmenistan; and in the same way, with the cooperation of the Tudeh, the coming to power in Teheran of a progressive Government would be encouraged, this Government to be in close alliance with the Soviet Union.[24]

It was chiefly to prevent the possibility of this last idea becoming fact that made Roosevelt hasten to take his seat at the Tehran Conference table.

He was to become the key figure in Iran's chessboard future. In many ways he and the young Shah seem to have got along and understood each other well. Roosevelt's earnestness of manner, and in particular his great interest in afforestation – he even suggested that when his term of office was over he should return to Iran to act as an adviser in this very field – seem to have partly surprised, partly delighted the Shah.

Roosevelt was staying at the Russian Embassy, where the conference meetings were held. With his physical disability, it was understandable that Roosevelt should ask his host to visit him, rather than that he should himself travel to see the Shah. But in Iran etiquette can have political consequences. It was Russia, the Communist bear, who received full marks for courtesy. Only Stalin visited the Shah in his own palace. (Stalin's birthplace, Georgia, had indeed still belonged to Iran in the early nineteenth century.) The Shah hid even from himself the humiliation felt at having to ignore the discourtesy of those who knew no better when he was invited to visit Roosevelt. But he allowed a hint of disapproval to escape in his memoirs: 'It seemed a curious situation that I had to go to the Russian embassy to see him, while Stalin came to see me.'[25]

Stalin came close to getting what he wanted. He was, the Shah recalled later, 'particularly polite and well-mannered, and he seemed intent upon making a good impression on me'. How soothing this was to the pride of the twenty-five-year-old Shah who was a ruler without power.

Stalin had not come unprepared. 'He went so far as to offer me a regiment of T34 tanks and one of fighter planes, and in view of our desperate shortage of modern arms I was most tempted,' said the Shah. 'But a few weeks later, when his offer was stated in more specific terms, some onerous conditions were laid down. Russian officers and NCOs would have to come with the gifts.' The writing on the wall was plain. 'I declined with thanks.'[26]

The Americans had read the message too, and they acted promptly. The Tehran Declaration at the end of the conference promised the future independence of Iran. Also, General Arfa states laconically, 'About this time the US Persian Gulf Command was organized.'[27] In fact it had been formed in 1942, but it was now that the US realized the importance of topping up this force and keeping its strength obvious. It grew to comprise nearly 20,000 men, and although it did not comprise fighting units, and had in theory to be nominated part of the British occupying forces – since the US had not participated in the Tripartite Treaty with Iran signed nearly two years before – it was a vivid reminder to the increasingly active Russian forces that in taking any liberties with Iran's future Russia would have to reckon with the US.

At the age of twenty-five the Shah had shown that if he and his country had once more to drink from the bitter cup of humiliation and occupation he could sweeten the drink with the sugar of Persian adroitness, adding the promise of US intervention so that any after-effects would be less toxic. By having so many tough problems at the very outset of his career, by being forced to bend in so many opposing directions, balancing the weight of outside powers round the fulcrum of his own intelligence, he was developing a resilient pliability that would ensure his survival as man and Shah. But this internal growth of his had to be paid for, both now and in the future. An undue sensitivity to criticism, voiced or suspected, was beginning to flare in his deepest nature. Any Persian is a naturally suspicious man: when he is Shah suspicion becomes part of the defence of territory, and is at once more resonant and more exploitable. More than thirty years ahead his character and his country would bear the marks of the Second World War, some of them good, some bad, and many capable of being put to variable use by the unscrupulous. He was a man who, as it now began to be seen, had been born for the times in which he was to rule.

On 1 July 1944, Tehran radio broadcast the news of Reza Shah's death in Johannesburg. The news must have brought home to Shah Mohammed Reza more sharply than anything else had done the fact that he was now solely responsible for his own and his country's future. From now on he would have to be his own father and philosopher. Now there was no one to react against. The future stretched ahead, empty and limitless.

Nearly four years' separation made this final separation easier to bear. It was some years now since he had feared his father at a conscious level. The four years of rule had provided an emotional cushion against the old man's love, as well as his domination. The Shah might break down and weep when his father's coffin was returned to its homeland, the exiled bones at least in peace. But he, Mohammed Reza, was already established as Shah in his own mind. He remembers: 'Well, he was outside the country. I felt . . . I felt *bad*, but again – probably this is because I have got to be the way I am – well, life was not finished, I had to carry on.'[28] If any thought echoed in the sad chambers of his mind that night as he tried to sleep at the palace, it was probably his father's telegram: 'Your Majesty, fear nothing.'

Chapter 9

Oil and Politics

Mohammed Reza Shah Pahlavi and his country both suffered
identity crises at the end of the Second World War. Iran was like
a chessboard with the so-called Allies already beginning to vie
with one another for influence, adroitly manoeuvring their own
pawns. But it seemed that nobody was taking very much notice
of the King, the Shah himself:

'Our democracy was imposed upon us by the British. And
how could you have democracy in a country where 99 per cent
of the people were illiterate? You just wanted that because you
could manipulate the Deputy [Persian Member of Parliament],
the Parliament, and this and that – a King really firmly seated on
his throne could not be handled as easily as Deputies who will
have to be re-elected every now and then. Because of your
influence with some segment of our population you were mani-
pulating those things so you wanted this kind of a régime. Why
did you want that? Because on the other side the Russians were
for the Absolute Monarch who was leaning to the Russians. But
it's true that there was tendencies everywhere – even in Turkey
and Iran – to having some kind of democratic system, because in
those days democracy was meaning much more, meaning much
more . . .'

'And you were influenced by your education in Switzerland?'

'No doubt; no doubt. And also there was nothing else to do
in those days, because the Occupying Force, the British and the

Russians, wanted a very weak monarch. And I was very young. So obviously then I was even less than a constitutional monarch, because even that could not be applied exactly because again the British and the Russians wanted a weaker monarch than even our Constitution allowed. So obviously in those days I was called a playboy and a weakling, that my twin sister would have been a much better man than myself. . . . Then the more we could take ourselves away from the foreign influence the more we had authority in the country: again it's normal and natural. Because any country, foreign country, who wants to have influence in another country tries to create complete disorder and – you know, divide and rule! So by the order of things in the normal way the less there was foreign influence the more the King re-asserted himself, in the eyes of his people, which is for us a normal thing. They have always known that, for 3,000 years of history – for us it's normal.'

'But I wonder if you were at all disappointed that your own hopes of perhaps ruling an ideal state in an ideal way couldn't take effect immediately?'

'Well, I was, I think *not completely blind and fool*, to believe that you could have an ideal state in a country where you have 99 per cent of illiteracy: how could you have that? How could illiterate people decide what – how to rule themselves? So it has to come, gradually, in the future. But in an orderly way, an orderly manner, I do not want this country to experience what I call the permissiveness of the Western societies. Why should we? What *good* would it make?'[1]

To add to his gall, not all of this subterranean interference was foreign based. The Russians had made inroads into the country through the Tudeh Party. The British still had the strength of the Anglo-Iranian Oil Company to play with, and were also accused of stirring up tribal resentment and discontentment; they were also thought to have links with the *mullahs*.

The United States had her own master-plotter on the scene. This was Colonel H. Norman Schwarzkopf (whose daughter was later to become famous as Elisabeth Schwarzkopf, the singer). He was a former Chief of New Jersey State Police, known simply as 'the Gang-basher'.[2] He arrived in Iran in 1942 to reorganize the Gendarmerie, a task which he and a team of Americans accomplished in an extremely thorough way and an incredibly short time. They were not popular. On 17 July 1944 one of the leaders of the opposition rose in Parliament to criticize the Americans. 'Their behaviour is rough and rude,' sneered Amini.

Nor were Americans tactful in their judgments or in the way they voiced them. Dr Millspaugh's book on his experiences on his second-time-around administration of Persian finances, covering the years 1943–45, said: 'The Persian government has always ranked as one of the most corrupt in the world. . . . It appears to me much more corrupt than it was in 1922.' And it was in a state of flux. In his sphere of finance alone he found himself working under four Prime Ministers and seven Finance Ministers in 1943–44, 'to say nothing of two or three extended interregnums when we had no Minister'.[3]

Dr Mossadeq also stepped into the limelight. Born in or around 1880 (he is believed to have varied the date for political convenience, in particular so that he never became too old to serve in the *Majlis*) he was the son of Mirza Hedayat, a former Persian Minister of Finance, and Najmos-Saltaneh, who was a Qajar princess and a cousin of Nasr ed-Din Shah. He was exceedingly rich, and one of Iran's leading landlords.

In the past he had had a few modern ideas of his own. Not all of them had been altruistic, and after one misdemeanour in his teens when he was a provincial governor under the Qajars he was sentenced, in spite of his princely birth, to the *bastinado*. This traditional Persian beating knows no class boundaries as far as its severity goes – when one Shah went to sleep forgetting to tell the two men who beat the prisoner to stop his own son had died by the time he woke again – but for those of high birth the blows are perhaps psychologically softened by the fact that the punishment is carried out on a silk carpet.

He was twice exiled under the Qajars, and took advantage of his time abroad to round off his education in France and Switzerland. He held a law degree. In 1922 he became Minister of Finance, and cut the salaries of all Deputies and bureaucrats including his own (he was rich enough not to notice the difference) which led to yet another period of exile while Reza Shah was Minister of War and effectively running the country.

From then on he frequently crossed swords with Reza Shah,

whom he accused of being a traitor in building the trans-
Iranian railway that was put to their own use by the Allies in the
Second World War. This had led to the period in prison which
had broken his health, leaving him with ulcers and a famous diet
of cakes and tea. Released at Mohammed Reza's instigation, he
was re-elected in the fatefully muddled *Majlis* of 1943.

He was to become one of the foremost figures in foreign
cartoons, using whatever extravagant, even self-hurtful, weapons
he could bend to bring his cause fame in his passionate but short-
sighted patriotism and his resolve to return Persia to a past where
her oil was her own, her princes many, the Pahlavis gone. He
would often fall into a dead faint after his speeches in the *Majlis*
and have to be carried out feet first. He received ambassadors
and foreign correspondents alike in bed, clad in pyjamas, his
high-domed almost bald head and frail body (encouraged to
stay so after his sojourn in prison) making such levées a spectacle
between obscene and ludicrous – but worth it all to him, because
unforgettable.

This was the scene, this the cast of characters when in 1944
the experts noted that Iran was now the fourth largest oil-
producing country in the world. Late in September 1944 the
Assistant Commissar for Foreign Affairs of the USSR, Sergei
Kavtaradze, arrived in Tehran. A few days later he revealed that
his real purpose was to demand an oil concession for the Soviet
Union which would cover the five Northern Provinces. On 16
October 1944 the Prime Minister Saed announced that the
Iranian Government was rejecting all applications for concessions. The US Government, through her ambassador in Iran,
supported the Government's right to refuse oil concessions to
foreigners.

Soon afterwards Dr Mossadeq made his first dramatic excur-
sion into oil politics when he introduced a Bill that would make
it an offence for any Cabinet Minister to grant an oil concession
without the prior approval of Parliament. Sir Clarmont Skrine
noted that 'it was at this juncture that Dr Mossadeq first became
a national figure'.[4]

It was the beginning of the Cold War between the Allies, and
a period of extraordinary internal difficulty for Iran. The Shah
had been concentrating all his energies on maintaining as much

as possible of Iran's integrity and independence. Now he realized how dangerous the internal situation was becoming: and the popular feeling that Dr Mossadeq had at once aroused did not escape his closest attention.

The Shah's account of the methods he used to try to use Mossadeq's growing energy and power to fuel his own resources deserves study. It gives some idea of the paramount fluidity and flexibility which surround the inner core of the Persian personality, acting as an essential lubricant in all relationships. It is this purpose-concealing ambiguity that epitomizes the Iranian attitude to politics and policies.

The Shah summoned Mossadeq and offered to appoint him Prime Minister, on one condition: that he then called for a fresh general election, and made sure that it was held 'without alien influence'. Certainly, replied Dr Mossadeq, but, on *two* conditions. The age-old Persian process of bargaining was under way once more. The Shah merely asked what these might be. Mossadeq replied that, first, he would need a bodyguard. The Shah agreed. Secondly, said Mossadeq, he would need the prior approval of the British *to the whole plan*.

The Shah was astounded in view of the motive he had just explained to his father's old adversary, and no doubt, was both serious and satirical when he asked him 'What about the Russians?'

'Oh, they don't count,' he replied. 'It is the British who decide everything in this country.' The Shah remonstrated with him, and reminded him of Reza Shah's successful nationalism, but to no avail. What gives great insight into both the Shah's own nature and attitudes, putting concern for his country before any personal feelings, was the Shah's next move. 'I found this attitude disturbing and dangerous,' he confessed later. 'Yet I had to take into account the delicate situation in my country. . . . In a crisis Mossadeq's patriotism and popular appeal could be invaluable.'[5]

He knew, in other words, that he was sitting at the top of a house of cards still more flimsy than Persian society so often over the centuries had proved to be. The energies of one of his greatest potential adversaries would have been doubly useful to him in the position he suggested. He also doubtless had a feeling of personal security when discussing international affairs with

Mossadeq, for though the latter was virtually intoxicated from imbibing his fellow countrymen's ambitions, whose well-known rhythms virtually made his own blood hum with power, he was a non-starter in the international field, in which the Shah had been educated for almost twenty years.

To comply with Mossadeq's demand for British approval while of course appearing not to comply with it (a *sine qua non* in an Eastern ruler, let alone a Shah), the Shah asked not only the British for their opinion of the plan for a new Prime Minister and elections, but also the Russians. The Soviet Ambassador had no objection, but the British Ambassador said new elections would be upsetting just then.

The Shah telephoned Mossadeq and reported these results to him. '"Thank you very much," he replied,' and the Shah added drily, 'and there ended the conversation and his interest in holding new elections.'[6]

The end of the war in Europe in May 1945 meant the beginning of a period of great danger for Iran. Russia was now one of the world's two greatest powers. Both the Shah and members of the *Majlis* were still in the relatively early stages of learning how to govern in the wake of Reza Shah's autocratic methods and the Allies' interventions, and British, American, and Russian troops were still on Iranian soil. The Tripartite Agreement had stipulated that British and Russian troops must leave the country no later than six months from the end of hostilities.

The period that followed was something of a political free-for-all. No Iranian, including the Shah, was absolutely certain of whom he could trust in Iran, let alone outside the country. For the first time since its very early days, the *Majlis* began to show signs of realizing that it did in fact wield power. It voted to grant no further oil concessions until all foreign troops were withdrawn.

On 19 May 1945 Iran demanded of Britain and Russia that they withdraw their troops.[7] Both countries stated in their replies that they had no legal obligation to evacuate soldiers until six months had elapsed from the end of hostilities. The date for the departure of British and Russian forces was finally set at 2 March 1946.

Britain, however, did begin to withdraw her troops, and this gave the Iranians extra fuel for an argument that now choked the diplomatic channels between Tehran and Moscow. At last in August 1945 the Russians left Tehran; but they showed no signs of leaving the north. This was thus, in practice, under Soviet domination.

In November 1945, with only three months left to go to the deadline for the evacuation of foreign troops from Iran, the blow fell: Soviet sponsored 'People's Republics' were proclaimed in Persian Azerbaijan and in Kurdistan. On 17 November, the second day of the coup, the Iranian Central Government informed the Soviet Embassy that it would be sending a military force into the area to quell the 'rebellion'.[8]

The Shah's forces set out to dislodge the takeover, but when they reached Qazvin, at the border of the Soviet zone, on the way to Tabriz, they were halted by Soviet troops. The Shah immediately protested to all the Allied Powers. Ernest Bevin, then British Foreign Secretary, suggested that a committee of the three Allies, the Soviet Union, Britain, and the United States should consider the position of Iran and settle privately the fate of Azerbaijan and Kurdistan. Not unnaturally, this incensed the Shah.

The US Government protested on 24 November, but in mild terms, suggesting that all Allied forces should be withdrawn from Iran by 1 January. This was not enough for the Shah. On 11 January 1946 the Iranian Government appealed to the United Nations Security Council, complaining that the USSR was interfering in its internal affairs and endangering Iranian security. The US finally voted for a resolution which recommended that Iran and the Soviet Union should solve 'the difficulties' by direct negotiation: meanwhile the Security Council would keep the complaint on its agenda.

The Shah's decision to bring the question of relations between Iran and the Soviet Union to the arena of world interest was of crucial importance. But, in the words of Alan Ford, 'the main credit for extricating Iran from a dangerous situation must go to the Iranian government itself, and especially to its new Prime Minister, Ahmed Qavam'.[9]

Qavam was a polished man: and a loner. He was voted into power by a margin of one vote on 26 January 1946. The last months of 1945 had been spent, as Peter Avery sums it up, in lulling Russian suspicions in Tehran by 'various accommodatory moves, typically in the Persian tradition of trying to placate an enemy or make him think that there are no real grounds for hostility and that his position is granted'.[10]

The Russians, and indeed the Shah himself, seem to have believed that Qavam's installation in the Prime Minister's chair would mean further real concessions to the USSR. Qavam had been helpful to the Tudeh candidates in the elections of 1943. A special Soviet plane flew him to Moscow for top-level discussions.

At the beginning of March the last 600 British troops were withdrawn. On 10 March Qavam returned from Moscow – but with no undertaking that Soviet troops would be withdrawn.

Qavam suggested that Husain Ala, the Iranian delegate to the United Nations, should withdraw Iran's complaint about the Russian occupation. Instead, Ala at once reported to the Security Council that direct negotiations between his country and the Soviet Union had failed. The new President of the United States, Truman, was forced to take notice. He sent a message, virtually an ultimatum, to Stalin, demanding that he honour his commitments under the Tripartite Treaty.

On 24 March the Soviet Ambassador told Qavam that complete withdrawal of Russian troops would begin that very day: but he gave no date for when the withdrawal would actually *end*. However, Mr Gromyko, the Soviet delegate to the UN Security Council, suggested that the withdrawal might be completed within five or six weeks 'if no unforeseen circumstances occur'. But eventually Gromyko walked angrily out of the Security Council.

Next the USSR promised to withdraw all Soviet troops in return for the long-desired oil concession in the north. On 5 April the *Majlis* approved this agreement on condition that Persian Azerbaijan should be free of Russian troops within six weeks from 24 March. The agreement provided for the combined Russo-Iranian oil venture to be submitted to the *Majlis* within seven months from 24 March – a vital date, chosen with particular Persian precision, for by then a new *Majlis* would be sitting.

G

The Russians were outdone. Convinced, as indeed his own
Shah was, of Qavam's sincerity in his friendly dealings with
them, they began to withdraw their troops, and the last Russian
soldier left Iranian soil on 9 May 1946. The Azerbaijan and
Kurdistan republics collapsed, and after a year and a half of
masterly procrastination the new *Majlis* finally refused ratifica-
tion of the promised oil concession by a vote of 102 to 2.

While recognizing his skills, the Shah seems never to have
felt sure of Qavam after these negotiations with Russia. Whether
the older man's sleight-of-hand made him feel youthfully in-
adequate, or whether he really believed that Qavam had been
prepared to betray Iran, he was on his guard. He judged publicly that Qavam, in spite of the brilliant outcome of the negotiations, 'seemed to be under the influence of the Russians'.[11]
But was this really patriotism – or pique?

Just before the signing of the final agreement with the
Russians, Qavam sought an audience with the Shah and, in tones
reminiscent of Reza Shah, suggested that Iran could not have
two rulers: either Shah Mohammed Reza Pahlavi must take all
the decisions, or they should be left to himself, Prime Minister
Qavam. It was a difficult, and in some ways a humiliating, moment. The Shah, now aged twenty-eight, had impressed the
'Three Bigs'. But the footwork of the victory over Russia was
being worked out by Qavam. A false move, a proud move, at
this moment could have left Russia in control of northern Iran.
Shah Mohammed had to bow to fate, and to Qavam. He
granted the Prime Minister's request for complete authority until
the fifteenth *Majlis* was convened. Small wonder that, in spite of
the successful outcome of Qavam's masterplan, he could never
really forgive him for what he had achieved.

Tudeh organized agitations among the oil-workers in the
south-west led to a general strike among the Anglo-Iranian Oil
Company's workers in Khuzistan. The disturbances were so
serious and the Central Government felt itself to be so weak that,
to add to the Shah's anger, the British Government decided to
send a brigade of troops from India to Basrah to protect the
AIOC's installations: their presence was sufficient to quell the
riots. This was the last use of forces from an undivided India
under British direction.[12]

But from November onwards the Shah began to assert himself, to become a more evident power. The Tudeh later admitted that part of Qavam's success in duping them so easily had come from the fact that they had expected him to be more severely hampered by his bad relations with the Shah.

In December Iranian troops gradually moved throughout Azerbaijan province. The quelling of Tudeh resistance had been bloody and had lasted for months. But at last, six months later, the Shah could enter the province which for centuries, as the training ground of successive crown princes, had held slightly aloof from the Central Government and which had so nearly fallen totally under the Soviet spell.

Many of those who might have resisted him still were dead. From the living came a rapturous welcome. His car was frequently blocked by crowds of cars. Sheep, bulls and cows were slaughtered in his honour. In one village a peasant had dressed his son in white and crowned him with flowers. He wanted to sacrifice him in honour of the Shahanshah, and had to be firmly prevented from carrying out his intention. The Shah returned to Tehran and said:

> The warm and affectionate sentiment which I observe in the people encourages me more than ever in my desire to serve. However selfish I might be, I realize fully that the power of Kingship depends upon the power of the nation. And the pedestals of the throne have their security in the hearts of the people. My wish is that every Iranian will benefit equally from his national and social rights and that the sacred principles of the constitution and real democracy are perfectly established in my country.[13]

It was his wish, but remembering the tragedy of Iran's past and still shuddering inwardly at the vision of Azerbaijan poised, as it had been, on the verge of the Soviet precipice, he knew that it might be a long, rough and ruthless road to the realization of his wish. If necessary he would use force to see his dreams for his country come true.

Chapter 10

First Assassination Attempt

THE Shah's private life had brought him no more happiness than affairs of state over the past few years. His closest companion was his twin sister, Ashraf, whose fiery temperament offset his own reflective nature. Soraya, who was to become the Shah's second wife, later wrote that Princess Shams told her, soon after she arrived in Tehran, 'It was Ashraf who ultimately was responsible for the break-up of Fawzia's marriage. I must warn you against my sister. She is an ambitious, scheming person.'[1] But outside influences seem only to have fanned the flames of what was a spontaneous combustion of incompatability. The war itself must take part of the blame: the young couple could not travel, the Shah had no real outlet for his ambitions for his country and for his talents, and they were driven back on a relationship enclosed in an enforced proximity. The palace was their mutual prison.

By the end of the same year, 1947, Fawzia had had more than enough: and with the war over there was nothing to prevent her leaving Iran. She decided to return to Egypt, and was there by the end of the year. Moreover she took their only child, Shahnaz, with her; the Shah was not to see his daughter again for five years – a sad reflection of what had happened during his own adolescence for very different reasons.

Fawzia demanded a divorce, and it was granted on 19 November 1948. The Shah was once more a free man, and for a time he indulged once more his old pursuit of night-clubbing, as well as keeping up his riding and other sports. There were many rumours of the different young women who accompanied His Majesty on his various excursions. As Princess Soraya, who had several years to study his inclinations, was to write later, the feminine and female type 'that appealed to him most was the European'. But, she added, 'so far as I know he never considered marrying any of these other women. He had far too much common sense for that'.[2]

Suddenly, on 4 February 1949, something happened which changed Mohammed Reza's view of himself and made him desperately conscious of the total isolation with which a Shah is always surrounded. Someone tried to kill him. And they came within inches of succeeding.

As usual, snow lay deep on the ground in Tehran at this time of year, 4 February, and the journey from the winter palace to the University of Tehran, where he was to attend the annual commemoration of the founding of the university (one of Reza Shah's greatest achievements) took some little time. The twenty-nine-year-old Shah was accompanied by his half-brother, Gholam Reza. Unlike Mossadeq, it had never occurred to him that he needed a bodyguard. And no one else had thought to insist that he should be provided with one.

Mohammed Reza Pahlavi did not provide the easy target that his father would have done. He was of little more than average height, fairly slim, and kept in excellent physical trim not only by his love of sport – particularly horse-riding and tennis – but also by daily exercises and an unadventurous diet. He was also, and this was to prove still more important, extremely mentally alert and he had swift and self-confident physical reactions.

Shortly after 3 p.m. the Shah was about to enter the Faculty of Law at the university. He was followed by his half-brother, his royal entourage, and high-ranking military officers. He descended from his Rolls-Royce and started walking along the red carpet that had been laid along the path newly swept clear of snow. Those invited to the ceremony felt their excitement mount. Ahead of him a crowd of photographers began to raise their cameras: flashlights glittered and shutters clicked.

Then the sound of four shots tore the cold air. The reports followed each other so swiftly that the Shah did not have time to feel the fear of apprehension, or the panic of indecision.

Almost as quickly as he identified the reports as shots from a revolver he must have realized that he was still on his feet. He was wounded: one shot had passed through his right cheekbone and came out under his nose. Blood was streaming down his face, but of this too he was probably unaware in that frozen moment of realization.

He was to discover later what became of the three other shots he had heard: 'fantastic though it may seem, three of them passed through my military cap without touching my head. But the gunman's fourth shot penetrated my right cheekbone and came out under my nose.'

He had now identified his attacker. He stood where the photographers had been standing, but instead of a camera he still held a revolver, which was now aimed straight at the Shah's heart. And he was standing virtually alone: at the sound of the shots, panic had broken out around him and his victim. Police, guards, ministers, members of the university, and army officers vied with each other not to save their sovereign but to get out of the line of fire and away from the scene of political disaster. Probably it seemed to each of them that the further he could run from the sound of those shots the more likely he was to survive not only with his life, but with some sort of future in terms of a career. Only bewilderment and curiosity and the physical difficulty of pushing a way through the throng kept some spectators in place.

Two men did not run, but stood, as if eternity itself would find no change in them.

One was the gunman: the other was the Shah, who later said 'both he and I were sufficiently apart from the crowd for me to know that he had a good clear field of fire. At such point-blank range, how could he miss?'

Had he been an older or even a bigger man, he might not have survived to continue: 'I can still remember my reactions at that instant. I thought "What should I do? Jump on him? But if I approach him, I shall become a better target. Shall I run away? Then I shall be a perfect target to be shot in the back".' No doubt these were reflexes rather than conscious thoughts, even though at such a moment of crisis time seems to bear no relation to ordinary life.

What the Shah did was purely instinctive and faultless. His sporting instincts, every fast turn on a dangerous road, every moment of danger in a stalling plane, every near-fall from horseback, came into its own to support the will to survive.

'So,' he says, 'I suddenly started shadow-dancing or feinting. He fired again, wounding me in the shoulder. His last shot stuck in the gun.'[3] For, if his later memories of these moments were as clear and accurate as they seemed to him later to be, he had not only been wounded twice and had three bullets pass through his military cap but he had been able to count the shots. Five of them. Perhaps he had not yet really felt his wounds: but he had heard five shots. And the revolver must hold six. One left.

In retrospect it sounds almost unbelievable that he had such presence of mind: perhaps the frozen moments were relived more analytically later, but he realized, at least, as the split seconds followed each other that his assailant, standing aggressive before him, was still dangerously armed: and if he had not been able to count with total accuracy, he must also have known that the bullets were running out. Survival now could only be a question of seconds.

'I had the queer and not unpleasant sensation of knowing that I was still alive,' he says.[4]

The trick was to stay that way. Fortunately the man's last shot had stuck in the gun.

Mohammed Reza Pahlavi, the twenty-nine-year-old Shah of Iran, was not only alive; he was safe.

What happened next had its political uses as well as being personally infuriating for the Shah, who above all would have liked the gunman to be captured and brought before him for questioning.

'The man then threw down his gun and tried to escape, and in their fury at this assassination attempt, some of my young officers unfortunately killed him,' said the Shah later.

Not for nothing had Mohammed Reza Pahlavi spent the last twenty-three years, since he was six, in hard training for his task as Shah. The moment of ultimate danger past, he suggested that he should simply carry on with the scheduled programme for that afternoon. With difficulty his half-brother Prince Gholam Reza persuaded him that it was essential to have his wounds examined in hospital. Five physicians and surgeons examined the Shah. They were astonished: the two bullets that had reached him had done little damage, no bone was fractured in his face and his shoulder was still mobile. The wounds were stitched, and at 4.40 he was once more at home in his palace. He felt better than the incumbent Prime Minister, Mohammed Saed, who had collapsed on hearing the news. A communiqué was published by the Imperial Court confirming that the Shah's injuries were very minor.

That evening, at 7.30 p.m., a state of emergency was announced. It was back to martial law once more. The arrest of Communists began again, as it had taken place regularly under Reza Shah. And the next day a second decree issued by the Government accused the Tudeh Party of 'preparing the way for revolution in our country'. Consequently, 'the *traitors, who will be recognized as such by the documents presented against them*, should be punished according to the law as a result' (my italics). From that night, and still today, it was to be a criminal offence to be a member of the Communist Party in Iran.

The Shah also used the assassination attempt as a golden opportunity to strengthen his position as constitutional head of the state. Among the very important decisions made soon afterwards by the *Majlis* at his instigation was one that the Senate, provided for in the original constitution of 1906, should be convened for the first time; and another stating that the Shah should have the power to dissolve both the Senate and the *Majlis* on condition that when he did so he simultaneously issued a decree for new elections to be held.

Among the handwritten notes said to have been found in the would-be assassin's flat was one reading 'I belong to the Tudeh party and I devote all my activities to it. I know very well that it is the Russians who back this political party and that they know their success in Iran depends upon this.' Small wonder that the Shah commented: 'He must have been a curious character.' But the still more curious political alignments were to prove quite useful to His Majesty, who said simply: 'We discovered that he had been friendly with various arch-conservative religious fanatics, yet in his flat we found literature of the Tudeh or Communist party.'[5]

If the young man's death precluded further certainty, it also created further suspicion. And the mystery and suspicion had their uses in a society where alliances and alignments are so constantly shifting. The question of who was behind the would-be assassin, and why, was never to be fully solved. According to Sanghvi, 'some evidence during a later investigation pointed to his connection with the *Fedayan Islam* [an Islamic extremist group]; other evidence suggested that he was connected with the Tudeh; and a further source of confusion was evidence of his frequent visits to a foreign embassy'.[6] Thus, almost anyone or any group who became unpopular could be tarred, heavily or lightly, with the suspicion of having taken part in or known of the plot.

The curfew was ruthlessly imposed. A more sinister and much longer-lasting restriction was also envisaged: there was a move to curtail the freedom of the Press. It was suggested that whenever either the Shah or one of his immediate family – his wife, child, mother, father, brother or sister – was insulted in the Press, the police should have powers to arrest the writer concerned and his editor, and to confiscate the newspaper altogether. An outcry burst forth from the Press. *Kayhan* pointed out that if the proposal became law 'anything the papers write could be considered defamatory and could have the paper in question closed down. No form of criticism will be possible.' In the end, instead of confiscation of the entire paper, prison sentences of from one to three years for those responsible for the publication of material considered damaging to the Shah and his immediate family became law. However necessary this may have seemed at the time it has given rise to a curiously erzatz journalistic tone in Iranian newspapers today.

At the same time, the Shah's move to inaugurate the Senate with some members nominated directly by himself, gave him extra powers.

On 28 July 1949 the first budget to be passed for six years was accepted by the *Majlis*. Next, the seven-year development plan was launched. The announcement was made in the same month as the signing of the new terms with the AIOC, and there was an attempt to make the latter more popular by suggesting that increased royalties would be used to pay for the plan. Great publicity was given to the unanimous passing by the *Majlis* of a Bill which transferred those parts of the Shah's land inheritance which he had not already distributed to the Pahlavi Foundation. Sensing a certain reluctance on the part of the *Majlis* to passing reform measures, the Shah did not hesitate to castigate them: 'Keep going, gentlemen. You cannot expect me to be shot at each week to keep you on your toes.'

The next step in the Pahlavi plan was clear: he must marry and produce an heir.

Chapter 11

SECOND MARRIAGE:

Soraya Esfandiari

'In 1950 I heard of a girl named Soraya Esfandiari, and I was much impressed by what I learned of her,'[1] the Shah wrote coolly later about the first of the two great loves of his life: a passion that was to transform many years but to come second, in the end, to the superhuman love of his life – his country.

Matchmakers had been compiling lists of suitable brides ever since his divorce from Fawzia. He had looked at countless photographs and studied endless dossiers. When in doubt he had consulted his old friend the gardener's son from Le Rosey, now installed in Tehran as his Personal Secretary and confidant. But it was Princess Shams whom the Shah sent to England, where Miss Esfandiari was then staying, to form a personal impression of her. She was immediately attracted by the presence and personality of this girl, eighteen years old, with dark hair and beautiful green eyes, and she sent the Shah a 'glowing account' of Soraya.[2]

Princess Shams invited Soraya to visit Paris with her: they would go shopping. The fact that His Majesty was also hoping to do a little shopping, by proxy, on the same trip had not escaped Soraya's notice: her cousin had explained to her why he had been asked to take so many photographs of her. But she seems to have had a fund of common sense and a keen notion of the ridiculous. 'I did not take any of this seriously,' she said later.[3]

But, although she was not of pure Iranian blood, on examination Soraya was not unsuitable. Her mother was a German, but her father was descended from a long line of chieftains in the great Bakhtiari tribe. He studied politics and economics in Germany, and when he was twenty-nine he met Eva Karl, a sixteen-year-old girl whose father, born in St Petersburg, had worked for some time as a factory manager in Tsarist Russia, and had returned to Germany at about the time of the First World War. His wife had been born in the Baltic provinces of Germany. Like her future daughter, Eva had striking green eyes, and fifteen months after she met the Iranian they were married, in a Muslim ceremony. He was still a student, but when he had finished his course they went to Iran and settled for a while in Isfahan.

They had been married for six years when Soraya was born on 22 June 1932. Eva Esfandiari was frightened that her baby daughter would catch one of the skin or eye infections rampant in Iran at that time, and early in 1933 she took her to Berlin. She was brought up in the Muslim religion.

Four years later, when Soraya was five, they returned to Iran, where her father was now running a school. A brother was soon born. In 1947 the family moved to Switzerland, near Zürich. Soraya went to boarding school in Montreux, and then to Les Roseaux in Lausanne in October 1948, when she was sixteen and a half. When she arrived in London in 1950 she already spoke German, Farsi (Persian) and French; now her mother felt that English would be the finishing touch. Evidently Eva Esfandiari had a very strong personality, and people had violent feelings about her. But in the Shah's opinion Soraya's 'was a real Persian girlhood'. To some extent this was true, and it explains why there was a striking affinity between them that defies rational analysis.

Although her family had its great tribal origins, Soraya was acutely aware that, in comparison with the Shah himself and with his first Empress, Fawzia, 'I did not come from a Princely family'.

But she had a stern education in tribal love. One day when she was six years old her father took her out on horseback for a picnic. They left home at 8 a.m., to ride across the broiling desert. By 11.30 Soraya was so parched that it must have been an effort even to ask, as she did, for a drink. But drinking is supposed to weaken one under such conditions, and tribal traditions encourage a peak of physical fitness and courage. One can imagine her father's aghast reaction to his young daughter.

'No Bakhtiar woman is ever thirsty,' he finally told her. And they rode on, without drinking, until they reached their lunchtime picnic spot.

By the time she had spent a few days in Paris with Princess Shams, Soraya was doubtless beginning to believe the possibility of what her cousin had said to her. One day as they were walking through the arcades in the rue de Rivoli the doubts ended. Princess Shams suddenly turned to her (she had just received a message from her brother in Tehran) and began talking about the Shah's great loneliness, his need for companionship and a happy family life. 'Ah!' she exclaimed, 'it would be wonderful if a young woman like you would be willing to share the life of Mohammed Reza!'

So it was arranged that she should go to meet His Majesty. She flew to Iran. On her first evening in Tehran she was invited to dinner by the Dowager Empress, together with Princess Shams and Princess Ashraf. Then, to her utter astonishment, a footman usher announced 'His Majesty the Shah'. Soraya was amazed; but the little subterfuge had saved her any panic.

Soraya formed an impression that was to be confirmed increasingly throughout the coming years and was going to cause her some considerable unhappiness. 'Unquestionably the head of the whole dynasty was Tadj-ol-Molouk,' she said later. 'Her ideas still remained those of the harem world in which she had grown up . . . the Tehran Court was fundamentally a women's court. . . . Sometimes I had the impression of living in a thorough-going matriarchy, at the head of which was the Dowager Empress.'

All seems to have gone well that evening. The Shah, who was wearing the Iranian Air Force Uniform (his favourite) was apparently as pleased with the sight and sound of Soraya in the flesh as he had been with her on paper. The conversational ice was broken with the subject of Switzerland. At 7.30 they dined. Afterwards, Soraya was somewhat surprised to find that parlour games formed a substantial part of evening life at the Imperial

Court. These lasted until about 11 p.m., when she left the palace.

As soon as she reached home her father questioned her: did she like the Shah? Yes. Enough to marry him? Even for a spirited adventurous and attractive girl who has been brought up to hope for a good marriage there must have been a moment of fright. Had she been a little older, she might have dared to delay. Going into a royal marriage with a Muslim could obviously turn out to be more like going into a prison than nearly any other alliance. She wanted time to reflect, but her father said: 'The Shah has asked for a reply this very evening. As soon as you have given it I will go and see him.'

'Yes,' she said. And so, on the evening they met, the bargain was sealed.

Iranian diplomacy can postpone an event for years, or can bring it to instant fruition. Another Iranian understands that.

Soraya's Farsi was of course perfect. And one thing that had struck her as remarkable was that the Shah addressed his mother in the second person plural. His brothers addressed him as 'Your Majesty'. Perhaps she thought at first that this formality was for her benefit: but this was not so. Wearily, she wrote later, 'Perhaps it will cast some light on the whole atmosphere of Court when I say that never did the Shah and I address one another in the intimate second person singular.' This remained so even when her temper made her an unpredictable force in Court circles. Even though Soraya herself gradually penetrated the royal shell, she knew that it would snap shut again the moment someone else joined the two of them. 'I never saw him completely relaxed and open if there were a third person present,' she said.

But she did not lack a whirlwind courtship. She saw the Shah nearly every day (sometimes official engagements precluded a meeting). He took her driving in his super-fast sports cars, took her up with him in some of his aeroplanes, went riding and swimming with her . . . and she was impressed. 'Had he not inherited the Persian throne he would surely have been a great sportsman and have won Olympic gold medals for Iran,' she said. He seemed to her a born athlete. She noted that, though not a strict teetotaller as a true believer in Islam should be, he was more than moderate in his drinking. After his doctors warned him not to smoke more than ten cigarettes a day, 'he always consulted his watch before lighting a cigarette'. He was, she concluded, an ascetic; and in many respects this was a fair assessment. She noted that he was well read, and interested in agriculture. But Soraya was above all a woman, and she responded above all to one of the qualities that is rated highest in a man, the quality that Winston Churchill said 'guarantees all the others': courage. Later she found him as fearless morally as he was physically, and as evidence of this she cited the fact that, though he might some-times find it hard to come to a decision, and would discuss all angles of it, 'when he had made up his mind however he was as hard as steel'.

Again, she was to find an exception to this rule of moral courage: the Shah is consistent in nothing so much as an occa-sional inconsistency. His weakness as far as courage went was 'a marked reluctance to telling high dignitaries that they were dismissed', a great impediment in court life. He preferred to inform them of their fate through an intermediary, because 'he would have found it disagreeable to witness the disappointment on the dismissed man's face'. How very, very Iranian: those who do not revel in cruelty (and Mohammed Reza, whatever his faults and whatever the rules of régime, surely does not do that) find it offensive even to contemplate closely the results of some decisions they have made. To Westerners, it is a distinction bound to seem dishonest, and some who received this treatment thought him two-faced.

Soraya soon realized that, though she was promised as the Shah's bride, theirs was not to be a fairy-tale existence. In all fairness she has admitted that her husband-to-be had warned her in the very earliest days of their acquaintance: 'Don't believe that I can offer you an easy life. I hope you have no illusions about that.'

Her first shock came when she was taken to see the Ekhtessassi, a modern villa opposite the Marble Palace where Mohammed Reza had lived in the early 1940s. This was to be their home. It comprised a guardroom, dining room and three sitting rooms on the ground floor, two bedrooms with bathrooms and a dressing room, and two upstairs drawing rooms. As she walked through

the twelve tattered rooms she realized that it was barely fit for
habitation by ordinary people, let alone a ruling monarch and his
consort. 'Many of the chairs were damaged, the upholstery
and curtains torn, the kitchen quarters in a deplorable condition,
and the servants rooms mere primitive cells.' Somewhat timidly,
she asked if she could not organize some repairs, a 'little renova-
tion'. 'Why? Don't you like it?' demanded her monarch and
husband-to-be.

The wedding date was set for 27 December 1950. But after
she had been in Iran for only eighteen days, Soraya returned
home one evening from a day with her fiancé feeling more than
usually tired and hot. She had a high fever and it quickly became
plain that she had contracted typhoid. She was looked after with
the very greatest of care and the Shah asked for doctors to come
from abroad to treat her. In the end it was the Shah's personal
doctor, Dr Karim Ayadi, who got the credit for saving her life:
he used Aureomycin, then a new drug, which was flown in
from America.

Soraya now saw a new side of her fiancé. He was not only
dashing, exciting and accomplished; he was also kind and con-
siderate. He visited her every day. He had a projector installed in
her room; he was also assiduous in his selection and sending of
gramophone records and flowers. Conventional perhaps, but
there is a limit to what even a Shah can do. That he was sincerely
in love with his bride-to-be no one doubted any more. It seemed
plain that they would be far better matched and happier than he
and Fawzia had been.

The Shah was anxious that the wedding should take place the
moment Soraya was strong enough to stand the strain of the
ceremony. He pressed the doctor to tell him how soon they
could fix the date. If the marriage did not take place before the
Muslim period of mourning lasting from mid-February until
May, it would mean waiting another five months or so. Finally
it was agreed that Soraya should be well enough on Monday 12
February. Royal astrologers told the Shah: 'The stars are particularly favourable for Your Majesty that day.'

But Soraya suffered a relapse. She ate some chocolates sent by
well-meaning friends from Switzerland, forgetting that typhoid
is an intestinal disease: for three days her life hung in the balance

5 The Shah's first honeymoon. When he was nineteen and still Crown Prince his father arranged his marriage to seventeen-year-old Princess Fawzia of Egypt

6 The Shah's second marriage to nineteen-year-old Soraya Esfandiari in 1951

again. Once more it seemed that the ceremony would have to be postponed: but the Shah was frantic. In the end it was decided that most of the entertainments planned to accompany the marriage (banquets, balls and festivities lasting for four days) would be cancelled; and the ceremony would be simplified.

The Golestan Palace, where the wedding had been due to take place, was impossible to heat, so workmen set about trying to take the chill off the Marble Palace. When the day dawned, bitterly cold as usual, Soraya had to wear thick woollen underwear beneath her fabulous Dior gown. The gown weighed over 40 pounds – far, far too much for her. She was also weighed down by a coat of imperial ermine, a present from Stalin, and the not inconsiderable weight of a diadem and emeralds borrowed from the Imperial Iranian Crown Jewels. She was, however, permitted to sit with her betrothed on a sofa.

The combination of the ceremony, the emotion, the onlookers and the weighty apparel suddenly became too much for Soraya, who felt faint. The Shah ordered the ladies in waiting to cut off as much as possible of the heavy petticoats she was wearing underneath the embroidered gown; then she was almost carried to the car. How she managed to endure the grand dinner for 300 people she had to attend that evening at the unheated Golestan Palace is almost unimaginable. It was in truth no easy life. Even their honeymoon had to be postponed because of the country's political problems.

Life as the Shah's wife had most of the disadvantages of an ordinary marriage: and very few real advantages.

The Shah rose at 7 a.m. leaving his wife to sleep on until 9 a.m. Her own day began around 10 a.m. They met for the first time, usually, for lunch, when after drinking their coffee they would listen to the news, read the papers and talk. This was probably the cosiest and most relaxed moment of their day. Dinner was at 7.30. But there was a snag. 'Almost every evening the entire family was present,' she lamented later. After they had eaten, the routine varied between games of bridge or other cards, and watching films in the palace cinema. At the beginning it is not surprising that Soraya felt like an outsider, listening to the private jokes that were bandied about but which she did not fully understand. And even when she had spent long enough at

H

Court to take her real place as one of the family, she still felt the lack of human warmth and simple sincerity that she had valued with her own family.

Warned by one sister-in-law against another, and aware of her mother-in-law's powerful influence, it cannot have been an easy existence for a girl of eighteen. Nor was it only the family she had to contend with: she began to feel a deep personal hostility towards Ernest Perron, still the greatest male influence on the Shah. He posed, she says, as 'poet and philosopher', and, now, as Mohammed Reza's Personal Secretary, played what she considered to be a 'sinister role' in the Shah's circle. 'He was as slippery as an eel,' she concluded, and 'despite his humble origins he was said to be Mohammed Reza's closest adviser. He visited him each morning in his bedroom for a discussion.'

Not even in their bedroom, in the privacy of the marriage bed, was there any sanctity. Soraya might be Empress: but she had already found that she had to share her husband not only with his country, with his Court, and with his family, but even with a secretary whom she regarded as interfering and malicious.

She must very quickly have realized that the land of roses and the nightingale might for her prove to be a land of thorns and darkness.

Chapter 12

Confrontations

THE attempt on the Shah's life had been only the peak of the mountain of Iranian discontent.

Just over a year before, in January 1948, martial law had been lifted in Tehran. It had been in force since 1941 – since when, on the ironic swings and roundabouts that typify Iranian life, the Press had enjoyed a freedom that had been curtailed under Reza Shah.

The end of martial law reflected the Shah's hope that the situation was better. But the attempt on his own life, and the successful murder in the same year (1949) of Abdul Husain Hazhir, who had been Prime Minister in 1948, showed that this was not so. Hazhir, who was young and was considered by many to be enlightened and sincere, had been on good terms with both the Shah and the British. Therefore his assassination could be read as both a revenge and a warning to anyone who was sympathetic to the Shah and his Court, or who was thought to be influenced by the British.[1]

Rather like the Loch Ness monster, this was only the latest sighting of a mysterious and dangerous element in the substrata of Iranian political life. The trouble had its roots in the distant past, in the Qajar division between Shah and people, in Court jealousies, in the great poverty that was still endured by more than nine-tenths of the population, in the illiteracy that led in turn to easy inflammation of the people by word-of-mouth (the only message they could easily understand), and by new ambitions seething in the soul of every Iranian – ambitions fostered by the Shah himself (in a comparatively realistic way) and by his people (in ways that varied from the ignorant through the vapid to the fanatical): that Iran should take her rightful place among the powers of the modern world, and should reap the benefits of what were, after all, her own resources.

One of the immediate triggers of the troubles that infested the years 1948–53 was another shortage of bread. And there were, as usual, echoes of these economic difficulties in the unstable political situation.

Shortly after the dramatically successful outcome of Qavam's strategy in dealing with the Russians, several of his Ministers resigned. A few days later, unable to form a satisfactory new cabinet, he tendered his own resignation. The fruits of success in Persian politics have for centuries carried the seeds of bitterness within them.

By November 1948, Qavam had been succeeded by no less than three Prime Ministers. Money was obviously needed to shore up Iran against her northern neighbour once more if Russia were not to seek to take advantage of the situation. In April 1947 President Truman had already announced the new US policy of an international 'Containment of Communism'. Then in June 1947 the US gave 26 million dollars to arm the Iranian Army.

But money was also desperately needed for internal reasons. In 1946 Iran's first Labour Law, limiting the number of hours people could work, had been passed; in addition, a draft seven-year development plan had been worked out. When in 1947 the Iranian Government asked for a loan of 250 million dollars to begin work on the development programme it was turned down flat. Oil then was the obvious answer. The Government could no longer ignore the stream of revenues that was pouring into the British Treasury.

In April 1948 the *Majlis* passed a law instructing the Government to restore Iranian sovereignty over Bahrein. This was a revival of an old claim. The Bahrein Archipelago is a sheikhdom, inhabited mainly by Arabs, with complete internal autonomy: successive agreements with Bahrein in 1880, 1892 and 1914 gave

Britain a protectorate over her, which the Iranian Government claimed was a violation of *their* territorial rights. Under Reza Shah, repeated claims about the question were made to the League of Nations throughout the years 1928–36.[2]

In the 1949 elections Dr Mossadeq's National Front Party won eight seats out of a total of 136 in the *Majlis*. And though a small group, these eight were so fervent, so united, and so well organized that they were to dominate Iranian politics for the next few years.

In October 1920 the British envoy in Tehran described Mossadeq as 'honest, intelligent, well-educated, capable and very friendly to us'. But now he was not even moderately friendly. His National Front Party's xenophobic rejection of every attempt to implement a compromise with the Anglo-Iranian Oil Company, interims of a 'Supplemental Agreement', met with such a response in the *Majlis* that every attempt to ratify this compromise met with failure. In addition the British refused to discuss a fifty-fifty formula for the sharing of profits. The British attitude doubled Mossadeq's appeal, and from 1950 onwards he was swept forward by a surge of national feeling.

In June 1950 General Razmara became Prime Minister. He was personally and socially very viable, having links with many sections of Iranian society, and he was a highly intelligent man. Unfortunately he was believed to have the support of both the Americans and the British, which in the present circumstances did not augur well for his future. But what he realized, and the British unfortunately did not, was that 'the real problem was not economic; it was, and is, a political problem'.[3] In spite of a very clear warning, the British Foreign Office was to refuse, over the coming months, to intercede in negotiations between the Iranian Government and the Anglo-Iranian Oil Company.

Extra pressure was put on the need for the revenues and on the Razmara Government by the aftermath of the Shah's visit to the United States in the autumn of 1949, in yet another bid to find funds for the Seven-Year Plan. His enormous disappointment ('I received a friendly reception but returned home completely empty-handed') led him to a conclusion quite startling to Eastern minds: that America was 'determined to aid only those countries which showed a desire to clean house at home'.

Reacting to the challenge he launched an anti-corruption campaign, and announced that his own Crown lands (many of which had been acquired by his father under a long-standing Persian tradition concerning uncultivated land – a legal act that had nevertheless earned the Pahlavis many enemies) would be distributed among the peasants. In February 1950 he announced many other reforms that were to be undertaken. They were particularly aimed at eradicating corruption. On 26 June General Razmara issued a press release detailing many of these reforms: provincial, village and district councils were to be set up, unemployment eliminated, the judiciary guaranteed independence, and the budget balanced.

Meanwhile Dr Mossadeq had been made chairman of a Special Majlis Oil Committee which was asked to report to the *Majlis* on the course of action it thought the Government should take. On 19 February 1951 he presented to the Special Oil Committee a formal resolution for the nationalization of the Iranian oil industry. Thus, softly, softly, began the underground explosion that was to rip open economies and send prices sky-high in the 1970s.

Prime Minister Razmara had to declare himself on the issue of nationalization, and said it was probably illegal (according to the terms of the setting up of the Anglo-Iranian Oil Company) as well as certainly impractical – it was run almost exclusively by British engineers who could not be replaced for many years by local workers. He ordered a paper to be read in the *Majlis* explaining why nationalization was not in the best interests of Iran, and the 'technical arguments and the style of this declaration, although written in Persian, led to a belief that it had been prepared by the AIOC'.[4]

Now the confrontation between the two sides was open. On the one side were the Shah and Razmara, in favour of land reform and against nationalization of the oil industry. On the other side were Mossadeq and the National Front, xenophobic over the question of oil and landed traditional rights as far as landowners were concerned.

On 7 March 1951, Razmara was murdered. The assassination took place at the Shah Mosque during a funeral, where he provided an easy target. Eight days later the *Majlis* passed a bill nationalizing the Iranian oil industry. As a final and typically Persian piece of irony, the *Majlis* asked in August that Razmara's assassin should be released from prison. This was the people that Mohammed Reza, who had so narrowly escaped assassination himself, had survived to govern: and this was Soraya's introduction to her role as his consort.

Chapter 13

Realism and Nationalization

THE Shah's attitude to the oil question was more realistic than Dr Mossadeq's. Brought up among the modern machinery of the West, he wondered how Iran's oil industry could be run without the help of the British when she had so few engineers of her own. Emotionally, he believed, as Mossadeq did, that Iran should reap the benefits of her own natural resources. Had not Britain and her Allies in the words of Curzon, 'floated to victory on a wave of oil'? And could not Iran expect some gratitude for this?

Apparently not: and when he realized this, the Shah's attitude towards Britain had inwardly stiffened, although he remained outwardly much more tractable than Mossadeq, and was in favour of a compromise. In the words of his official biographer, Ramesh Sanghvi: 'Like his father, he had been dissatisfied with the Company's conduct for some time, and now a Labour Government in Britain seemed to be supporting conduct more appropriate to the era of gunboat diplomacy.'[1]

Discontent was spreading. Not long after this *The Economist* wrote that:

> The . . . nationalism of thirty years ago, which was reared on the pap of missionary education in Syria and educated on President Wilson's fourteen points, was a mixture of xenophobia and of religion, but it was conditioned and shaped by an ancient social order. Today nationalism remains anti-foreign but with this

distinction: whereas its forerunner was merely hostile to the foreigner on the spot and regarded distant powers such as the United States as genial and tolerable, the nationalism of the fifties is directed against all foreigners, westerners and Russians alike. Likewise, it is still fired by religious emotions, as is evident in the strength of the Moslem Brotherhood and in Mullah Kashani's power in Persia; but it is also propelled by a third and new force, social discontent.[2]

Kashani was the leader of one of the two small and fanatical religious groups which were whipping up nationalistic feeling in the country: but they were also opposed to the secular resolution of political problems and therefore anti-Shah, and pro-Mossadeq.

Razmara's death concealed for a while publication of a suggestion that might have saved him: he had just received from the British a proposal for a fifty-fifty split of the oil revenues; in other words the British were now themselves proposing a solution they had earlier rejected. But Razmara, in spite of advice from one adviser (the Shah?) that he should announce the proposal in an effort to reduce tension, preferred to wait until passions had cooled a little. 'This decision may have cost Razmara his life,' the Shah later commented. 'But the British proposal was in any event too late, for Persian nationalism had become thoroughly aroused and public sentiment favoured nationalization.'[3]

This was due to Mossadeq's singlehanded campaign to keep Iran's revenues at home. But she still obtained only 16 per cent of the receipts while Britain took 84 per cent. 'He shouted that he would wring £300,000 – nearly 1 million dollars – a day from the Company,' the Shah remembered. 'In fact, how could anybody be against Mossadeq? He would enrich everybody, he would fight the foreigner, he would secure our rights. No wonder students, intellectuals, people from all walks of life, flocked to his banner.'[4] There were anti-British riots and demonstrations, in which three Britons and eight Iranians were killed, and scores of people injured. At the oilfields, the workers themselves went on strike. Abadan was now the world's largest refinery,[5] but it soon came almost to a standstill. The country had taken the bit between its teeth.

On 28 April 1951, the day after Ala fell, Dr Mossadeq accepted the post of Prime Minister. Shah and Parliament had little choice. After the fall of five successive Governments in eighteen months, there was no one else with an appeal that would move both *Majlis* and masses. But Mossadeq had accepted the post *on condition*. He said his policy for the immediate eviction of the Anglo-Iranian Oil Company must be supported. With the pistol of possible national disintegration at his head, the Shah 'endorsed the project submitted to the *Majlis* for the enforcement of the Nationalization Law and expropriation of the Company'. It was approved the very day after Mossadeq became Prime Minister: on 29 April.

What Mossadeq did next was, the Shah said, 'catastrophic'. When the British company again repeated their willingness to enter into a fifty-fifty agreement for the sharing of the oil revenues, Mossadeq refused to countenance the idea, or to consider any variation on it.

This move from the British came only after relations between the two countries had been further strained. Although nationalization was, of course, one of the very major election planks which the British Labour Government had used as a springboard to power, it was a different matter when another country considered following the same course. They instantly took the dispute to the International Court at The Hague. The Iranian Government riposted by questioning the authority of the Court to deal with a matter concerning only a sovereign state and a company seeking a concession. Thus they hoist the British by their own company petard. As an interim move the Court advised that the matter should be settled by negotiations.

Nor was the atmosphere improved when the Iranian Government's offer to allow the 2,500 British workers to stay on for the new employers, the Iranian Oil Company, was refused and they were evacuated under the protection of the cruiser *Mauritius*, while in Cyprus a battalion of paratroopers who had been flown in from England stood by in case of a further emergency. The Iranians had promptly responded by sending forces to Abadan and Khorramshahr.

President Truman began to wonder whether it was possible to break the deadlock by using an outside umpire. With this hope in mind he sent his Foreign Policy adviser, Mr Averell Harriman, to Tehran. He arrived on 15 July to find both the Iranians and the British less than overjoyed to see him. Sir Francis Shepherd, the British Ambassador, openly said that there was 'not much point' in his coming because of the fixed attitude of the Iranians.[6] The next day he withdrew this remark. As for the Iranians, they showed again that intrinsic wiliness and resilience that has enabled them to survive aeons of change by staging protests in the guise of the Tudeh movement, already outlawed and illegal, but plainly still under strong and determined leadership. Some of the worst demonstrations Tehran had ever known took place on the day of Mr Harriman's arrival: twenty people were killed and some 300 injured in clashes between Mossadeq's National Front party and the Tudeh Party outside the *Majlis*.

On 16 July the now familiar martial law was proclaimed once more, only to be cancelled six days later. Meanwhile the police began a general arrest of the Communist demonstrators and confiscated the Communist presses.[7] The oil question and the Tudeh agitation combined had stirred up a hysteria in the country that no one person could control, and that was to sweep the originators of discontent on to their own eventual destruction.

After some weeks of advice, Harriman withdrew from the scene. Next a British Government mission headed by Lord Stokes, Lord Privy Seal and Minister of Supply, arrived in Tehran on 4 April 1951. He submitted proposals to the Iranian Government again incorporating a fifty-fifty oil revenue sharing plan: this was really a window-dressed repeat of the AIOC's earlier offer; and again it met with rejection. But at last the British were beginning to admit that the problem was larger than a company affair.

Lord Stokes stated on 22 August that 'I have no alternative but to regard the discussions suspended and go home'.[8] On the same day the AIOC announced that by the end of August 16,000 Iranian employees would be dropped from the pay rolls, and that unless oil sales from Abadan were resumed, a further 60,000 would be dismissed in the near future. On 30 August Mossadeq rejected the joint proposal of Truman and Churchill.

who had failed to notice, or at least to accept, the *fait accompli* of nationalization.

All attempts at working out a further compromise failed, and at dawn on 27 September Iranian troops seized the Abadan refinery and refused admittance to all but ten key British technicians: President Truman warned Britain that the US would not support the retaliatory use of force by the British.

The next day, 28 September 1951, the British Government announced that it had asked the United Nations Security Council to intervene in the dispute. Meanwhile the remaining British staff at Abadan were evacuated, peacefully, and on 1 October the Security Council met to consider the British application. Mossadeq quickly warned the Security Council: 'Beware of taking a decision which may endanger international peace.'[9]

Britain had by now warned all customers for Iranian oil that it should be treated as the property of the AIOC. Anyone who bought it from the nationalized Iranian company would, they said, be sued 'for being in possession of stolen goods knowing them to be stolen'. Thus Iran's entire export market was cut off. On 10 September, Britain froze Iran's sterling balances, and at the same time, all British licences for the export of scarce materials from the United Kingdom to Iran were revoked. This was, as Sanghvi puts it, 'a declaration of economic war'.[10]

On 9 October, Britain submitted a second petition to the International Court, charging the Government of Iran with the violation of international law in having nationalized the oil company. Nine days later the United Nations Security Council rejected the British request for instant action, and held that until the International Court pronounced its verdict, the British Company should stay in abeyance. The US now held the balance in much of the debate between Iran and Britain; in particular, the American oil companies were crucial. Mossadeq 'had believed that the Western world was so dependent on Iranian oil that he could dictate his own terms'.[11] But instead of this, the production elsewhere in the Middle East had been stepped up to make good the loss from Iran.

In the Shah's opinion it was Mossadeq who was endangering the stability and the modernization of Iran.

'A prisoner of his advisers and even more of his own stubborn self, Mossadeq let his negative emotionalism rule out any chance of agreement,' the Shah wrote later. 'Instead of spending his time on reform and reconstruction, he devoted himself to bickering.' And, very sadly, he summed up:

> Think of the economic miseries and the political perils that the people of my country might have been spared if Mossadeq had been willing to enter into rational negotiations. I still fondly imagine that, in spite of his disastrous stubbornness, he at least had some desire to reach an agreement; but in the case of some of his advisers I am sceptical. I suspect that some of them fervently hoped that there would be no settlement; for that would mean economic collapse and, in turn the imposition of alien political control.[12]

This the Shah termed 'perverted nationalism': and he was plainly referring to the Tudeh Party. It was from this period that his real gut hatred of the Communists dated: to him there is no greater traitor to the state than a Marxist.

After Mossadeq's rejection of Lord Stokes's proposals, the AIOC and the British Government filed separate petitions with the International Court at The Hague; but the Iranian Prime Minister refused to recognize the Court's jurisdiction. And so it was that the British appealed to the United Nations Security Council.

The UN talks ended on 13 November 1951, the day on which the State Department issued a statement saying that 'while progress has been made, no new basis has emerged on which a practicable solution could be reached'. Mossadeq asked the US Government for a loan to make up the deficit due to the rundown in oil production, and as a temporary measure withdrew a vast sum from its deposit with the International Monetary Fund. On his return to Tehran he received a hero's welcome, and the *Majlis* gave him a unanimous vote of confidence.[13] He demanded, and got, approval of a plan for immediate elections, which would ensure more widely based support for his next moves. And he ordered the closing of all British consulates in Iran, as from 21 January 1952.[14]

But not everyone was with Mossadeq. On 6 December 1951 several thousand Communist-led youths rioted in the streets of Tehran in protest against his policies. They fought for five hours against police and supporters of Mossadeq's National Front Party: five people were killed and more than 200 wounded. Not unnaturally Mossadeq began to think in terms of gaining the support of the Communists, extraordinary though this seemed for someone of his background. Meanwhile opposition to his National Front Party mushroomed, since it was now regarded as responsible for so much unemployment and unrest; and two days later, on 8 December, a number of opposition deputies took refuge in the *Majlis*, complaining that they had been threatened by National Front extremists. Even then the riots continued, and two days later demonstrators entered the *Majlis* and Senate.[15]

Economic collapse drew inevitably closer and social chaos was rampant. Mossadeq seems to have floundered into a fury of frustration in which national suicide seemed better than any compromise whatsoever. On 12 December, while reporting on the results of his visit to the US, where his request for a loan of 120 million dollars had been turned down, he flew defiantly in the face of all reason and Iran's needs, and went on to deny that there existed any real need at all for a settlement of the dispute. He advised the country that it should stop all oil production and proceed on the basis that Iran had never in its history had any oil. In that way, he claimed, future generations at least would escape exploitation. In the same breath he had to announce to a nation already feeling the severe effects of economic stress that it was to enter an age of official austerity.

The Shah had every reason to be close to despair. As a final insult, Mossadeq had demanded the exile of the Dowager Empress whom he recognized as an extremely potent adversary. Furious at this attempted interference in his family affairs, the Shah ignored the suggestion. And as he reflected on the balance of power in his divided country, he realized that, while his family might be, as it is so often in Iran, his greatest support, there was that other strength that his father had relied upon and that Mossadeq had not won over: the Iranian Army.

Chapter 14

Mossadeq Rules

FOR the next eighteen months, until mid-1953, the positions of Shah and Prime Minister were the reverse of the traditional in Iran: Mohammed Reza Pahlavi was virtually the throne behind the power. It was a position he did not relish. He could not fulfil himself, however much he enjoyed such things purely as pastimes, in travelling or night clubs or fast cars. His strategy was simply to wait; and to wait in his own country. He realized that, more often than not, it is he who leaves the table who loses the game. This was a hard time and a hardening time. It scarred his soul as Shah and as an overwhelmingly proud man. It left furrows on his face and grey in his hair. It left pain in his eyes, which would never again see the world as peacefully and hopefully as he had done when he dreamed at school in Switzerland of what he would do when he became Shah.

The ferocity of his emotions at this time tempered his aims to a steely realism and this explains better than anything his habits as a ruler who is, however benevolently disposed, a despot by the standards of the Western world today. The battle lines with the Court one side and Mossadeq's National Front Party the other had already been drawn up: and they led straight to a duel between Shah and Prime Minister.

Mossadeq seemed bent on a course of economic destruction in 1952. He turned down proposals by the International Bank for Reconstruction and Development, to keep the oil industry going, because the Bank reserved the right to use workers from any of its subscribing countries, and Mossadeq refused to have technicians from Britain. On 13 July he told the Shah that he could not continue as Prime Minister unless he was given powers to govern for six months without recourse to Parliament, and became Minister of War. The Shah refused. Mossadeq resigned.

Ahmed Qavam, now an old man – and, incidentally, a cousin of Mossadeq's – was reappointed but the Shah could never feel wholehearted about him.

The Tudeh Party, which seemed more powerful than ever now that it was an underground party, was joined by Mossadeq's supporters in riots and demonstrations. The Prime Minister appealed to the Shah for the troops to support his position. He received, indirectly, an answer to the effect that the troops had orders to remain in barracks. The message was very plain indeed: the next day, 22 July, after Qavam's resignation, Mossadeq was once more installed as Prime Minister.

It must have been a period when His Imperial Majesty the Shahanshah felt between the devil and the deep blue sea: for he had never trusted Qavam; nor did he trust Mossadeq, who was certainly wily. He threw his whole personality dramatically and melodramatically into the cause for upholding oil nationalization. Seeking *bast* (sanctuary) in the *Majlis*, as those who had reason to fear the Shah in former times sought *bast* at the head of the sovereign's horse, he had his bed moved into the Parliament buildings and announced from it: 'I will not move until I have attained complete victory.'

On 22 July the judgment of the International Court on the oil dispute reached Iran: the Court had upheld Mossadeq's contention that the matter was outside its jurisdiction. With this triumph behind him, his power escalated and at the beginning of August both Senate and *Majlis* granted him the extra powers he had demanded. Yet he never gained the full support of the army.

Bills were signed for the prosecution of the former Prime Minister Qavam and the confiscation of his property: the old man refused to budge from his house, and, in the event, the confiscation was never completed. 'It's especially true in Iran that blood is thicker than water,' one commentator explained, 'and as Mossadeq was his cousin he knew he was safe.'

bove: After seven years of child-
marriage to Soraya the Shah's
for an heir led to divorce. This
re was taken during their last
together

ght: When the Shah returned to
ountry after the attempted coup
953 loyal Iranians prostrated
selves before him

9 *Above:* A peasant kisses the Shah's hand after receiving the deeds of his land at the outset of the Land Reform programme

10 *Left:* The Shah on a pilgrimage to Mecca in 1957

In October the Iranian Government officially broke off diplomatic relations with Britain; but Tehran was only just in the process of getting its water supplied from a mains system which was being installed by a British firm. Mossadeq was furious at the thought of them leaving, and so these British engineers stayed on – astonishingly, unmolested.[1]

When President Eisenhower took office, he and Churchill proposed a fresh basis for settling the dispute in order to get the oil and money supply flowing again: but again Mossadeq rejected the proposals. He also remained as relentless in his hounding of the Court. In October 1952 he demanded the removal of Princess Ashraf's Egyptian husband, Ahmad Shafiq, from his post as Director of Civil Aviation. Following this Princess Ashraf, the Dowager Empress and several of their friends had gone into exile. The Shah then knew that he must act positively against Mossadeq. But when?

> Worst of all, from my personal point of view [he remembers], was the strain and suspense of waiting for the proper time to take counter-action. I had detailed reports on every phase of our critical situation. . . . But my father had bequeathed to me at least a little of his marvellous sense of timing, and I knew that premature action might be worse than none at all. To strike too soon might merely seal the doom of a country that was already heading towards disaster.[2]

It was now two years since his marriage to Soraya, and their delayed honeymoon to Europe seemed unlikely ever to materialize. The era of austerity proclaimed under Mossadeq affected palace life too. There were no great banquets, and whenever there was a formal occasion requiring that the royal family should borrow some jewels from the collection of Crown jewels kept in the vaults of the Melli bank, Mossadeq demanded that a receipt should be given for each item. If everything was not returned to the vaults first thing the next morning there was a great fuss.[3]

So, bereft of any true function, the Shah and his wife passed the time of day riding, swimming, and playing handball. And like Nasr-ed-Din Shah, who had started his reign very well but withdrew into Court games and practical jokes when the situation

I

of Persia *vis-à-vis* Britain and Russia became too much for him, Mohammed Reza gave way completely to a childish streak in his nature and indulged to the full his desire for pranks at the palace. He would slip unobtrusively out of the room where his guests were .Then, 'during the showing of a film there would be a terrific barking of dogs. The startled guests would all turn their heads,' remembers Soraya, 'before they realized that their Emperor in the next room was a superlative dog imitator.' On another occasion, a bridge evening, all the ladies suddenly leaped to their feet screaming – for 'horrible green spiders and frogs were climbing over their laps'.⁴ They were toys brought back from the United States. Possibly Soraya realized that such 'jokes' were a simple way of releasing tension. She began to read books on psychology, especially the classics by Jung and Freud, and believes they 'helped me to console the Shah who nowadays suffered frequent bouts of gloom'.

It seemed that Mossadeq had almost won. After the US Ambassador, Mr Henderson, had visited the Shah in May 1952 with proposals for solving the oil dispute, and the Shah had promised that his Government would consider them closely and earnestly, Mossadeq raged openly 'What does His Majesty think he is doing? A Shah's job is to reign and not to rule!'

The Shah began to suffer from increasing bouts of anxiety and loss of self-confidence. He could not sleep properly. He interrogated his wife whenever she had met anyone as to the exact degree of loyalty they had displayed: 'How deeply did X bow to you?' 'Did Y kiss your hand?' 'Did Mrs Z's curtsey seem to you spontaneous or deliberate?'⁵

Worst of all, bereft of his executive powers, he seems to have felt that the divine right to rule, and therefore his divine protection, was leaving him. One day he made three attempts to land his plane, and each time pulled the nose of the plane up again at the very last minute. His dilemma was solved when an officer in the control tower said simply, 'If Your Majesty has enough fuel it would be better to circle for a quarter of an hour or so until you are feeling more yourself.' He did so while some of his passengers took out their copies of the Koran and prayed: at the fourth attempt he made a perfect landing.⁶ Soraya hoped against hope that events might enable them to leave the throne and enjoy a simple life somewhere as husband and wife. 'My wife thought less of politics than of our being together,' the Shah said later: and doubtless in one way this was a help to him.

The Shah had finally been compelled to extend Mossadeq's plenary powers. He was still hoping for complete control over the Executive and the army.

Early in February 1953 Mossadeq asked that all the property the Shah had inherited from his father should now be handed over to the Government: its worth was estimated at 680 million rials or about £7,400,000. On 11 May the Shah did formally transfer estates inherited from his father to the Government, in return for a payment of 60 million rials annually to the Pahlavi Foundation, which, though a charity, never discloses details of its income or expenditure. Meanwhile rumours that he was thinking of leaving the country became more and more numerous. He seemed to be losing the battle for power.

But if the Shah himself had been weakened by the exile of members of his close family, by the pruning of that part of his income derived from his father's estates, and by the replacement of some ninety key military figures by men, many of them Tudeh members, whom Mossadeq trusted (and yet through whom he *still* failed to gain ultimate control of military power), his country itself was still weaker in the absence of any revenue from oil. Some of Mossadeq's supporters began to waver. In the bazaar, the merchant class, which had grown under Reza Shah and had recently favoured the Prime Minister's policy, was beginning to have grave doubts that the country could hold on for long enough without foreign funds. The Ayatollah Kashani was concerned at the growth in the power of the Tudeh and at the mounting danger signs of an economic collapse which would hit the entire nation. Many people including the police, gendarmerie, schoolmasters and all the lower ranks of the civil service, had been carrying on with their jobs without receiving salaries, living on 'tick' and the old Persian tradition of making do: stale bread was damped with hot water to make it just edible once more, and many members of the middle and some of the upper classes were becoming used once again to doing without meat in their diet, as they had so often had to do in the past.[7] But for how long was this situation to be welcomed?

The eve of the Shah's departure dawned. An emissary secretly approached the Empress Soraya, and delivered a message: the Ayatollah Kashani begged her to use all her influence to change the Shah's mind about leaving. The next day, 28 February 1953, the Prime Minister arrived at the palace to say goodbye to his sovereign and enemy. He wanted to savour the moment of ultimate triumph. Suddenly, to the surprise of both men, a crowd was heard outside. Mossadeq urged the Shah to leave while his life was still safe. But when Shah and Prime Minister listened to the chants of the crowd, they were able to make out the phrases 'Long live the Shah!' and 'Down with Mossadeq'. The disappointment and outrage were too much for the Prime Minister, who fainted. When he came to, it was the Empress who led him by the arm to a back door leading to adjoining gardens from where he could make a safe get-away.

The Shah himself had been almost as astonished by the unexpected turn of events as his Prime Minister. But Mossadeq pushed on with consequences that were finally to prove disastrous to himself. In a broadcast on 6 April 1953, he accused the Court of supporting plots against his life; and he again accused the Dowager Empress and Princess Ashraf of conspiracy against him. He had already persuaded the *Majlis* to disband the Senate; now he suspended the functions of the Supreme Court. He ordered his own supporters to stay away from the *Majlis*, thus depriving it of the attendance necessary for a quorum. He extended martial law, and set up a committee to examine ways of curtailing the Shah's powers.

One of the first signs of resistance to Mossadeq came in a typically sinister form towards the end of April 1953. On 20 April the Chief of Police, General Afshar-Tus, disappeared. He had formerly been an instructor at the Military Academy; but even there, he had earned a reputation for brutality. For a few days no one could be sure what had happened to him: when they found his body a few days later it was obvious that slow retribution had been taken for his former cruelties. The murder was much more than the elimination of a hated Mossadeq supporter: it was a symbol of the bloodshed that would follow if there were an open confrontation between the Shah and his Prime Minister.

Dr Mossadeq continued to try to chip away at those loyal to the Shah, but attempts to undermine the monarchy no longer had a united backing, and when a Bill designed to limit the Shah's powers came before the *Majlis* on 7 June 1953, there was uproar and hand-to-hand fighting broke out in the Chamber. The Ayatollah Kashani, who was now President of the *Majlis*, himself accused Dr Mossadeq of acting unconstitutionally.

The Prime Minister's position was further weakened when on 29 June 1953 a letter was sent by the new US President, Eisenhower, rejecting Mossadeq's appeal for loans until the oil dispute was settled. Any hopes Mossadeq might have had of dividing the Americans from the British were now seen to be vain, and without her former 'exploiter' Iran was not better off than before, she was far, far worse off.

On 14 July twenty-five National Front supporters resigned, and, stung by this desertion from his own side, Mossadeq called for the dissolution of the *Majlis*. A referendum to settle the fate of the lower house was held on 10 August 1953. General Arfa told how Mossadeq 'arranged that there should be two tents in all polling stations, one for those who intended voting as he wished and one for the few bold enough to brave the threats and insults of the hefty young Communists stationed before its entrance, who had assurance doubly sure by destroying the dissentient votes, the police having been ordered not to interfere'.[8] This was intimidation and manipulation on a bigger and more brutal scale than even the Iranians were used to. In one provincial town where the population was about 3,000, some 18,000 votes favouring dissolution were counted. In previous elections the Pahlavis themselves had not been slow to influence elections, but even the Shah was breathless at the announced results and said later 'it seems that the dead had voted'.

On hearing the result, another twenty-five deputies who previously had been amenable to Mossadeq's policies broke with him: and so, finally, did the Ayatollah Kashani. Thus bereft of his right-wing religious support and more liberal followers, Mossadeq was left with the banned Tudeh as his power base. It looked as if it might be sufficient. The next day, 11 August 1953, the pro-Mossadeq and Tudeh newspapers denounced the Shah with bitter attacks. All pictures of the Shah in Tehran's shops, cinemas, government offices were torn down. The Shah's Imperial Guard of trusted men was disbanded, and replaced at the palace gates by infantry soldiers unknown to him. Dr Mossadeq had already boasted publicly, 'I have muzzled the Shah'. Now it looked as if he had confined his sovereign to kennels.

Chapter 15

Exile

WITHIN a week of each other during that hot summer of 1953 two powerful personalities arrived at Tehran airport and were allowed through immigration unnoticed. This was to cost Dr Mossadeq dear, although one of the visitors stayed only for two days and the other for three.

Only 25 July Princess Ashraf arrived. Unseen by any of her enemies, she slipped quietly into a taxi and a few hours later she was with the Shah, to (in Soraya's words) 'encourage us to act'.[1] By next morning Mossadeq had learned of the Princess's presence. He demanded her immediate departure.

Princess Ashraf had been in close contact with Allen Dulles (brother of John Foster Dulles), the director of the CIA who was 'on holiday' in Switzerland – where the Princess was also spending some time that summer. The next day, Mr Dulles told journalists of the growing Communist danger in Iran.

The second visitor was Norman Schwarzkopf. He had not lived in Iran for fifteen years, since 1948. He stayed for two days, and was gone again before, a week later, the *New York Times* reported that he had come to Iran 'to see a few friends'. One of the friends he saw was the Shah.

The other friend was already in hiding from Mossadeq's revenge and the possibility of assassination by his henchmen. This was General Fazlollah Zahedi, described by Soraya as 'half swashbuckler and half Don Juan'. He was as impassioned in his dislike of the Communists as he had previously been of the Allies. He was, in fact, just the man one would choose to set up a coup – he was ruthless and manipulative, and had twice been chief of police in Tehran.

Looking back over this period the Shah's official biographer, Ramesh Sanghvi, wrote: '*That the CIA did some work during those fateful days is not denied:* however, all Iranian sources to whom I talked underlined the basic point that if there had not been simultaneous risings in Tehran and other cities, Dr Mossadeq, in control of the armed forces, would have easily crushed the CIA agents'[2] (my italics).

The Shah may have decided a few months previously that he wanted to act: but all the outside evidence points to the fact that by now he felt almost unable to do so. His will had been half-paralysed by Mossadeq's manipulations, and his sense of divine mission seems to have almost deserted him: hence his deep depression.

Since the day six months previously, in February 1953, when the mob had gathered outside Mossadeq's own home, he had strengthened the guard there. Twelve tanks now surrounded his town residence. This had meant weakening the defence of the Saadabad Palace where the Shah and the Empress Soraya had been living. As this was set in very spacious grounds, the palace was extremely vulnerable. Fearing an attack by the Tudeh, the Shah and Soraya had therefore travelled north, and divided their time between a villa Reza Shah had built on the shores of the Caspian Sea, near Ramsar, and a hunting lodge at Kelardasht, in Mazanderan, the region where Reza Shah was born: both practically and psychologically these were safe places.

As soon as the result of the referendum of 10 August became officially known, Mossadeq declared that the *Majlis* was dissolved. On 13 August 1953, acting on advice received from the CIA, who had been studying the Iranian Constitution and looking for legal ways of obstructing Mossadeq, the Shah at Ramsar issued two *firmans* or decrees stating that he appointed General Faz-lollah Zahedi Prime Minister in place of Dr Mossadeq. Zahedi was still in hiding, and Mossadeq was living inside his strong ring of protection. So how was the change to be made? He decided to use Colonel Nematollah Nassiri Commander of the

Imperial Guard (later rewarded by being made chief of SAVAK) as a messenger. He carried news of his appointment to the hidden Zahedi.

Zahedi took control of the next stage of the operation, and instructed Nassiri to arrest three of Mossadeq's closest advisers. Zahedi told Nassiri that he should try to deliver the decree to Mossadeq personally, so that he could not deny that he had received it. Before midnight on 16 August 1953, Colonel Nassiri, accompanied by two officers, drove from the Saadabad Palace to Mossadeq's house in Tehran, and walked coolly through the ring of tanks and troops up to the front door. 'The Colonel had judged correctly that the tank crews and other troops knew him so well, and were so accustomed to respecting his authority, that they could not bring themselves to shoot him down,' the Shah said later. Considering the darkness, it must still have been courageous to rely upon one's personal identity as a safeguard for survival.

Nassiri's request for a meeting with Mossadeq was refused: but at about 1 a.m. a receipt for the *firman* was handed to him. It was, he could see, in Mossadeq's own handwriting. Nassiri was told that the chief of the army's general staff under Mossadeq wanted to see him at the War Ministry. With no choice, he made his way there under escort, and was arrested. His driver managed to get away unnoticed, and returned to the Saadabad Palace with a message from the Colonel to be transmitted by radio to the Shah at Kelardasht.

Two days had now passed since the Shah gave Nassiri his orders. Now in his headquarters at Kelardasht, he waited impatiently for the news that never seemed to come. 'I recall vividly that for two nights I hadn't slept,' he recalls. Minute after minute, hour after hour passed, and still there was no news. At last, before dawn on Sunday, 16 August, Mossadeq came on the air telling the people that the Shah had plotted to overthrow him, and had failed. A few minutes later Nassiri's message was transmitted, and the Shah learned of his imprisonment. It did indeed seem that they had failed.

Following a prearranged plan for this contingency, the Shah and the Empress at once flew in a single-engined plane to Ramsar. From here they were flown on to Baghdad in a twin-engined plane by the pilot, Lieutenant Khatami (later to become the Shah's brother-in-law). As luck would have it King Faisal of Iraq was expected to return from a trip that morning, and the Minister for Foreign Affairs was waiting for him at the airport. When the Shah's plane landed unannounced, the Iraqi minister recognized his unexpected guests. Piles of clothes had been thrown in onto the plane seats, together with a few suitcases, a briefcase, and a jewel box. The Shah's pale blue suit was crumpled, and the Empress, dressed in a brown linen dress, looked wan and exhausted. Even in the shade the temperature was nearly 40°C.

The officials improvised and did all they could to make their unexpected royal guests comfortable. They were taken to the White Palace. Not until it was diplomatically safe did King Faisal see them. Ironically he and his family were to be assassinated in a palace coup five years later while his royal 'refugees' survived. Two days later, amid endless speculation from the Press that the Pahlavi throne was lost for ever, the Shah and Empress travelled on to Rome, where they felt they would be safer from possible kidnap or violence. His Imperial Majesty's Ambassador in Rome failed to welcome the man who now looked like a deposed monarch. There was more to come. 'I recalled that my personal car was at our Embassy,' said the Shah later. But, 'Our then Chargé d'Affaires actually refused to give me the car keys.' But individual strands of loyalty are as much a part of Persian tradition as fickleness and opportunism: among the Embassy staff was one long-term loyal employee who quietly brought the keys to him.

They drove to the Excelsior hotel. On the Tuesday night a shocked Shah and Soraya heard on the radio in Rome that the Iranian Foreign Minister, Fatemi, had made an impassioned speech denouncing them and demanding that all the Pahlavis should be hanged.[3] Yet according to CIA reports, 'Mossadeq, although popular with the masses, had never been able to undermine the young Shah with his people.'[4]

Events were balanced on a sword-thin edge: who would win?

When Mossadeq first announced that he had imprisoned the Shah's messenger, Colonel Nassiri, a mob had demonstrated in the streets in favour of Mossadeq's revolt and his plain intention of overthrowing the Pahlavis. But his announcement that the *Majlis* was dissolved had lost him the support of the liberal and intelligent majority. The Ayatollah Kashani had already withdrawn his support: now Mossadeq felt the draught as many less influential but solid men withdrew. He was left with virtually no one in his favour among the Muslim right wing or in the bazaar. He could only count now on the Tudeh, the Communist party: and for all his anti-Pahlavi violence he was a traditionalist. The situation was two-edged for the Prime Minister, who appeared to be going to throw his country to the dogs of mob rule. All was nearly ready for the proclamation of a republic. 'It appears', writes Peter Avery, 'that . . . on 17 August, the Tudeh Party was under careful instructions, efficiently passed to its members with great rapidity and succinctness and possibly emanating from the Russian Embassy, to participate in the crowd's acclamation of Dr Mossadeq.'[5] On 18 August the Tudeh decided to destroy all the statues of Reza Shah in Tehran, then set out to desecrate Reza Shah's mausoleum at Hazrat Abdul Azim, some eight miles away. But when they began to loot the mausoleum before settling down to destroy it, they met with unexpected resistance from the local inhabitants.

The next day, 19 August 1953, there was an astonishing turnabout. The streets of Tehran were suddenly filled with highly keyed and disciplined troops who made their orders felt and had them obeyed.

Nine hours of street fighting followed. Members of the Tudeh seemed to be obeying a general order to stay indoors. A new element was seen in the *bazaari* mobs now on the Shah's side. They were led by Sha'aban Bi Mokh (Sha'aban the Brainless), who ran a Zurkhanah, a 'House of Strength' or gymnasium in Tehran. A former champion athlete, both his sympathies and his ambitions were on the side of the monarchy, and, with his strong-arm followers, he persuaded, frightened or paid those in the bazaars to demonstrate and fight for the Shah. Gangs of young men walked through the streets distributing piles of banknotes, mainly 10-rial amounts, to anyone who shouted 'Long Live the Shah'. They distributed 10 million dollars.[6]

Unaware that the tide was turning in his favour, the Shah was at this time shopping in Rome, trying to forget his anxieties and what still looked like a desperate outcome to his and the Americans' hopes of saving Iran from Mossadeq and the Communists.

By noon, according to General Arfa, 'Most of the town was completely in the hands of the loyalists, the Ministers having all disappeared'.[7] General Zahedi, the Prime Minister who had spent the first three days of his appointment in hiding, emerged at about 2.30 p.m. and broadcast to the nation. The end came when a tank manoeuvred into position in a narrow alley behind Mossadeq's house and fired a single shot which demolished half the building. Mossadeq climbed a ladder to get into a neighbour's garden, and from there escaped in a lorry. He was arrested within forty-eight hours and later brought to trial for treason and lèse-majesté.

The throne was once more ready for His Imperial Majesty the Shahanshah Mohammed Reza Pahlavi. American money, the CIA network, the Shah's supporters, had won the day. The next month, September 1953, President Eisenhower announced an immediate allocation of 45 million dollars in emergency economic aid, distinct from the money already available under the Point Four Plan, to make up deficits in the Iranian budget. The wall against Russia must be strengthened.

Chapter 16

Counter-coup

ROME at lunchtime on 19 August 1953: the Shah and the Empress Soraya had little appetite. What they wanted was not good food, but good news. While they were drinking their coffee a reporter from the Associated Press Agency ran up to their table with a tape which read 'Tehran: Mossadeq overthrown. Imperial troops control Tehran. Zahedi Premier.' The Shah went white, and Soraya burst into tears. Dozens of people crowded round their table. For once the Shah was almost completely off guard, and as he looked up into their expectant faces he cried simply: 'I knew that they loved me.'

It was the cry of a man who realized that the sacrifice of his youth, the terrible turmoils and disappointments of his twenties and thirties, the arduous training, the humiliating deference to Allies whom he had sometimes regarded as mannerless upstarts, the dedication of his life and the hopes for a golden future for his country, had not been in vain. He was vindicated, by popular acclaim. Small wonder that at that moment, a moment of pure emotion, he regarded his sudden victory as spontaneous and almost unanimous; small wonder that later he chose to under-estimate, both publicly and in his own mind, the part that the CIA had played in the restoration of the monarchy.

Recovering his composure a little, he added, 'It is a revolution, but a just and honorable revolution. We finally have a legal Government. Now everything will be for the best.' Then, to Soraya, he said simply: 'We will be going home.'

Upstairs, he grew calmer and realized that it would be wise to wait for confirmation of the Imperial victory from General Zahedi. When this came it was decided that the Empress should go on to Switzerland until Iran was considered safe enough for her presence. Finally the Shah took off in a specially chartered KLM Constellation. On the flight he sat with his shirtsleeves rolled up, chatting to some ten or so journalists whom he had allowed to accompany him. They celebrated together, opening bottles of champagne on the flight: it was perhaps the most informal moment in the adult life of Mohammed Reza Pahlavi as each hour brought him hundreds of miles closer to his destiny as Shahanshah once more. After a night in Baghdad, he flew back to Tehran in his own twin-engined plane.

In Tehran everything had been done to disguise the ravages of the past few days. Wherever possible the statues of Reza Shah which had been torn down by the Tudeh had been hastily set up on their plinths again and repaired; others were covered with carpets or flags. Troops, alternately facing the road and the buildings lining it, were stationed every fifty yards from the Mehrabad airport to the palace, and the whole area had been closed to the public. The Shah's portrait was once more displayed as prominently in as many public places as possible. Also prominently displayed was the picture of General Zahedi.

As the Shah left the plane to the strains of the Iranian National Anthem several Ministers who had remained loyal to him ran forwards and threw themselves on the ground to kiss his feet. The Shah lifted them to their feet and walked on. By midday on 23 August 1953 he was home in his palace, and the end of an almost classic example of coup and counter-coup, played according to Persian rules, was being celebrated. The Empress joined him two weeks later.

Only twelve days had elapsed since Mossadeq's 'referendum'. But in those twelve days the Shah had suffered terribly, and the scars of those wounds would stay with him forever. Now, at the end of it all, he was back in power: but it was in fact a new Shah who was welcomed home that day, a changed man who would never again trust either his subordinates or his destiny. From now on he would seek to control power as absolutely as was possible in his country: he would keep as tight a rein on the executive as was practicable; he would allow no alliances of different groups to join against him; he would believe that no man had been sufficiently moved by his trust or mercy to remain absolutely loyal to him in all circumstances. From now on Mohammed Reza Pahlavi would walk through his life alone, suspicious of every so-called friend, of every Minister thought trustworthy, of every servant deemed discreet, of every shadow judged insubstantial.

The events of this fortnight in August 1953 could be read two ways. Publicly, he declared from his palace: 'Until now I was a hereditary king but now I am an elected one: by your actions, you have given me the chance to believe that you have elected me.' This was partly, indeed, true: but at a deeper level he made a final, private, decision. Never again would the Shah of Iran have to thank a President of the United States for giving him back his birthright. Iran must be shown to be his, and to be glorious. More than twenty years later, in 1975, he told me: 'And myself, you know, I have this deep belief that I am pre-destined to do things. It's already set, it's already decided. And I will be around as long as what will be decided will not be accomplished.

'I take a little credit for myself still. But I have great faith.'

'But you think the number of years you will live is pre-ordained?'

'Oh, I think so. I think so, otherwise I should have died many times.'

'Your father, you said, Your Majesty, had such an imposing personality that it virtually shut the door on close friendships, and you said "I often wondered if he was lonely". In your own position you *must* take great care in choosing friends . . .'

'It's the same. Not that I create some awe in people, but I cannot open myself. I have no friends.'

'What about the General, your brother-in-law, General Khatami, who was killed very recently in the hang-gliding crash?' [General Khatami had piloted the Shah's plane to safety when Mossadeq tried to overthrow the regime in 1953.]

'That was no *friendship*.'

'No friendship?'

'No friendship at all! [almost angrily] No. I *have* no friends –
I . . .'

[I was told later that the Shah had been deeply distressed by
Khatami's death.]

'In the family, do you feel your brothers are friends?'

'Not what you call friends.'

'Your wife?'

'Well they are all dear ones – they could be very close. But the
question of *confiding*, discussing and . . . *this* does not exist.'

'Even in the marriage you can't . . .?'

'Well with her it's much more than others.'

'But you always feel you have to – really there's no one you
can turn to in difficulty and doubt, you have to make up your
own mind and solve your own problems?'

[With a sigh] 'This has been the case so far.'

'But then you feel you can turn to God?'

'Oh yes [in a voice that seemed to me stylized] otherwise this
would have been impossible to do.'

Chapter 17

The New Régime

THE last quarter of 1953 paved the way for policies to which Iran still adheres today. On 26 October 1953 the Shah celebrated his thirty-fourth birthday: but in some ways he was already an old and sad man, burdened with a knowledge of the darker side of human nature. From this knowledge came increased political acumen in the international scene, where pride and determination combined with flexibility to make him a first-class negotiator. But on the home front his experiences nurtured suspicions and repression, and led him to encourage the system of spying, and spying on spies, which eventually led to the setting up of the Secret Security Organization, SAVAK, and to an alienation within society of many of its most valuable members, and of group from group, which ideally, in a country completely loyal to him, he would have liked to see united.

Talking about the Iranian nation a few months later he dropped some hints of the thoughts that had been in his mind since he flew home in triumph: 'The Iranian nation is firmly resolved to smooth over the difficulties in its way of progress. . . . After the bitter experience of the past it has discovered the truth, that the attainment of goals is not possible except by relying on the racial virtues and ancient qualities, that is, an adoration of Iran, and unity and self-sacrifice.'[1] So he turned to look back in his search for the path forwards; and he turned not only to the glories of the Persian Empire at its height, but to the controls

K

used by Reza Shah to subdue those who were unruly when he
came to power.

In some ways this was, in the short term, not only expedient
but sensible. Unfortunately judged by a longer time scale some
of the harsh measures he would introduce over the coming
years would have a backlash, stirring up unnecessary resentment
against him both in his own country, among many who otherwise would have been devoted to his aims, and, increasingly,
in the West.

It is easy to understand how many of the policies which
originated in the 1950s seemed eminently practicable: and how
hard it was to envisage that, twenty-five years later, they would
have widened rather than healed the rift that was now apparent
between the Shah and many of his people, from some of his
ministers and a large proportion of the Muslim clergy, including
the landowners, and also a proportion of the peasants (though
if all his aims had been achieved with magical swiftness, the last
group would have had much to thank him for).

But to try to move a country – and, more important and im-
measurably more difficult, the various societies within it – forward at breakneck speed, inevitably produced symptoms of
unease. The progress made in Iran in half a century took the
country from a feudal to a modern technocratic society, a
transition which had taken countries in Western Europe perhaps
ten times as long. Iran's past is thus of paramount importance
when considering its present, and as in many societies where the
written word is not understood by more than half the population,
and the literate half has no great training in reading, memory
speaks much louder than facts.

The greatest example of reform and the complications and
difficulties attendant on it concerned land, its inheritance and
ownership, and the profits from its proceeds. The Shah's own
scheme for selling his Crown lands to peasants had been interrupted by Mossadeq when he was Prime Minister. Mossadeq
feared a 'landslide' where all great landowners, of whom he was
one, would be forced to distribute and share their land and wealth
with their tenants and others. Mossadeq had introduced instead
his own rural improvement decree, under which landlords had
to pay the peasants an extra 20 per cent from their share of farm

profits; half this extra amount went directly to the peasants and half to a village council.

The ultra-complicated question of reform had been nibbled at since Malkam Khan, who died in 1907, proposed it in an essay; but theory was slow to be put into practice. Now that Seyid Zia ed-Din Tabatabai had returned from exile, Mohammed Reza often saw[2] and consulted this former rival of his father's. It was an alliance no stranger than many other unlikely relationships in Persia.

During Reza Shah's reign much new *Khaliseh* (Crown Land) had been acquired, mainly from the confiscation of estates belonging to rebels and tax-defaulters. Reza Shah also acquired large areas of land for use as his personal estates, and these were administered separately from the *Khaliseh*. When he abdicated in 1941 these personal estates, comprising over 2,000 villages or parts of villages, were transferred to the state by a decree dated 11 September. The next year a law was passed for their return to their original owners and courts were set up specially to arrange these transfers. In 1949, those estates which had not yet reverted to their original owners and the ownership of which was not *sub iudice* became instead the property of Mohammed Reza, and were constituted into a *vaqf* (land immobilized for some purpose, usually religious or charitable) which was to be administered by the Pahlavi Foundation for social services. This *vaqf* was said to comprise 'between 1,500 and 2,000 villages and various other items of real estate.'[3]

After his visit to the United States in 1950, the Shah emphasized that steps must be taken to establish social justice. Direct taxation must be levied, so must inheritance taxes, and capital must be distributed more evenly. On 15 January 1951 the newspaper *Darya*, edited by Dr Arsanjani, pointed out that although it was nine years since Reza Shah had abdicated, no positive steps had been taken to modify the distribution of wealth.[4] A *firman* arranging for the sale of the royal estates to the local peasants was issued on 28 January, but there were legal difficulties in implementing the scheme, and opposition to the Shah's decision quickly sprang up among the landowning classes, who claimed the sale was a betrayal of Islam.

Proposals were made in the *Majlis* for the purchase of large estates by the Government who could then distribute them: but since it was known that funds for such a project were not available, this was actually a step to impede land reform by a stalemate.[5] On 16 March 1951 the first actual distribution of land from the Pahlavi estates took place, and in September 1952 a development bank was set up to carry out development work in the transferred villages, to set up cooperatives, and to collect money due from the peasants, who were in fact buying the land at low prices and on easy terms. But in the spring of 1953 the sale of the Pahlavi estates was suspended by Dr Mossadeq's Government.

Only four days after his triumphant return to the battle-torn city of Tehran, the Shah said that he would continue distribution of his estates to the peasants. This he did, but other landlords showed no tendency to follow suit: he had once more roused the ire of the landlords who had, in Qajar times, been close to the throne. Indeed, in those times the thousand families who now under Mohammed Reza Pahlavi comprised the majority of large landowners had mainly been related to the Qajars, and this was often how they had gained their wealth and power.

But there were many reforms which were easier to set in motion. In November 1954 the United States promised Iran a further 127 million dollars. Now the development plan could really make headway.

In September 1954 an initial agreement was reached on the difficult question of oil revenues. This was based on the idea of an international consortium. The United States began by securing the agreement of the five major American companies to the idea, and then presented a plan for the approval also of Britain, the oil company itself, and the Tehran Government. Under this the parties would combine to explore, produce and export Iranian oil. In compensation for the company's nationalized assets, and of the claims and counterclaims of both parties, Iran undertook to pay the AIOC £76 million. The income was to be divided into two equal parts. Iran's share, plus a royalty of one-eighth on crude oil, was to be half of the oil income before the payment of taxes from foreign governments:[6] in practice she would receive nearly 70% of the profits. By the time this agreement was reached Iran was almost bankrupt and therefore totally dependent on the aid she was receiving from the United States.

The Shah was no longer satisfied with the sharing of profits, but in her present state Iran was not in a position to impose its will on its partners and customers. The new agreement was ratified in October 1954, and the flow of oil began once more. In 1952 output had been only one million tons: five years later it was thirty-six times greater. Cooperation with the West proved lucrative: in 1955 the United States loaned Iran another 150 million dollars. Western technology was also available: a British firm was engaged to supervise a £30 million road reconstruction project; while American, French and West German companies supervised the building of 770 agricultural schools, 780 art and technical training centres, 245 health centres, 400 village clinics and 160 hospitals.[7]

The Shah also instructed General Zahedi and his Government to open talks with the Soviet Union on both frontier and financial problems. A new atmosphere had prevailed from this quarter since Stalin died in 1953, and on 2 December 1954 agreement was reached on the demarcation of Russo-Iranian frontiers in Iranian Azerbaijan and in Khorassan. One question remained: whether Iran should join the Baghdad Pact, as the United Nations hoped she would but Russia hoped she would not. In October 1955 the Shah had decided that Iran would join.

If international relations were thus changed all round from 1953 on, and internal development plans speeded up, there remained an area where progress was ambivalent. Aggression was no longer, for the moment, turned against Iran's old imperialist enemies or against those she considered exploiters of her oil and other resources, it was directed instead at some of her own population: those who were, or might become, dissidents. Martial law was extended in Tehran for another two years or so after the Shah's return to overall power in August 1953.

An anti-Tudeh drive was only to be expected after the events of the summer, and this had many side effects. Before long 'it was no longer possible for writers and artists to meet in cafés opening off one of Tehran's most thronged streets, as throughout the

War and for nearly a decade after it they had been in the habit of doing,' Peter Avery noted.

> Until 1951 Sadiq Hedayat had been of their number and was generally to be seen, at about six o'clock in the evening, chatting with friends in a teashop or one of the bars in the centre of the city. When his brother-in-law, Razmara, was murdered, Hedayat decided to leave the country; he wrote to the author saying that the 'vileness' and political 'obscenity' of Tehran had become intolerable. There was, he said, no hope any longer that political freedom or decency might prevail; he was leaving never to return.[8]

Most significant of all was the proclamation of General Teymour Bakhtiar as Military Governor of Tehran. He was a relative of the Empress Soraya's, since he was the son of a leading Khan of the Bakhtiari tribes. Bakhtiar had been educated at French schools and the military academy at St Cyr, then entered the Iranian Army and rose through the ranks to become a general. The marriage of Soraya to the Shah in 1951 had enhanced his chances of success, and although he played no part in Mossadeq's overthrow his promotion to the Military Governorship of Tehran, and as Director of Army Intelligence, was a clear indication of the Shah's great trust in him – great, but not undying.

One of Bakhtiar's first objectives was the location and elimination of Tudeh groups and members, and of those individually sympathetic to Mossadeq. The Shah has said that 640 officers were arrested after the Mossadeq crisis.[9] The number of other categories arrested has never been published. But between 1954 and 1956 Tehran was a city ruled not only by the Shah, by his Prime Minister, General Zahedi, and by his Military Governor, General Bakhtiar: it was also a city ruled by the curfew, and by suspicion and fear. The price of bread seemed less important than the names of those who had just been, or who rumour had it were about to be, arrested.

It was perhaps now, and not during Mossadeq's tenure of office, that the Shah should have been interrogating his wife about the sincerity of their guests' bows and curtseys: now, Soraya noted, they were much more obvious and deeper than they had been before; but it was perhaps before that they had been more genuine.

On 18 November 1953 Dr Mossadeq was brought to trial before a military tribunal. He used the courtroom as a theatre to question everything: the Shah's régime, the competence of the court to try him, the patience of his audience. Sometimes he spoke for five hours non-stop; at others he ranted so rapidly that it was impossible to take notes of what he said. It was a deliberate and memorable swan song.

After forty-three days, on 21 December 1953, the tribunal announced that for all the crimes cited (which were in effect that he had acted unconstitutionally in defying the Shah) he 'had been condemned to death according to the law', but that because of the Shah's own intervention the sentence was commuted to three years' solitary confinement. The Shah did not want to make a martyr of him. And, as he told Soraya, 'if it hadn't been for him our oil would probably still be in the possession of foreigners'.

After his release he returned to his estate at Ahmedabad, near Tehran. Not long afterwards his home was attacked by a mob. Mossadeq telephoned and asked for police protection. It arrived, drove out the mob – and stayed itself, never allowing Mossadeq to leave his estate again.[10] He died fourteen years later, in 1967.

THE SHAH

Part III

Chapter 18

Questions of Succession

'HAVE all Your Majesty's marriages been happy?' I asked the Shah.

'Not all of them.'

'The first one wasn't?'

'Not even the second.'

'No?'

'Not *happy*,' he insisted.

'Because of the children aspect?'

'Yes, and all the things that this created – maybe complexes on the other side, and people all around chattering and – you know . . .'

'She felt that she was failing you?'

'Well maybe – and obviously there are always very, *very, very* nice people around who will [acid laugh] obviously take the opportunity to be as mean as possible when there is a situation like this.'[1]

Perhaps no one was really surprised that Soraya did not show any signs of having a child by the end of her first year of marriage in 1951. Two years later expectation had changed to curiosity and then to suspicion. The couple were quite obviously still in love with each other: indeed, Soraya would have rather had her husband to herself, with no throne, than have to share him with the entire Iranian nation. The Shah had already fathered a daughter by his first wife, though according to the Constitution

Princess Shahnaz, as a woman, was not eligible to inherit the throne. The fault then – and fault it was certainly felt to be, nothing less, particularly in an Islamic society – must lie with the Empress Soraya.

The Shah bore the brunt of the speculation and rumour that surrounded them at this time. It was easier to approach him about his lack of an heir, it was less of an apparent insult since he already had a child, and reminding him of his duty to the state was an excuse for opening the subject with him. To someone as proudly sensitive as he is, the questions must have started as an irritant and gradually become almost intolerably insufferable. Soraya too must have begun to wonder if all was as it should be. It not, what would happen? Since all the Shah's younger half-brothers had Qajar blood in them (on their mothers' side) they were also ineligible, according to the Constitution, to inherit the throne. The only person whom the Shah could name as his heir, therefore, was his only full bloodbrother, Prince Ali Reza, two and a half years his junior.

Prince Ali Reza had perhaps read enough of Persian history to know what was good and what might be bad for him, politically. But at any rate, Soraya remembered later, 'His only passion was hunting'.

The Shah was extremely fond of his younger brother, and had a high regard for him. He often mused, 'Ali has a far better character than I.'[2] But he found it hard to show the affection he felt.

The Prince was determined, as usual, to join the annual family party in honour of the Shah's birthday – his thirty-fifth – on 26 October 1954. That week he was at a cotton plantation he owned on the Caspian coast. On the afternoon of the 26th itself he had instructed his pilot to prepare to fly him back to Tehran, but when the time for departure came, the pilot tried to persuade him to cancel their flight. The sky was black and a storm threatened. The Prince was still hesitating when some peasants staggered onto the airfield carrying a stretcher on which one of the plantation labourers lay desperately ill with pneumonia. They begged the Prince to take the invalid with him to hospital in Tehran: it was his only chance. He agreed and at six o'clock in the evening the twin-engined plane took off for the short flight over the Elburz mountains. But it did not land in Tehran as planned and the Shah's birthday dinner was not as gay as usual.

The next day the fact had to be faced: inquiries at all of the country's airports had proved fruitless. The plane was lost. Various search parties were designated and set out to look for it, no easy task considering the huge mountainous area that would have to be searched.

In charge of one group was Mr Alam. 'I myself was at the head of a group searching the Eastern side of the mountains. We were all looking for it, and another group found it. We brought back the body to Tehran, and His Majesty was very calm. He didn't show any emotion or crying or weeping – but after a while I learned that he couldn't sleep these nights.'

I pressed Mr Alam: how could he be so sure? The Minister of Court looked at me speculatively, as if balancing in his mind how much of the palace secrets it was worth revealing in order to prove his point. Finally he said: 'The butlers told me that he couldn't sleep.'

So it is true in Iran too that no man is a hero to his valet; that, like Napoleon and George III, the Shah of the most secretive society of all is really perhaps, known best by his servants. Mr Alam explained that apparent lack of emotion. 'He doesn't show anything in his manners when this sort of bad thing happens,' he said of his monarch. 'You cannot read anything in his face – he doesn't show it. Even one thinks that he does not regret it much – but at the bottom of his heart he's very sad. I know that he's not a "show-off" man so he doesn't show his emotions at all – that's very clear. But the after-effects of events show that he has been very very injured, even if he hasn't shown it.'[3] With his wife, the Empress Soraya, the Shah was apparently less able to keep up the brave front that he managed to maintain in public. She said later, 'I have never known the Shah so sad.'[4] And, with an insight that may well have been extremely accurate, and was perhaps based on some remark that the Shah let slip, she added, 'I believe he reproached himself for never having let his brother see how much he had loved him.'[3]

Nineteen fifty-four must have been the year of personal heart-searching, as 1953 had seen the peak of the political crisis. But the Prince's death was politically important too: he was the only person whom the Shah *could* then have named to succeed him. A *frisson* of foreboding ran through the country. What would happen to the country if anything happened now to the Shah? Revolution or anarchy would seem inevitable.

The question of the succession to the Peacock throne had now clearly become a public, a constitutional, issue. Ernest Perron, now the Shah's Private Secretary, tried interrogating the Empress Soraya about the most personal aspects of her marriage. She had never liked him, and now dislike turned to repugnance and fury. In an Islamic society a barren woman is virtually disgraced, even if she is an Empress.

To Soraya's chagrin, the Shah refused to comply with her wish that Ernest Perron should be banished, or at least dropped from the royal household. She had to go on enduring the fact that he spent hours each week closeted with the Shah: and now that the succession was a public issue it was inevitable that she was under discussion.

Tadj-ol-Molouk was not her daughter-in-law's greatest fan, and since there was no sign of a grandchild some began to feel an open hostility in the atmosphere. Soraya began to understand that life at Court was a perpetual series of deceits and disappointments: no sooner did one grow fond of someone, or grow to trust someone, than they either had to leave under a cloud of suspicion or proved themselves totally unreliable. Yet there was one person who could be trusted, who was loyal and strong enough to stand by her, to turn away from the questions and reprove the malicious tongues, to scourge the gossips for her and to do all he could to protect her dignity and her feelings: it was the Shah himself. It is hard to find anyone who can fault his behaviour in his marriage during this time of intense personal strain.

'They were in love,' Mr Alam says simply, in a phrase that conveys all to many Western ears but would receive a less understanding reception in the East, and in the Middle East. It was true. The Shah was still in love with the Empress, as she was with him. He realized that a tide of unpopularity was rising against her. Although she had done some social work in the country she kept outside the political arena. Comparing her with the present Empress, Farah, Mr Alam comments, 'She was a different type. And besides she did not have the opportunity.'[5]

Perhaps all the criticisms made the Shah feel still more protective. As a man he would have liked a son, but it was only as a Shah that he *needed* one. It would be two and a half years more, before he would finally admit that this was one problem he could not solve.

Only one month after Prince Ali Reza's funeral the couple arrived in New York and were immediately admitted to the Presbyterian Medical Centre in Manhattan for 'check-ups'. The former Empress recounts that the specialist who examined her said, 'We can find no reason why Your Majesty should not become a mother. You must just be patient.' She asked if any treatment might accelerate the possibility of conception, and was told, 'No, it is pointless, it's simply a question of time.'

Reassured, they stayed on to see something of the United States, with the aid of an official introductions service. This perhaps shows better than anything else how different attitudes towards Iran are today.

While he continued to travel with the Empress, the Shah was receiving regular reports from his various spies at home in Iran. And, in the words of one observer, 'It may be noted here that the Shah had several intelligence organizations working for him, each reporting to him independently; he also made himself accessible to a variety of unofficial informers. Thus there was no prominent person who was not reported on by someone.'[6]

Soon after they returned to Iran the Empress Soraya witnessed a scene that seemed utterly extraordinary. She and the Shah were taking tea one afternoon at the palace when the Prime Minister Zahedi was announced. The Prime Minister bowed low to the Shah, and then said something that astonished Soraya:

'Your Majesty, the burden of my office has become too heavy for me to bear. May I have your permission to go on sick leave? I should like to spend it in Switzerland.'

The Shah's expression was one of surprise as he replied: 'I am truly sorry to hear this, General. But if you think that your health needs attention, then perhaps it would be better if you were to go abroad for a time.'[7]

Zahedi thanked the Shah, and departed. He flew at once to Geneva. It was only afterwards that Soraya found out the truth behind that tea-time encounter. It had been a charade, a classic example of palace pressures and Persian politics. The Shah suspected that the General was becoming too powerful. The Shah's position was extremely vulnerable: apart from having no heir, he had been abroad recently, and Zahedi, of course, was well situated at the centre of power not only to give orders to his old friends in the army, but to seize control of the *Majlis* and of the country itself.

The outgoing Prime Minister was offered an ambassadorship. The present Shah is admittedly much softer-hearted than his father was, but it would be a mistake to attribute his different decisions to this temperamental difference. This was a deliberate policy.[8] He later wrote:

> A number of Tudeh party members, including those who had tortured or murdered non-Communist citizens, were executed or imprisoned. I later extended clemency to those among the prisoners who showed a clear desire to become loyal citizens. Such ex-Tudeh members are not permitted to hold regular government posts, but the Government does find them other employment; for example a number of them are now working for our semi-autonomous Plan Organization.[9]

This was all in the spirit of the Persian proverb: 'Handsomeness with friends, moderation with enemies.'

In the same year six of the army officers sentenced to death for the Tudeh Army Plot of 1954 were executed, though the sentences of thirty others were commuted to life imprisonment.[10] Some estimates put the number of those killed during the coup of 1953 and the ensuing purge at around 5,000.[11] Without the Shah's new and sophisticated system of cooption it might plainly have been very much higher.

Meanwhile the economic situation of the country was giving the Shah cause for concern. There had been a budget deficit of 10 million dollars in 1955. The problem facing a country as vast and underdeveloped as Iran, with a population scattered over such difficult terrain, was circular: to educate and build, accommodation and services were needed; and how could these be provided, without first having staff, accommodation and services for them?

Another development plan was approved by the *Majlis* on 23 March 1956, allotting 33 per cent of the money available for communications and transport, 26 per cent each for agriculture and for social services, and 15 per cent for industry. The plan was reflecting more and more of the Shah's own aims and interests for his country and it was plain to all who were concerned for it that he was gradually centralizing power here as elsewhere.

Nor was he neglecting relations with other countries. In 1956 he visited Turkey and India and he accepted an invitation to visit Iran's former exploiter, the USSR, which resulted in a notable relaxation of relations between the two countries.

Chapter 19

The White Revolution

THE build-up to the next crisis came so softly that the Shah doubtless expected the very opposite of what transpired: a shock that led to the dismissal of General Teymour Bakhtiar, and so, incidentally, to the confirmation of this powerful man as an enemy, instead of an ally and kinsman, of the Shah's.

Both the Shahanshah and his country seemed slightly more relaxed than for many years at the end of 1956. With the exception of Iraq, with whom the Shatt-al-Arab frontier provided a constant line of dispute, Iran was on better terms with her neighbours, especially Russia. Now that oil was once again, and more than ever before, a vastly profitable export, and now that friendly relations had been restored with Britain, and American friendship and funds could apparently also be relied on, it seemed that a new era of prosperity and peace was dawning. The Iranian Government even felt secure enough to gainsay Reza Shah's 1935 edict that the country must be called Iran: from now on, it announced in 1956, either Iran or Persia would be perfectly acceptable. And if economic progress in the country as a whole was painfully slow, a rural Institute of Social Reform and Village Development had been established, and the capital at least was able to enjoy its notable new luxury: piped water.

At the beginning of 1957 the Shah began quietly but insistently to gather more power into his own hands, to increase his own direct say in matters of policy and action. In April martial law ended in Tehran and in several provincial centres. But order was to be kept in a different way. General Teymour Bakhtiar, who had been Military Governor of Tehran, exchanged his post for a new one in a new organization, SAVAK, the State Security and Intelligence Organization, which now replaced the security services in the hierarchy of the Shah's policing of his people. In April 1957 too, the trusted Prime Minister Ala was himself replaced by someone who would show himself still more amenable, more publicly obeisant, to the Shah: Mr Eghbal.

Mr Eghbal had already served His Imperial Majesty as the Minister of Court: and that position has always been a crucial one in the Iranian power system, allowing unrivalled daily access to the Shah and his most private plans. In his address to the *Majlis*, Dr Eghbal emphasized that he was there not only as Prime Minister but, as such, as the servant of the Shah, there to carry out policies given from above, and that he would be loyal to the *n*th degree. 'Using the Persian word, *chakir*, for servant, the Prime Minister himself told all and sundry that he was the servant of the Shah: the office of Prime Minister had finally been captured by the throne.'[1]

The *Majlis* found that some new features were to its own advantage: its mandate was extended from two to four years, and its numbers increased from 162 to 200. There were even two parties now: for in May 1955 Mr Alam had been given the task of leading the so-called People's Party, the Mardom Party. The 'two-party' system was to survive for twenty years, and did from time to time provide a genuine forum for conflicting views, but these still tended, as formerly in Persia, to follow personal rather than party lines.

In August 1957 the National Iranian Oil Company signed an agreement with an Italian company, a new step, and in April 1958 another agreement was signed with the Pan-American Petroleum Corporation, which in addition to Iran's 50 per cent share of *all* profits gave Iran 50 per cent of Pan-American's profits: thus Iran was to receive 75 per cent of oil revenues – a shock for the oil world and a victory for Iran.

Perhaps because of the Shah's increasing power, 1957 also saw the crystallization of the succession problem. The Shah had now lost hope of an heir by the Empress Soraya, and the matter was openly discussed by them at last. The Shah decided to consult the Council of Elders, who met to consider the subject in January 1958. Soraya left for St Moritz while her future was under discussion.

On 14 March a divorce was announced. Those who heard the Shah broadcast about his decision to end the marriage because of its failure to produce an heir for the country he had decided to put before his personal interests said that his voice shook with emotion. If Soraya's lack of interest in politics and the tensions produced between them by the question of the succession had slightly dimmed the lustre of their first years together, he remembered too that she had loved him, unquestionably, for himself, and had perhaps even hoped in 1953 he would be simply a husband, not a Shah. In a way that was the highest compliment that anyone had ever paid him. He would not forget it. They remain on good terms nearly twenty years later. The business of searching for a new wife began almost at once, but his advisers found for a while that the Shah had no heart for the idea.

Meanwhile Soraya settled in Europe, and remembered the conditions of poverty that remained for the Shah to fight: the annual per capita income was only some £40 a year. In the country, many small farmers were more like serfs. 'These conditions were not of the Shah's creation,' she wrote. 'For example, he was blamed because humans and animals often shared the same room and because most Persians slept on the floor. But one must not forget that these were immemorial customs. All Persians used to sit, eat and sleep on the floor. My own grandparents still slept on the ground. It is not possible to change such conditions overnight.'[2] Fifty-six per cent of cultivated land belonged to a small group of rich landowners, some of whom owned up to 100 villages each. Meanwhile the cost of living was again rocketing, and Iran's loans and grants from abroad were some 25 per cent down on the two previous years.

In spite of this reduction in aid from the West, or perhaps because of the incipient weakness it was thought to show, the USSR regularly transmitted special anti-Iranian broadcasts, threatening that if Iran continued as an ally of the US she might be destroyed by Soviet missiles. President Eisenhower visited

Tehran in December 1959. The financial crisis reached a peak in 1960, when the budget totalled 390 million dollars and the country's deficit totalled 145 million dollars. It seemed that the time was ripe for reform.

Two acts of strong resistance to corruption had already taken place in the passing, in October 1958, of two Bills which sought to end corruption both inside and outside the *Majlis*. One of these forbade all Government employees, Deputies and Senators and members of the Imperial family to hold interests in firms having or seeking Government contracts. The Shah planned to inaugurate more land reforms, and on his instructions a Bill was drafted incorporating these.

Elections were held in August 1960. Dr Eghbal was leading the Melliyun Party, and Mr Alam the Mardom Party: when the results were announced, it seemed that Dr Eghbal had won 79 per cent of the seats.

No one believed it, and the resentment and talk of corruption was so widespread that the Shah advised the newly elected deputies to resign. The Prime Minister also resigned, and was replaced by an engineer, Mr Emami. Unrest continued and new elections were held in January 1961, but many groups boycotted them, and widespread student demonstrations meant the closing of Tehran University, while the National Front sponsored an 'ominously successful' general strike in the capital.[4] On 23 February there were further student demonstrations, and although it was six months since Dr Eghbal had been Prime Minister, his car was burned in the ground of Tehran University.

Royal displeasure was now felt to be mounting against the entire Eghbal family; his brother was cashiered from the Ministry of Foreign Affairs and Dr Eghbal himself, having had a promised Ambassadorship to the Court of St James's cancelled, fled the country. He was later *formally* charged with illegal interference in the elections and with giving away illegal tax concessions, which had cost the treasury 500 million rials (over 7 million dollars). But as an ex-Cabinet Minister he was safe from actual prosecution, and by the time the law had been amended to allow for this he had been appointed (of course, by the Shah) Iranian Ambassador to Unesco and was thus once again saved by diplomatic immunity, though twenty-five minor officials were sentenced to fines and imprisonment for their part in tampering with the elections. Dr Eghbal was a virtual exile, but one in supreme comfort: as Marvin Zonis notes the same post served as both punishment and reward. It was a brilliant display of Persian political virtuosity.[5]

In May 1961 further demonstrations broke out. They began with Tehran teachers demanding higher salaries on 2 May, and the next day serious clashes broke out between the teachers and security forces. The January demonstrations had resulted in about 300 people, students and police, being wounded: but on 3 May a teacher was killed. The Shah acted swiftly to defuse the situation and to prevent more bloodshed: Mr Emami, who was, according to his experience, more suited to supervise a factory than to run a country, was removed from office, and in a radio broadcast on 9 May the Shah announced 'a series of strong and efficient reforms in all parts of the country'.

It is a measure of the Shah's cool ability to judge his own and his country's situation objectively when this becomes essential, that he now named as Prime Minister a man for whom he himself had no warm feelings at all, but rather dislike and distrust. This was Sorbonne-educated Dr Ali Amini, former Ambassador to Washington and Minister of Finance under Dr Mossadeq. He was an outspoken forceful critic of the malpractices in Iranian society. He favoured limiting the power of the throne and was an ardent fighter for civil liberties.

In his investiture speech on 12 May 1961 Dr Amini said:

> Every country that is run in this way inevitably ends up in total chaos, with enormous bloodshed. Too much money has ended up in the wrong pockets. Too many millions of dollars have ended up in secret Swiss bank accounts or in the United States. . . . I solemnly warn the nation: those whose interests will be damaged by my reform programme will intrigue and do everything to bring me down.

He warned that the Government deficit had risen from ten million dollars in 1955 to 500 million six years later. 'The treasury is empty,' he warned. 'The nation faces a crisis. I dare not say more lest I create a panic.'

Corruption had been widespread, in spite of the sincerity with which the Shah had pushed through the anti-corruption law in 1958, popularly known as the 'Where-did-you-get-it-from' law. Two men who had prospered greatly in recent years were General Alavi Kia, Chief of Army Intelligence, who had a budget of some 1½ million dollars to run a department, consisting primarily of himself, which produced reports on the Shah's popularity. General Bakhtiar himself now lived in a million-dollar mansion in tree-lined Kahke Avenue. He also had a country retreat on the Caspian, eleven farms, three estates, and five more villas dotted round Iran, three residences in Europe, and substantial funds abroad.[6]

Many former Ministers were also suspected of having appropriated funds, or having received bribes in exchange for accepting contracts from foreign countries. The 'Where-did-you-get-it-from' law needed more strict enforcement it seemed. Both generals were dismissed.

Others were not so fortunate: some 32 generals and 270 colonels were in prison in June 1961. Prime Minister Amini felt that General Bakhtiar should also be arrested and tried: but when he heard rumours of what was afoot, Bakhtiar sent a terse message to Amini: 'I'll shoot anyone who comes to arrest me.'[7] Dr Amini decided instead to ask the Shah to order Bakhtiar abroad, to Europe, for 'a vacation'.

The Shah went with the Empress Soraya for a visit to Norway while Amini continued to push through his 'revolution from above' and to weed out corruption. They returned, three days early, to a strange reception: 'they stepped into a closely and heavily guarded Rolls Royce and sped through the streets where no crowds cheered. The silence was so embarrassing that a Government radio announcer tuned in "canned applause" to simulate a popular welcome.'[8]

Nor was Amini himself a particularly popular figure it seemed: he had apparently succeeded in antagonizing most powerful sections of society: 'the army was against him because he had cashiered hundreds of officers, the politicians were against him because he had persuaded the Shah to dissolve Parliament; the newspapers 'freed' by Amini were against him because he had threatened to cut editors from the public payroll. Most of all Iran's landowners, the so-called 'Thousand Families'[9] were up in arms – for Amini, a landowner himself, had warned them that they must distribute land or face a revolution from the peasants. One man, a self-made millionaire who owned thirty-five villages and an estate larger than Switzerland, raged, 'I can build up another fortune with my sweat and bare hands even if I am stripped and left in the desert':[10] but many felt less confident of their future.

Dr Amini's new Minister of Agriculture, Hassan Arsanjani, was not to be put off from reforms he had been planning since 1945. Within two weeks of his appointment he said: 'One can no longer continue with this system from the Middle Ages. . . . In these land reforms we are facing the reactionary front which has wasted fifty years of the Parliamentary régime and have now confronted us with the choice of a "red" or "white" revolution. If the country remains in its present state, it will explode.'[11]

As members of the *Majlis* and Senate naturally tended to be drawn from the literate and landowning classes (the literacy rate in rural areas was still under 15 per cent) the Shah chose a breathtaking way to announce that the reforms would take place. On 11 November 1961, when neither House was in session, he announced that he had a right under the Constitution to initiate legislation. 'This claim has been disputed but nevertheless government by decree was inaugurated.'[12] On 15 January 1962 it was announced that the Land Reform Bill of 9 January had become law by royal proclamation. Each family could retain one village, regardless of size: the peasants in the extra villages would receive title to the land they were then tilling; peasants should make annual payments to the Government for fifteen years, after which they would own their own land; ex-landlords would be reimbursed for their lands with fifteen-year Government interest-bearing bonds; the Government would establish rural cooperatives to help the peasants carry out their new agricultural responsibilities. (A new *Majlis* was not elected until the autumn of 1963.)

To overcome the landlords' resistance to reform and to give impetus to the programme from the very top, the Shah renewed the distribution of Crown lands, which were removed from the aegis of the Pahlavi Foundation. In April, in a ceremony at the Marble Palace, the Shah gave the deeds to their lands to 2,600 farmers from forty villages along the Caspian coast: the last of the 518 villages he had once owned.[13] By the end of the year, 500,000 hectares of land had been distributed to 35,000 peasant families and 1,080 peasant cooperatives had been established.[14] It would be hard to put the clock back to the Middle Ages after this.

But the strengthening of the position of the Central Government was also inevitable if the reform continued. Partly because of this, the year had been a fateful one for Prime Minister Amini. In January an announcement of cuts in Government scholarships had been followed by unprecedented unrest at Tehran University: students poured through the streets shouting 'Down with Amini, down with corrupt and vicious government'. At first sight the Government's reaction is astonishing. The events of 22 January 1962 were described by Dr Ahmad Farhad, the University Chancellor, who at once resigned, in a letter to the Prime Minister:

> At 11.00 a.m. soldiers and paratroopers had occupied Tehran University. There was no reason or excuse for the violation of the rights or regulations of the University.
> Soldiers and paratroopers after entry attacked boys and girls indiscriminately. . . . Many of the students were beaten to the point of death.
> I have never seen or heard so much cruelty, sadism, atrocity and vandalism as on the part of the Government forces. Some of the girls were criminally attacked in the classrooms by soldiers.
> . . . troops [were] fighting unarmed students without interference from their officers.
> Even the University Hospital was not immune from the soldiers.[15]

Afterwards the University was closed down. The fighting had left one dead, and 218 injured; 300 students were in prison, and Dr Amini said 'If we run short of cells we will build new gaols.'[16]

The Government's motive for these violently disproportionate reprisals were analysed two months later in a pamphlet signed by the Students of the Freedom Movement of Iran, dated March 1962, entitled 'The Fate of the University':

> The intention was to close down the University because the University had become the last bastion of the national struggle, it

had replaced the Bazaar as a political centre. In the old days, the Bazaar could resist the Government because it was economically independent and it enjoyed clerical support. But the centralization of Government and the establishment of banks . . . robbed it of its independence. With the economic depression [beginning in 1960] the intimidation of the police finally was able to completely suppress the Bazaar voice. The clergy were similarly silenced. The civil service restricted. The press muzzled. The Majlis nonexistent. They had left only the University. . . . It was this last voice that had to be silenced.[17]

But gradually it began to appear that the students had vastly oversimplified events. Zonis comments: 'As the investigation continued, more of the guilt was reputed to centre on Bakhtiar. It appeared that he had instigated the military attack in order to embarrass the Shah, bring down Amini, discredit the National Front and have himself – the choice of the military – promoted to the premiership.'[18] Four days after the violence in the University, Bakhtiar was summoned to the Marble Palace. When the former General emerged from his face-to-face encounter with the Shah, he went to the airport, and flew to Switzerland. Some 300 army officers who were thought to be sympathetic to Bakhtiar were placed on permanent retirement: the Shah had not forgotten how his father had risen to power on the crest of a military wave.

A budget crisis in the summer led Dr Amini to press the Shah for cuts in military expenditure and the size of the army. When the Shah refused, Amini tendered his resignation. Now the Shah proclaimed as Prime Minister his old friend, former royal estates' steward and former Minister of Labour, Mr Alam. And to placate the National Front an astonishing offer was made: they were invited to join the Government, to hold cabinet office. But they would do so only on condition that the Shah's powers were reduced, and negotiations were broken off.[19]

It was absolutely vital now for the Shah to have a Prime Minister whom he trusted implicitly. Moreover Mr Alam was extremely sophisticated and urbane, and capable of dealing with every group of supporters or opponents on their own terms. 'It is madness,' he told journalists when he heard of his appointment. 'I am too lazy for the job.'[20] All his sophistication and suppleness would be called to the fore now, for as usual in Persian politics, the reforms hid many different motives. One of them certainly was the Shah's genuine concern for the most poverty-stricken and miserable of his people, and the desire to bring the nation up from a prostrate position at least to its knees.

But the reforms also meant more power for the Central Government: and it was this above all that united so many strands of the opposition. While some peasants agitated because reforms had not yet reached their areas, others felt that the reforms would impede a complete takeover of landowners' assets by the peasants. On the other side the wealthy, the land-owners, the religious leaders (who stood to lose most of their vastly profitable *vaqf*, religious lands) and the merchant classes were determined to stand firm against any further implementation of reforms.

Mossadeq's referendum had failed, but it had given the Shah an idea, and reminded him of the only man in Europe who held an amount of undiluted power in his hands that, if not as potent as his own, had nevertheless impressed him: General de Gaulle, like his father a man who had assumed supreme power from a military base. He would follow his example. Six items were to be approved:

1. The land reform law, to divide state, religious and land-owners' estates among the peasants cultivating them, with compensation for the former owners.

2. The sharing of profits by workers in the industries in which they were employed.

3. The nationalization of forests, with compensation for former owners.

4. Electoral reform, including the right of women to vote and to be elected.

5. The eradication of illiteracy by using conscripts to educate during their term of social (instead of military) service.

6. The transformation of state-owned industries into share-holding companies in which the public could invest.

It was a double blow for the *mullahs*, who were not only to lose their lands but to see women enfranchised. This they claimed was a violation of Islamic law. The tremendously influential religious leader, the Ayatollah Khomeini, who had once boasted, with probable truth, 'I can summon a millon martyrs to any cause', was arrested. He had allegedly issued pamphlets stating that land reform was contrary to Islamic principles. In March, theological students at the religious city of Qum demonstrated: their leaders were arrested, and SAVAK members occupied mosques, shrines, and theological schools. With the heat of summer and the religious festival of Moharram, mourning the martyrdom of the Shi'a saints Hossein and Hassan, passions once more began to flare. On 4 June, Khomeini was arrested.

Within two hours, crowds had begun to gather round the bazaars in Tehran to protest against the arrest of the holy leader, and by ten in the morning the troops were firing on them. Rioting spread to Meshed, Qum Isfahan and Shiraz but was put down after three days. Estimates of those killed varied widely, someone sympathetic to the demonstrations believing that between 5,000 and 10,000 Iranians had died throughout the country, while Mr Alam, now Prime Minister, told the *New York Times* that 86 people had been killed and 150 injured.[21]

In October 1975 I asked Mr Alam, Minister of the Imperial Court, if it had greatly distressed the Shah to have to use the army to fire against their fellow-countrymen. 'Indeed it did,' he replied, 'but at the time it happened that I was Prime Minister; it was a very serious business, it had to be or not to be. . . . There was a very severe collation against the Government: that was from the clergy who were losing their profits and the landlords who were losing their land and the Communists who were losing their fertile ground for propaganda.

'The referendum showed afterwards that the University and the people were 99 per cent in favour of this [land] reform. But when the University reacted against the reform it was only those inspired by Communists and *mullahs* – His Majesty called this the "Unholy Alliance", between clergy and Communists and landlords. And it was *serious*. Therefore when I proposed to His Majesty "Do you allow me to shoot? To order shooting?" he said "Yes, not only I allow, I back you."

'Of course it was a very bad event, but altogether only ninety people were killed – *only* – and about 200 injured; not more than that [in Tehran]. In the provinces we had more; we had not only rebellion among the tribes we had rebellion in other towns than Tehran, so everywhere – the whole country – was boiling.

'And His Majesty was as a rock. I could really feel that I can rely on that rock.

'For example in the worst period of the event a group of people including my predecessor the Minister of Court with five or six people went to His Majesty just when we were having trouble all over the country – our rebellion in Tehran – in the third or fourth day they went to him and asked him to get rid of the Government and make another Government to be just of some more lenient character and to make some reconciliation with the *mullahs* and things like that. He not only refused but he threw them out of the room. He not only did that but he immediately summoned me and ordered me to detain all of them and put them in gaol.'[22]

The Shah had decided on reform once and for all, and reform he would have, even if it had on occasions to be imposed by force: it was a peculiarly Persian problem, and the solution, like some herbalist's painful remedy, may have drawn criticism and scepticism from the West, but it was largely effective locally. When the Ayatollah Khomeini urged the boycott of elections in October 1963 he was arrested for the second time. This time he was detained by SAVAK for seven months, until May 1964, when SAVAK claimed to have reached an 'understanding' with him. No sooner was he released than Khomeini claimed the understanding had been extracted under duress; therefore, as a true Shi'ite, he had been entitled to rely upon *taqiyah* (dissimulation): as he was now to speak the truth, and renounce the 'understanding'. A few days later he was taken by the police, put on a plane at a military airport and taken to Turkey; there the Turkish authorities cooperated with SAVAK and he was kept under house arrest.[23]

SAVAK now took the extraordinary step in view of the prisoner's exceptional rank and following, of issuing a statement 'Since . . . Mr Khomeini's attitude and provocations have been considered contrary to the interests of the people and to the security, independence and territorial integrity of the state, he has been exiled from Iran effective November 4, 1963.'[24] No formal charges had been brought against the Ayatollah: yet he had been exiled and was held a prisoner.

Iran was shocked. What to many foreign observers may have seemed, in comparison with some of the treatment meted out by SAVAK, a comparatively mild chastisement was, to the faithful Shi'ites, drastic action. Never before had a religious leader been treated with such disrespect. This meant more ammunition for the forces who opposed the Shah's White Revolution, and above all for Bakhtiar who, it was said, had flown from Switzerland to Baghdad at the time of the riots in 1963.

SAVAK's new head was General Hassan Pakravan, whose name means 'pure soul'. He was known as a softly spoken, pipe-smoking intellectual:[25] the sort of person who, in England, might relax by solving *The Times* crossword puzzle. The puzzle in Persia was not so simple: how to maintain a vigilant watch and control over a man who was not even in the same country. It would take seven years to solve it.

Chapter 20

Plots and Counterplots

THE official figures given out after the referendum on the Shah's six-point White Revolution were highly gratifying to the régime, in spite of a manifesto urging boycott of the referendum which had been issued by the National Front. This concluded: *We must say NO to the arbitrary rule of the Shah, his interference in the affairs of the state, the rule of terror and SAVAK atrocities, colonial domination of the country, police violations and gendarmerie oppression and the overlordship of government officials in towns and villages.*[1]

This rejection of overtures made to the National Front which followed the sacking of the head of SAVAK, and of the army, and their replacement by 'officers reputed for their liberalism'[2] was more than the Shah's tolerance and temper could take. National Front leaders were rounded up. The Shah himself went to Qum, the religious centre which had been the womb of so much of the *mullahs'* entrenched opposition to him, and attacked the *mullahs*, or 'black reactionaries', whom he now regarded as '100 times more treacherous than the Tudeh', or 'destructive red elements': 'the Black reactionaries and the destructive red elements . . . have chosen the Egyptian government as their leader and want Iran patterned on Egypt.'[3] (Egypt had been a republic since President Nasser ousted King Farouk, the Shah's former brother-in-law.)

Arrests continued as the year went on. Some who were charged with activities against the security of the state in January 1964 had been in prison for up to a year. The first elections to take place since the Shah dissolved the *Majlis* in May 1961, had been held in October 1963. *The Times* commented in a leader: 'Critics say that they were rigged, and to a large extent the critics are right. . . . But to write the whole episode off as a hoax is absurd. However chosen, the new Majlis is very different in composition from its predecessors. It contains a more varied cross-section of the people, including for the first time women.'[4]

The Shah now had yet another Prime Minister: the youthful intellectual Hassan Ali Mansur. Mr Alam had resigned from office on 15 May 1964, and had been invited to go for a while to Shiraz, as head of Pahlavi University.

On 21 January 1965 Prime Minister Mansur arrived at the *Majlis* in his car. He was to seek party approval for new agreements recently signed with five international oil companies.[5] As he walked towards the doors three bullets hit him. They were fired by a twenty-year-old theology student, Mohammed Bokharai, who was seized with his two accomplices. Mansur was rushed to hospital where surgeons operated and removed two bullets from his throat and one from his stomach. The Shah flew back from a skiing trip to his bedside. For five days it looked as if he might recover, but then he had a sudden relapse, fell into a coma and died. He was buried in the mausoleum normally reserved for the royal family.

Meanwhile under interrogation the assassin had named Bakhtiar, now in Baghdad, as an instigator of the plot. The Shah began to wonder if, after all, exile provided a sufficient deterrent and, still more, enough control over the enemies of the régime.

Two months later, 10 April 1965, came the second organized assassination attempt on the Shah's own life, in what came to be known as the 'Marble Palace Plot'. The Shah had just walked into his office with his head of protocol at 9.30 that morning, and the door had barely closed behind them, when gunfire sounded all around. When the Shah opened his office door three corpses were lying in the hall. One was a soldier, two were bodyguards. It took a little time to piece together what had happened.

The would-be assassin was the dead soldier, Reza-Shams Abadi, a twenty-two-year-old who was doing his national service in the Imperial Guard, and had run after the Shah from his car into the palace with a submachine gun in his hands. A gardener who had tried to stop him had been injured – one notices again the loyalty of the simple employees, as in 1953 in Rome – while two guards took to their heels. One of the Shah's bodyguards tackled him but was instantly killed by a bullet in the head. The second bodyguard, warned by the sound of gunfire, had time to fire a pistol at the soldier who was still advancing on the Shah's office with his submachine gun firing. Both bodyguard and soldier fell dead.

Physically the Shah had not a scratch. Emotionally too he seems to have been able to withstand this second attempt on his life with a composure that amounted almost to the blasé. He refused to cancel an audience with a French admiral later that morning, nor did he mention the incident to him; the admiral first heard of the attempt when he returned later to his embassy. And after lunch he played bowls. 'The will of God which had saved me on several previous occasions snatched me from the jaws of death.'[6]

Twelve young men were charged with complicity in the assassination attempt on the Shah.[7] Two were sentenced to death and ten to life imprisonment; later the death sentences were reduced to life imprisonment and the third ringleader's life sentence to ten years. Four of the other plotters were freed on the eve of the Coronation two and a half years later. 'They had committed a crime against me personally,' said the Shah, 'I had therefore a right to commute their sentences.'[8] Once again mercy avoided martyrdom. But once again Bakhtiar's name was linked with the plot.

Those accused of the assassination of Prime Minister Mansur were not so fortunate: members of the *Fedayan Islam* (Devotees of Islam), they were sentenced to death or imprisonment and on this occasion the death sentences were carried out. And at the end of 1965 fifty-five people were taken into custody and charged with plotting the overthrow of the régime and with trying to establish an 'Islamic Government', while fourteen Tudeh members were tried *in absentia* and sentenced to death.[9]

Two years later, on 19 May 1967, came yet another attempt

M

on the Shah's life when forty Commandos attacked his car: but
they chose a moment when he was not in the vehicle. Only
fifteen days later there was a fourth attack: the Shah was visiting
West Berlin when an Iranian student in Germany, Alikai Nadar,
tried to aim a car laden with explosives and directed by remote
control, so that it would collide with the Shah's car. This time
the trial had a particular interest: it was held in West Germany.
It was the first time that anyone accused of plotting against the
Shah had been tried outside Iran. The court sentenced Nadar to
only eight months' imprisonment. He freely admitted that he had
been masterminded, and that the money for the bombs and the
remote control with which the car was fitted had been supplied
by that mastermind: Bakhtiar.

Back in Tehran a dossier was being prepared against Bakhtiar.

'As he was a very ambitious man, he was also one of those
who was intriguing, from Baghdad,' Mr Alam summed up later.
'He went from Switzerland to Baghdad, and from Baghdad he
was intriguing against the Government of Iran. He was even
financially helping the rebels here to make difficulties for the
Government.'[10]

On 15 August 1967 the Office of Military Prosecution in
Tehran announced that Bakhtiar had made 'a vast fortune
illegally' while head of SAVAK. He was also charged with
'engaging in illegal activities . . . to further his own personal
ends' and so, in accordance with traditional Iranian justice,
'orders have been issued to confiscate all his properties. . . .' In
1969 Bakhtiar was arrested by the Lebanese in Beirut and sent
to prison for smuggling arms.[11] The Lebanese police had been
warned of the explosive contents of his car in a telephone call
from SAVAK in Tehran.

The Shah hoped for his extradition, but the Lebanese authorities refused to hand him over on the completion of his prison
sentence. As a result, on 22 March 1969, Iran broke off diplomatic relations with the Lebanon.

When Bakhtiar was released from prison 'by virtue of the
Lebanese traditions of hospitality' he was not handed over to
SAVAK but allowed instead to be exiled to the country of his
choice. In September 1969, he was tried by the Iranian authorities
in absentia for treason and the death sentence was passed on him.

It was now up to SAVAK to find a way of carrying out that sentence while Bakhtiar was outside their territorial limits.

An international campaign was started to try to gain a reprieve. Bakhtiar had chosen Switzerland as his country of exile and had landed at Zürich in March 1969. From here he flew secretly to Baghdad. He would manage to survive for another seventeen months. He relied partly on international politics to protect him: the old dispute between Iran and Iraq, which still smouldered, had proved extremely useful, as had his knowledge of the inside workings of Iranian Military Intelligence.

At last, in August 1970, Tehran newspapers carried a report of Bakhtiar's death. It was said that he had been accidentally killed by a member of his party while hunting game in Iraq, only twenty miles from the Iranian border.

At the outset of his reign in 1941 foreign observers had concluded that the young Shah, influenced by his Swiss education, was 'experienced and well-meaning', unlike the nineteenth-century Shahs who 'tended to come to the throne with traditional notions of a monarch's unfettered prerogatives, which they then had to modify or abandon as a result of the winds of change blowing from Europe'. The opposite had happened to Mohammed Reza Pahlavi: he had 'tried at first to behave as a constitutional monarch should. It was the experience of kingship which forced a change on him.'[12]

Chapter 21

THIRD MARRIAGE:

Farah Diba

IN May 1958, two months after his divorce from Soraya, the thirty-nine-year-old Shah went on a private visit to Paris. His ambassador there held a reception at which the best Iranian students in Paris were presented to him. Among them was a tall girl of nineteen, twenty years his junior, who was attending a course at the École Spéciale d'Architecture in the Boulevard Raspail. Her name was Farah Diba.

The extreme awe and reverence in which the Shah is held even by those courtiers and members of his household who are in daily contact with him seems only normal to the Persians. Compared with the near-servility shown even by his family in the last century to Fath Ali Shah, each of whose sons had to stand to attention in his exact place in the hierarchy, attitudes today are relaxed and even casual. But to a Western observer this deference, extending as it does even to those who carry out the Shah's will, seems sycophantic (when I came out of the Minister of Court's office with Mr Alam, I was astonished to see the hasty way in which a roomful of people turned to face us and bowed low, horizontal to the floor).

One can therefore imagine the consternation when this girl, who had never been in His Imperial Majesty's presence before, stepped forward and asked how Iran could make progress when grants for study abroad were being cut, while some

subjects were not yet taught in her own universities. It was a
protest and a question in one: a mode of addressing the Shahanshah that was most novel and one that Farah Diba would never
outgrow. Then the Shah smiled, and everyone relaxed. He would,
he said, look into the matter.

In 1959 Miss Diba returned to spend the summer holidays in
Tehran, and went to one of the Shah's ADC's, then the husband
of Princess Shahnaz, to ask for a bursary to pay her fees in Paris.
All three became friends and Shahnaz decided to introduce
Farah to her father. The Shah has since claimed to have no clear
recollection of their encounter in Paris and the Empress Farah
has often teased him about this.[1]

According to another story which they both ignore, the Shah
saw her leaving his son-in-law's office, and asked him, 'Who
was that?' The next day Farah received an invitation to visit
Princess Shahnaz, with whom she had been at school, and
when she arrived the Shah too was there. 'Before she left,'
[the story continues]

> the Shah had asked her to marry him. Farah refused, but so inno-
> cently and timidly that the Shah was not scandalized as he had the
> right to be in a country where his slightest wish is a command.
> Instead he invited the little student to tea every day at his daugh-
> ter's house. He did not mention marriage again but talked to her
> about her plans, about herself and his life until, finally he gained
> her confidence and then her affection.

A fortnight later he took her over the desert in his personal
plane and again asked her to marry him: this time she accepted
his offer.[3]

The Shah says he first saw a photograph of Farah.[3] He told
his daughter he would like to meet her.

They had their first 'good discussion' at his son-in-law's
house. About a week later, the Shah proposed to her, and she
accepted. 'Of course,' he adds, 'we then had a number of further
meetings.'[4]

'I was a little bit in the clouds, you know – I couldn't realize
what was happening to me,' the Empress told me. 'I can't
remember what was my first reaction when he proposed to me ...

'In a way . . . it seems that it must have been done like this.

Sometimes you think that things are arranged from before or even – destiny.

'When we met first of all I was anxious. But when we started to talk I was natural. . . . I was myself in such a state that I couldn't see how he was! But I think inside him he is maybe a little bit shy – sometimes it comes out: not in work, not in his official duties, but on private occasions.

'When I first met him I was very anxious, and my heart was beating, you know – you meet a king and you have to talk to him and the thing was, now I think back, I didn't try to impress him. . . . For instance, to behave in such a way to please him so that he would marry me.

'You know – it was most natural. I mean he wanted to meet me and I went there and he met me and we talked!'

Did he propose the first day?

'No! No, no. Of course, we met a few times . . . I don't know how many times.

'My husband tells me – this I can tell – before we got married and during – when we were meeting each other – he liked in me my simplicity.'[5]

Farah Diba was born in Romania on 15 October 1938. She was a distant cousin of the Shah's, but from an untitled family herself. Her grandfather was a former Iranian Minister at The Hague, her uncle was an adjutant to the Shah. Her father, a diplomat, died of cancer when she was ten, and, her relationship with her mother, an ardent worker for health and social reform, naturally became still closer.

'I was the only one. But I grew up with a cousin of mine, a boy, we lived together so it was almost like a brother.'

In a Muslim society, had she felt at a disadvantage compared with her male cousin?

'No. Of course it's different you know because after all he was not my brother. But I didn't feel that at all – maybe because I myself was a tomboy when I was young.

'And my mother let me do many things which are very normal today but which were not twenty years ago. I was the leader of cub scouts [the Shah says 'she was Scout leader for a group of small boys from another French language school'] and we went camping, there were boy scouts with us and this relationship between girls and boys twenty years ago was much more difficult.

'I wanted to go to a public swimming pool and that was sometimes a question of argument in the family: whether my mother would let me go in the pool when there were boys around. Or let me go to Paris alone to study.'[6]

She had been to the Italian school in Tehran, and then, when she wast en, to the Jeanne d'Arc school in Tehran, run by the sisters of St Vincent de Paul, where she learned French and captained the basket ball team. She came twentieth out of 156 candidates for admission to the École Spéciale d'Architecture in Paris.

Mohammed Reza Pahlavi had refused to be rushed into a third marriage.

Now he had found someone whose qualities he felt were right. So, while speculation mounted in Tehran, Miss Diba flew back to Paris on 20 October 1959, ostensibly to continue her third year studies, but also to shop for her trousseau. The Shah told her uncle that she was to buy 'twelve of everything' she wanted. She ordered her wedding dress from Yves St Laurent.

On 23 November 1959, came the announcement of 'the engagement of His Imperial Majesty Mohammed Reza Pahlavi with Miss Farah Diba'. The wedding date was set for 21 December, two months after Farah's twenty-first birthday.

The bride-to-be had flown back two days earlier, saying goodbye to Paris and the somewhat limited freedom that an Iranian girl of good family was allowed. Now she lived an almost unreal life.

The evening of her engagement provided a double cause for celebration with 450 guests. The royal family was also celebrating the marriage of the Shah's youngest half-sister, Princess Fatemah, who was twenty-nine, to General Khatami, Commander-in-Chief of the Iranian Air Force. It was he who had flown the Shah to safety in 1953.

She was entering a turbulent society. 'But I did not know what was expected of me,' she admits. 'Now I think that I should have been more worried, or frightened. But I was not. When I went from our house all dressed up to go to the Palace to the ceremony in my wedding dress and people gathered in the streets, I was waving to them.

'The idea never came to my mind fortunately, that maybe they wouldn't like me or something like that. It was much later when I thought of that. . . . I didn't *try to be anything* and this is what helped me I think.

'Later on I realized that it's not an easy job, first, in a married life, to come to a family with their own traditions and their own way of life – there were brothers-in-law, sisters-in-law, mother-in-law; also there were court people, there was your duty as a Queen towards the nation. I took it so naturally that fortunately everything came by itself.'

Rumours about her predecessors' inability to get on with the matriarch Tadj-ol-Molouk have never been heard about the Empress Farah.

'She has got a strong character and sometimes she was maybe difficult,' she says. 'With me it was different: maybe she had changed a little bit. I liked her and really love her because for me she is a symbol of, you know, the eldest person in the family, and I was brought up with a sense of family and I always try to keep this sense.'

Her wedding coincided with political troubles, as Soraya's had in February 1951. Relations with Iraq that were strained over the double question of the Shatt al-Arab frontier and the Shah's support of the Iraqi Kurds. The president of the Iraqi Council, General Qasim, had suddenly renewed the Iraqi claim on more of the Shatt al-Arab zone.

Troops moved into position on both sides of the frontier; and the new Empress heard her husband say: 'My first duty is to my country.'[7] Their honeymoon was postponed: the public reason was 'a cold'.

A foreigner observed their 'dissatisfaction with the Shah's régime now seems more widespread and vocal than at any time since his 1953 exile'.[8]

In the same month (December 1959) President Eisenhower visited Iran. An American diplomat was quoted as saying, 'The Shah is in the very real sense of the word a nice guy. But as Leo Durocher once pointed out nice guys finish last.' Some Iranians were complaining that the Shah was not tough enough to rule effectively.[9]

Relations with Russia were also fraught: 'This cold war

lasted from March 1959 until the middle of 1962,' wrote General Arfa, 'Kruschev adding menacing personal declarations openly inviting the Iranian nation to rise and overthrow the monarchy.'[10]

The country was beginning to slide into a financial depression. The Shah's ambition of making Iran a 'modern stable state' by 1965 could not be achieved: but there were undeniable signs of great progress. Opium addiction and malaria, which till 1950 had been two of the country's major health hazards, had been virtually eliminated,[11] and new ports and dams were a sign of both efficiency and of confidence in expansion.

On 31 October 1960, ten months after their marriage, the Empress Farah gave birth to a son: The *Valiahd*, or Crown Prince Reza. 'I think he was very happy when his son was born,' the Empress says simply.

The future of the dynasty and of the country was no longer in obvious jeopardy. The Shah gained a new confidence: and in May 1961, when the Crown Prince was less than seven months old, he dissolved the *Majlis* and his reform programme, including the land reform, was imposed by *fiat* (decree).

But the early 1960s also saw the riots in the university and among the theological centres. The Shah burst out openly at a press conference when he was on a visit to the United States: 'Let me tell you quite bluntly that this King business has given me nothing but a headache.'[12] But gone were the days when he felt, 'I am still deeply in love with Soraya. I destroyed my personal life to save my country.'[13]

Asked if at last he had made a happy marriage, he replied: 'I think so, definitely. Because what do you seek in marriage? Love, it's true. But in addition to love the feeling of having a home. A companion who understands you, shares your sorrows and your pains and your joys. And also creates a family. In addition to my eldest child, my daughter [Princess Shahnaz] I now have a son and a little girl and we enjoy them very much.'[14]

People turned to the new Empress instinctively, as they had done more than 150 years previously to one of the many wives of Fath Ali Shah, 'the Queen at Shiraz . . .' who was accustomed every two years to take a journey to the King at Tehran. The British diplomat James Morier noted in those times of great cruelty and hardship: 'She enjoys a great reputation, and the affections of the people; for she is charitable to the poor and ready to do justice to the oppressed.'[15]

The Shah and the Empress quickly realized that this spontaneous reaction could help not only their people, but themselves as well. For Farah the need to help the unfortunate is inbred. If she took over from the Shah many of the inquiries into maladministration and charitable work, as well as following her own interests in the arts, she would keep both sovereign and family in closer contact with the public than the Shah himself dared. Because of his belief in a dignified image and the traditional belief about the Persian people expounded to Morier in 1808 that 'the better you treat them the worse they will treat you',[16] the Shah has followed the dictates of his natural reserve. He never mixes with crowds. The couple therefore fill complementary roles, whose results were soon seen in plain terms.

Shortly after the birth of the Crown Prince, the Shah proclaimed two holidays for the whole of Iran, 20 per cent reduction in tax, and an amnesty for ninety-eight prisoners. About a week before the birth of their second child (Princess Farahnaz, born on 12 March 1963) it was announced that the *Empress* had asked for an amnesty for 14,750 prisoners: this they duly received on the birthday. The Shah also gave much of the credit to his wife for the decision to spare the lives of those behind the Marble Palace Plot. 'He only asked for my pardon,' the Shah said later of the ring-leader. 'He was a broken man. As soon as he left the Empress came and joined me. Mansuri turned round – he looked so utterly miserable. I exchanged glances with the Empress and decided at that moment to pardon him.'[17]

If Reza Shah met his match in Tadj-ol-Molouk, Mohammed Reza Pahlavi met his in Farah.

'What do you think is the quality you need most of all in an ordinary wife and second in a wife who has to play the part of an Empress?' I asked him.

'Intelligence, patience . . . maturity. . . . Now I may be mixing things and thinking more of the Empress than women, because I was going to say "not to believe in the first thing that you hear". Because women have the tendency of immediately believing what they hear and then they have a prejudgment [prejudice] – that might be a handicap for them. It will take a long long time before they are convinced that what they have heard on this or that subject is wrong . . .! "This man has done that!" Then he's finished, dead.'

'If the woman is more intelligent than the man?'

'That cannot work. She will not have the respect that a woman should have for a man if a marriage is going to work. They will start to disregard and even despise the man – obviously this cannot work. But if instead of intelligence – well, personality, is important for instance. How could an intelligent woman accept to live with a man who has no personality? Kindness is not enough, I think that he *must* have something else to offer; otherwise, she will develop some kind of mother complex or daughter complex or something.'

'Do you feel that being the Empress has made her sacrifice a great deal of pleasure in life?'

'Oh – well, yes, although we have our vacations and she really likes *that* but she is working very very hard and [banging his clenched fist against his thigh in his only impulsive gesture I saw] *too much!*'

'You have two months' holiday a year?'

'Maybe just a little more, but they are not complete holidays. I work at least three or four hours even during my holidays. Maybe exceptionally one day I will have nothing to do. And she will sometimes get also the *courier* [mail] and do some work – but *otherwise* she *works* too *hard* – too *much!*'

How different he sounded talking to me from his attitude when talking to the brilliant Italian interviewer, Oriana Fallaci, two years before, when he said:

Women – well, let's put it this way, I don't underestimate them . . . but I wouldn't be sincere if I asserted that I had been influenced by a single one of them. Nobody can influence me, nobody at all, and a woman still less. In a man's life women count only if they are beautiful and graceful and know how to stay feminine. This women's lib business for instance – what do these feminists want? What do you want? Equality you say? Indeed. I don't mean to seem rude, but – you may be equal in the eyes of the law, but not, I beg your pardon for saying so, in ability. . . . You've never produced a Michelangelo or a Bach – you've never even produced a great cook. Women, when they are in power, are much harsher, much more

cruel, much more bloodthirsty. I'm quoting facts, not opinions.
You're heartless when you're rulers – think of Catherine de' Medici,
Catherine of Russia, Elizabeth I of England, not to mention
Lucretia Borgia with her poisons and intrigues – you're schemers,
you're evil, every one of you.[19]

It was an Islamic outburst. I asked the Shah whether the
interview had in fact been accurately reported. With startling
candour he replied: 'Er . . . I said those things. But she was
obviously trying to . . .' he corkscrewed his index finger through
the air, and I suggested 'Needle you?' 'Yes, that is the right
word. And she got those answers.'[20]

Before the arrival of Islam with the Arab invaders of Iran
in the seventh century there were two women rulers of Persia –
'though that was hardly our apogee', says the Shah. In the past
the role of the Shah's consorts (always plural until the present
Shah's serial monogamy) has varied between that of the harem
darling and that of the palace matriarch. A glimpse of the former
is seen in an account of the death of Fath Ali Shah, who had more
than 150 wives: '. . . becoming worse, he asked Aga Bihram, one
of the eunuchs, to sit behind him, as for a pillow, and he put his
feet in the lap of Taj el Dawlé, his favourite queen, and passed
a very painful hour. He afterwards spoke to Taj el Dawlé as
follows: "My days are finished, and now everyone of you must
think of himself."'

The Shah plans to hand over the reins of power to the Crown
Prince in or about 1988, while hoping (as Reza Shah planned)
to remain in the wings as a potential *deus ex machina* in the event
of unexpected troubles. How the balance of power would work
in practice between father and son it is hard to conceive. But
should any untoward (if not quite unforeseen) fate overtake the
Shah before the Crown Prince reaches the age of twenty, he will
step straight into a monarchical mould where the Empress acts
as Regent, and a council of state (similar to the former Council
of Elders but much better briefed) advises him. 'The financial
and economic sides of our country and all the defence and
security sides of our country – all the people responsible for
these things will brief the Empress and the Crown Prince on
what these questions are, and what is the matter with these, and
how things are dealt [with] today; exactly what is going on,

what the country needs, what is its geographical position, its geopolitics in the world, its importance, its strong points, its weak points.'

The future is blue-printed, with plans to meet all eventualities.

'Would you have rather had four boys?' (That very day a young Iranian had told me of his distress at having a daughter as well as a son: two daughters, he said would have been 'horrible'.)

'*Four* boys? No, no. They all believe that I have something against women which is not true. That comes from that interview published by Oriana Fallaci.'

'Where you are lucky as the Shah is in having a very happy home and family life –'

'That counts, that counts.'

'– because you can't show your feelings to very many other people.'

'No. That counts *a lot*. If one didn't have that it would be – so much more difficult.'

'Do you still watch a lot of films in the evening?'

'Yes.'

'There's quite strict censorship – for instance, *Last Tango in Paris* wasn't allowed to be shown here, was it?'

'We have less now, less and less, but I think some of these pictures, I don't know if they should be shown.'

'Who decides?'

'There is a board.'

'Do *you* go by the Board's decisions?'

'In *our* house? Oh no.'

'Have you seen *Last Tango in Paris?*'

'I have. I have.'

'Your opinion . . .?'

'Not much. Once you see a pornographic thing – maybe the first time, you are astonished or shocked or maybe even interested; then it's all the same thing. They try to make it more dirty and more exaggerated each time. Finally it has not got much interest. I think when there are nuances and you have got to guess a little, you have got to make your imagination work, it's much more thrilling than those things.'

' It was also a study of despair, wasn't it? The agony of this man?

'Oh yes, obviously you can explain it this way, but – er – then many other pictures were made, Italian or even British. You can always have some explanation. But it's not aesthetic, I don't know – you can't really get pleasure of the eye – you can eventually understand what it *means* but it does *not create* the pleasure of the eye.'

'What films have you seen recently?'

'Well personally I'm for either very famous novels which are now filmed or historical facts, made into films. For instance I liked very much what was produced by this famous French author, *Les Rois Maudits* [shown on television in England under the title *The Accursed Kings*]. That was very precise facts. I don't mind if his facts are romanced a little. And I like Westerns. But now today you must have at least one or two sex scenes and *lots of blood – lots* of blood. Everywhere you have got to have blood.'

'I suppose you are careful about the children – what they see?'

'Not especially, no; if this is the present world, OK; but they must also know that there are other things than that.'

'And they all go to school here, don't they? How is that arranged?'

'We have a school in our house, and other children are brought in to classes: the good, studious children of other schools. And they develop friendship with the young boys and girls, and I think they are treated absolutely equally. This is what we want and this is what they want too – the children themselves. No, I think they have a very healthy education.'

'Does the Empress ever feel now that *she* can advise *you*? Or do you always advise *her*?'

'Well, she is absolutely free to tell me exactly what she thinks, which she does.'

'She is a good critic, is she?'

'Oh yes, she can be very vehement and very [quick in] following up the critics; but it's good, it's quite healthy, I think. Then I will have to convince her, because she wouldn't give up before she is either convinced or she gets her point.' A silence followed. Then I asked:

'And sometimes she gets her point, I hope?'

'Sometimes, yes, sometimes, surely.'[21]

Any previous Shah would have been ruined if he had said as much. And even if some of the Shah's predecessors had been transported into the twentieth century and had been talking to 'one of *you Christian women*', as His Imperial Majesty Mohammed Reza Shah Pahlavi at one moment addressed me, it is hard to think of more than one or two who might have had the courage, generosity, honesty, and above all, the political flair to make such an admission.

Chapter 22

The Life of an Empress

AFTER seventeen years at the top of one of the world's most turbulent societies the Empress Farah looks very different from the simple girl of twenty-one who married the Shah. Yet she retains her warmth and determination beneath an elegant exterior.

Traditionally Persian women have a 'carnation on their cheek which is called the *namak* or salt of beauty, and which is the second requisite of female perfection. The first is large black eyes, with brows very much arched.'[1] The Empress, now the mother of four,[2] is rather pale beneath her reddish-brown hair. Her eyebrows are shapely but not exaggerated, and do not meet, or nearly meet, in the centre as they do in most paintings of beauties of the past. Her eyes are most eloquent – 'eyes like the stag', in traditional terms.

She looks very different in public and in private: on state occasions she looks hollow-cheeked and haughty; she appears to listen intently to the endless speeches at banquets, but at a display of gymnastics, her chosen expression is blank. In private her face is alive and luminous, ever-changing. With his professional eye Annigoni noted, 'She can be beautiful and she can be ugly. And so she is alternately it seems to me.'[3]

Her task has grown, and keeps her working about seven unremitting hours a day – not counting state functions and official dinners – with a staff of forty. It is not easy. 'I had a

11 The Shah and the Empress Farah whom he married in 1959

12 In 1967, when he had been on the throne for twenty-six years, the Shah arranged
his coronation. *Left to right:* Princess Ashraff, the Shah's twin sister, Princess Shahnaz
his daughter by his first marriage, Princess Farahnaz and Crown Prince Reza, two of
his children by Empress Farah, Empress Farah, and Princess Shams, his elder sister

normal life before my marriage and of course I miss it,' she admits. 'In a job like mine the most difficult thing is to remain oneself, not to be restricted to that "golden cage"; not to lose one's identity.'[4] Her own interests have suffered: 'I feel guilty if I read a novel.'[5] But her beliefs in social justice have not: 'A gift of money can be first aid. It is rarely a cure,' she says.[6] The responsibilities of her life have made her almost too wise for her age. 'You have to educate yourself, you have to find a kind of philosophy in life. I am not talking only about myself but anybody who really wants to find a way of life for oneself.

'. . . I didn't expect it to be the way it is today. It is much harder. You know when you are young you are full of ideals; but your horizon is closer and it took me years really, little by little, learning about my country and its problems, to find ways to solve them. . . . It's a wonderful challenge but it has also some disappointments. . . .

'I would like to be less sensitive: I don't mean become a rock, no, but to the point where it can't make me suffer a lot . . . For me each problem becomes a problem of life and death. . . . But physically and morally for one person it can't be possible: I can't go on like that. I don't know whether I will change or not. . . . To live without destroying myself – psychologically I have to make myself stronger.

'You know I believe very much in justice; and I believe very much in the *pride of people*. I believe that people should be equal, regarding law, as human beings. When I see someone stronger maybe pushing someone weaker or not being kind to him I get so angry and I am revolted – I can't stand that, that is really for me the hardest thing: to see people bullied. When I see somebody pushed by a policeman in the street I just can't stand it. In a case like that I go to the Chief of Police and say "This is the way I want it to be and this is the way which is good for you." I can understand for instance that your policeman is not educated, he doesn't realize what he is doing, and sometimes he behaves the way *people* [the public] behave because this is our society. You cannot expect to educate millions of people, but you can expect to educate a few hundred policeman: so you have to show the example. I want people to respect these policemen, so

N

they have to behave in a way so that they are of help in the street, like a father to a child who will come to him instead of being scared of him.'

She gets 50,000 letters a year. 'But sometimes – oh the expectations are unbelievable, you couldn't imagine it in your country or in America – just people who . . .! Imagine people asking what they ask from us! They don't want to move themselves, to do something first, to try to find work for instance, or to do something and *then* if they have a problem, *then* come to me. The first thing they think, without making any effort on their side, they just write to me. (Most of these letters are written by people who are in this business of writing letters.)

'Something that I want badly to be done – for instance there was some land that was supposed to become a park, and then there was a plan to build some housing there – you know, I go like an advocate to explain to my husband that this should be kept as a park, my throat goes tight and I want to find a lot of arguments.' [The Empress won her case: the land has since become a park.]

Does she ever feel there is a subject she cannot discuss with the Shah?

'No, no.'

One of her greatest personal successes has been the relationship with her mother-in-law, the formidable Tadj-ol-Molouk. 'With me she is too sweet sometimes. I have tears in my eyes she is so sweet with me, when I hear the way she behaved before.

'She understands, she realizes more things. We go twice a week to her house for dinner, and a few years ago sometimes I really couldn't always go for one night: either I was too tired or I was just busy, and she would say – not seriously! – "You don't come to hear me, you don't like me", or something like that. But now she understands, she says "I know you work too much, and you write, and you should rest" – you know.'[7]

Iran has changed fundamentally between their two generations, but both are strong characters and devoted to the good of their family and of their country.

She thinks family life in Reza Shah's time was 'less a problem of security: not so many bodyguards and security gadgets around. That's one thing which is too bad for our children. And for ourselves also! Fortunately one gets used to them, and they become part of the family, all these security people. But it's not normal, and this is what the children suffer from. They would like sometimes to have nobody around, but we try to arrange [that] when they go out and they go to movies and they go shopping. Some people even tell me that they do it too much. But I say, you can't do it too much with these children, you want them to become normal – I mean the circle gets closer and narrower round us. For us, well, it's different, but for the children it would be impossible. And sometimes my son says when we go to a restaurant he wants the guards to be far away and not to be noticed.

'*Our* time was much more simple. Suddenly after I came out of school it was another generation – a sudden change: we were much simpler and more natural, and then children and young people became more complicated. But you know in a way we had much more fun with simple things. We would enjoy family parties . . . and a little bit, the nostalgia, you know, that one has for the Good Old Times . . .

'One of the only things my husband likes in life is flying, driving, driving boats – speed! This is one of the few things he likes in life. He goes too fast also on skis. I love skiing but I am more cautious – I go for style and he goes for speed. But I tell him that for the country he should not take risks – in an aeroplane in bad weather. But he tells me "you don't know, it's *not* bad weather". General Khatami was the only one who could talk to him, and say "Your Majesty, if you want to fly a jet you have to do it at least once a week, or once every fifteen days, and not take it up after a few months without flying!" But you know it's a king, and other pilots don't dare to tell him; but I think they should – do the regular thing that any pilot must. His life is not his own so he must be more careful. It was a sad thing that happened to General Khatami.' (General Khatami was the loyal pilot who flew the Shah out of Iran in 1953 when Dr Mossadeq tried to depose him. In 1959 he married the Shah's half-sister, Princess Fatemah. He was killed in a hang-gliding accident in 1975, shortly before this interview.)

Could speed cheer the Shah up if he was feeling depressed?

'Yes, or riding also. He rides the most *terrible* horses: not a calm horse, not a kind horse. . . . He wants to have a horse who jumps all the time, who moves all the time with his front legs or . . .

'But he's not really *depressed*. He is worried, yes, he can be very worried. And he doesn't show it. Sometimes one feels that he doesn't even have the *right* to show that he is worried! Because you know if people around him see, everybody becomes nervous. . . . I don't know if it's love of danger. . . . Sometimes we discuss it and what I think is dangerous, he tells me it's not. For instance he loves driving fast and – fortunately in the traffic of Tehran he cannot do it! But driving very fast motor boats for instance – I'm scared, those motor boats, new ones, which really *jump* over the waves. And when I tell him it's dangerous he says, "It's not, because you don't realize – you are not technical enough." But I think it *is* dangerous.

'The same love is for my son – he loves flying, he loves driving fast, and I tell him "you are going fast" and he says "no it is not fast". The Crown Prince started flying when he was twelve, I was of course very anxious and very worried: then I thought that the pilots know if a boy can do this or not so I had a lot of confidence in them. Then when he wanted to fly solo it was different. Then we reached the point you know where we couldn't go back. If we had had to tell him not to fly it would have hurt his personality thinking that we don't believe in his capabilities. Or if we had told him "because of your position you cannot do that" – it wouldn't be good either. So we were forced to let him do it. My brother-in-law who unfortunately is dead now, General Khatami, flew with him twice that morning before he went solo and said "He's all right, he can do it", so I had a lot of confidence.'

What made the Shah happy or unhappy?

'Everything that is related to the country. The family less. I think that he was also very happy when the Crown Prince was born. I think he's happy when he sees his boy behaving the way he has done. There were different occasions when he proved that he was a responsible boy: that makes my husband very happy.

'I would like him [the Shah] to have – you know, more physical contact with the children. I myself am a person who likes hugging and kissing but he is not so much that. . . . He talks very much, he has patience, he has affection and love, but I always tell him, "But you *love* the children, why don't you take them in your arms and *hug* them and *squeeze* them and *kiss* them. But this is maybe something that because he didn't learn when he was a child – they didn't do it to him so – he is shy in that way. You know maybe he would *love* to hug them but he doesn't do – just to kiss like that. . . . He is better with the girls because they climb on him, but the boys are always dashing off to do something. . . . I believe that this is important – the physical contact with the parents.

'But people would be surprised if they knew some things. For instance, about little children weaving carpets, he said, "If an art must be developed with the fingers of little children working in bad conditions, working in humid places, or sitting all the time, which will damage their hands, then I don't want that art to exist, knowing that can happen."

'For him it's a sense of justice too. And he's very sensitive sometimes. When there are children involved, or friendship is involved, or human relations or animals involved, he could come to tears in a few minutes. That people wouldn't know! In official pictures he's always very serious and I always say, "Why don't you *smile*?" because he's got, I think, a wonderful smile and such *kind eyes* – but the moment it's official he goes too serious.

'Sometimes it *is* useful, I think *still* in our country it's useful. Because it's a question of education. Our people need someone to be strong with them, and severe, otherwise they lose – their place, or respect. You know, they wouldn't understand. For instance, I can be very kind to a person on a private occasion; but the next day he comes for an audience with me and he should remember, or she should remember, that now they are talking to the Queen – it's different. My husband sometimes gives this example: in America for instance it's very possible that an officer goes with a soldier in a *boîte* [night-club] they drink, they joke: but the next morning it's finished! They salute. But here it might be different – you might be kind to someone and then the next day he will come and put his arms around you, be too familiar. And that is why . . .

'It's so difficult, it's happening in my own life – to be almost equal with everybody, not to show [preferences]. That creates so much jealousy inside a family, among friends, among others. You know how it is. If, in front of everyone, the King talks privately to someone, it's very important. I remember that many years ago, with one of the other kings one of the Ministers went to him and said, "Your Majesty, I would like to come up to you and you can say whatever you like into my ear – Go to Hell, Drop Dead – as long as you say *something* into my ear, it makes my life different in front of the others that the King has spoken to me and said something in private."

'So you know it's sometimes difficult, we are not allowed to show differences; that we like this friend more than the other or this Minister more than the other, or that person more than the other. I think we have to be like that otherwise it creates too much of a problem.

'*Sometimes* I think it's difficult to understand him, but one *can* understand him; and one must know what he . . . He's not moody, you know. I always say it's fantastic for a leader in his position, it's wonderful to have such a strong character, you know, to be always the same. Of course, sometimes he's happier, sometimes he's worried; but he's just strong, and stable and – I sometimes say like a mountain, really, whatever happens. Contrary to me: sometimes I'm full of energy and enthusiasm and I'm up, up, *very up* – and then suddenly I go down.

'Sometimes he tells me that he envies me, because since he's stable his happinesses are less and his worries are less. Because when I am happy for a little thing, for a big thing I can be *very* happy! I can enjoy really simple things of life or enjoy things much more and then suffer the same way much more. He doesn't suffer over little problems: nor can he be quite as happy if some little thing happens. But no, he's not difficult to understand, and he's not had an easy life. This you have also to realize: his childhood, and becoming King in such difficult times, and suffering so much to reach the level that this country has reached today; and suffering also the *human* side of it, which is for a person who's in power now for over thirty years, believing in some people and then being betrayed by the same people and then believing in some other people and being betrayed again – you know this relationship with people, it's difficult! But he has developed a philosophy in his life. He knows people so much now.'[8] That has been the hardest education of all.

Chapter 23

Oil, Arms and Finance

IN 1852 Nasr ed-Din Shah, aged twenty, his jealousy aroused by envious courtiers, arranged for the assassination of his Prime Minister Mirza Taqi Khan, a brilliant administrator who had organized a paid army, resisted the influence of the British and Russians, and rationed the Shah's 'pocket money'. In 1881, remembering how he had been manipulated, the Shah instructed his private secretary to read a letter to all his Ministers:

> At the beginning of government in our reign, we appointed an independent and capable prime minister. Everyone indirectly and openly said that the existence of such prime ministers is a hindrance of the public good and to progress in the affairs of state. We divided the tasks among the ministers and ourselves assumed the over-all burden. It was complained that this arrangement does not permit preservation of the interests of the kingdom and the subjects. [The Shah then went on to recount all his many experiments and their failures.] The present state of the government and the arrangement of affairs is also a source of objection, and it is said that there is no organization, order, good, propriety or progress. We thus consider our opinion as inoperative, and we ask the ministers, on the basis of their considered, statesmanlike opinion, to tell us explicitly what we should do and how we should arrange affairs.[1]

No one dared to.

Almost a hundred years later, after a similar period on the throne, Mohammed Reza Shah Pahlavi had tried still more methods of governing than Nasr ed-Din. As a very young Shah he had seen his Prime Minister, Ahmad Qavam, outmanoeuvring the Russians. The sharing of power had been forced on him by Dr Mossadeq. After his return to power in 1953 he made sure that he assumed the 'overall burden'. Finally, the recession of the 1960s gave way to the oil boom of 1973, to be followed by the first drop ever in oil sales and the beginning of another deficit. And now Iran had only some thirty years of oil left to nourish the national body.

But in 1973 came a moment of supreme victory: Iran gained complete control over her own oil for the first time in her history. It was the beginning of a bonanza that lasted for two years before Iran learned that economics have their own stubborn rules. By the autumn of 1976 money was being borrowed on expensive short terms to pay for food imports, and Iran had an estimated trade balance of payments deficit of 3,000 million dollars.[2]

The Shah's realization that 'there is no economic power without military power'[3] made him determined about one thing: both inside and outside his country he would come as close as he could to absolute power. Signs of this new attitude were evident even before the birth of his heir. In November 1958 he was quoted at a press conference as saying that Bahrein was an integral part of Iran.[4] The next year he said that Iran would never grant military bases to any country.[5] The birth of the Crown Prince hardened his temper: since 1969 he has been noticeably more aggressive in his way of running his own country, in his foreign policy, and in his militant demands for higher oil prices.

SAVAK, Defence and Oil have become the three prongs of the Pahlavi trident, designed to transfix dissidents, enemies and would-be exploiters alike. On 22 September 1972 he made a speech to the Iranian Defence Academy on the theme that Iran would die rather than surrender.[6]

He offered a double warning to the West and to Russia when he said, 'Russia's military penetration of Arab countries has put a potential stranglehold on the West's oil supplies. You could be defeated economically without a shot being fired. But we have never cut off our supplies and will never be bullied into doing so. . . . If necessary we would fight to a scorched earth situation.'[7]

There are three main reasons for this increased aggression. One, and probably the chief one, is his intention of abdicating in favour of Crown Prince Reza in about 1987, when the Prince will reach the age of twenty-seven. This was first rumoured in 1971,[8] when the boy was eleven, shortly before the 'scorched earth' address to the Defence Academy. The Shah is a fond family man, one of the most loving fathers in a thousand years of Persian history, and the absolute antithesis of Shah Abbas, the great Safavid monarch (1587–1629) who murdered his eldest son and blinded two others to ensure they should not challenge his rule. He has no intention of handing his son a time bomb in the shape of the Peacock throne. This intention of handing over the reins of power (though he himself plans still to be in the wings to help in case of emergency) reflects his own father's intention of abdicating, which he planned several years before he was forced to do so by the Allied invasion in 1941.

The second main reason for the Shah's increased aggression is what he sees as the failure of his attempts to establish a more liberal régime in the 1960s. It is easy to understand the fury that must be felt by someone whose authority and desire for progress is constantly jeopardized by innate unreliability, the defect that Arthur Arnold doubted in 1877 would allow Englishmen to contract for oil with the Government of Persia.[9] Even the short-term visitor to Iran catches glimpses of the extraordinary multiplicity and unpredictability of the Persian mind and character, now loyal unto self-sacrificing death, now treacherous, now with matchless hospitality, now steeped in corruption ('let no man of rank be a tree without fruit', goes the Persian proverb).

One Persian aristocrat told me 'Persians are very immoral'. I asked why he thought that was. Very gravely he replied 'Because they have no sense of morality.' Elusive is perhaps the word that sums it up, and underlines the Shah's reason for believing in strictness. There is even a word, *dastan*, which 'commonly implies something that is neither fact nor fiction but lies somewhere in between'.[10] This may partly explain why, when Charles Issawi asked a Persian delegate at the United Nations in 1948 where he could find out about the Iranian economy, he received the half serious answer, 'The best source on the Iranian economy is still Herodotus.' (Herodotus was born a Persian subject.)

Finally the Sha'rieh, or religious law of the Shi'a branch of Islam, proclaims that it is in keeping with the faith for someone to lie when under pressure and to retract that lie afterwards: a device used by the religious leader the Ayatollah Khomeini in 1963–64, and known as *taqiyah* or dissimulation.

The third main strand of the Shah's inter-linked reasons for increasing the aggressiveness of his régime is shortage of time: Iran has only some thirty-odd years of oil left. The country must be largely literate by then and must be made to stand on its own two feet – industrial and agricultural. Not long ago Iran was self-sufficient in food, though its people lived simply on bread, cheese, herbs, rice, fruit, and occasional feasts of meat and tea. Today it is a massive importer of foodstuffs. But at one point when oil prices were rocketing (after the fourfold increase in oil prices which took place within a fortnight as an indirect result of the Yom Kippur War in October 1973) he declared that if the world tried to defy the new prices, his country would shut down the wells and 'go back to eating goat's cheese'.[12] It was a phrase reminiscent of Dr Mossadeq, and in fact at no time had the Shah more closely resembled his hated former Prime Minister than when he almost blindly and singlehandedly sought to drive through the united Anglo-American front against further huge increases in 1976, a battle from which he withdrew tired and defeated, but with typical realism.

Iran's own position is unique in both race and religion. As an Aryan nation she stands apart from the Arabs (though she has similar neighbours in Afghanistan and Pakistan); and as a Muslim one she is in many instances divided from them too in belonging predominantly to the Shi'a, not the mainstream Sunni branch of Islam.

The catalyst in Iran's aggressive defence of the Persian Gulf was Britain's decision to withdraw her forces from the area by the end of 1971, which the Shah welcomed as 'the right course and the only possible thing to do'.[13] This left Iran as the greatest potential peacekeeper: an octagonal patch of comparative stability in a patchwork quilt of ever-changing shapes and colours in the Middle East as the kaleidoscope of régimes and alliances were repeatedly shaken.

President Nasser toppled the Shah's former brother-in-law, King Farouk, from the throne of Egypt in 1952; the year when, in Iran, Mossadeq was at the height of his powers and the Shah was smarting most under the indignity of his position. Small wonder that he continued to see post-revolutionary Egypt as a symbol of 'There but for the grace of Allah . . .', and constantly reviled President Nasser for killing Muslims in the Yemen, for sending arms to the Cyprus Government for the massacre of the Turkish Muslims in Cyprus, and on any other possible occasion.[14] Relations with President Sadat are markedly better. The Shah describes him, with fellow-feeling, as 'a courageous man who can make decisions in a delicate and difficult situation. He has the courage to stick to his decisions'[15] – heartfelt praise.

The coup in Egypt was followed by many others: King Faisal of Iraq was murdered in 1958; in 1966 Sheikh Zeid of Abu Dhabi, one of the richest spots on earth in terms of per capita income, had deposed his brother (known as 'Jackpot' because he kept his money under the bed);[16] in 1969 Colonel Gadaffi seized power in Libya in a bloodless coup; the next year, 1970, Sultan Qabus of Oman, who had been kept a virtual prisoner for seven years in a fashion reminiscent of some Persian heirs, deposed his father, also in a bloodless coup. He began to introduce reforms, but soon his attention was distracted by attacks from the radical Popular Front for the Liberation of Oman. The danger of both another Communist enclave and of a supertanker being sunk in the Strait of Hormuz, which would block Iran's outlet for oil, led to immediate support from Iran: after the Shah's forces captured an important strategic position in Dhofar, in Oman, the *Tehran Journal* carried a banner headline proclaiming the victory and explaining that 'Iranian forces have been operating in Oman for some time now at the request of Sultan Qabus'.[17]

In 1973 the coup d'état in Afghanistan particularly upset the Shah: the King was deposed and replaced by a President. Relations with Pakistan, to whom the Shah had often previously complained about the smuggling of arms from Pakistani Baulchistan to rebels in Iranian Baluchistan, had improved when the Shah sent tanks and aircraft to Pakistan after their conflict with India in 1965.

Meanwhile in Turkey, student violence had disrupted the Shah's plan to persuade Western oil companies to construct a pipeline from southern Iran to the Turkish Mediterranean port of Iskenderun, which would have made her partially independent of the Gulf.[18]

'The Persian Gulf is a matter of life or death for my country. Perhaps I mean life *or* death',[19] the Shah said after he seized the tiny, barren, but strategically vital Gulf islands of Abu Musa and the Greater and Lesser Tunb which lie just behind the Strait of Hormuz in the Gulf, shortly before the British evacuated the Gulf. They had been under British control for half a century, and Whitehall ascribed their rightful ownership to the Arab Emirates.

Still the Shah was not satisfied. In 1973 Iran proposed a 'mutual security arrangement' among the Persian Gulf states to protect the oil lanes, to guard the states of the region against outside subversion and aggression, and to 'eradicate any excuse for great power interference in the region and the drawing of the Persian Gulf region into the orbit of great power rivalries'.[20] Two years later, when no agreement had been reached for putting these proposals into practice, he was growing increasingly concerned about the 'continuous build-up of US and Soviet naval forces'[12] in the Gulf.

To police the Persian Gulf, it was revealed by the *New York Times* that the Iranian Government had signed a secret contract with a big American defence contractor, Rockwell International, for a 'complete intelligence system' costing about 220m. dollars in computers, radio equipment, and planes, and that former employees of American Intelligence Agencies would man this[22] (while Iranian manpower was trained).

Since the Russians had established port facilities at Umm Qasr on the Iraqi shore of the Gulf, the Shah had dropped his earlier objections to the Americans doing the same at Bahrein. He had begun to speak of Iran and the other littoral powers' 'primary' instead of 'sole' responsibility for the Gulf, and let it be known that if the Russians extended the military facilities allowed them in the Iraqi treaty into bases, he would not be averse to the Americans following suit in the Persian Gulf.[23]

Tension with Iraq itself had been a constant factor for many
years now. A treaty concerning the boundary of the important
Shatt-al-Arab waterway had been signed by Reza Shah in 1937
when Iraq, as a client state of the Western powers, was in a much
stronger position than Iran. Constant guerrilla skirmishes and
the use of the Kurds as bargaining counters in the latent conflict
between the two states had followed Iran's unilateral abrogation
of this treaty in 1969. The Soviet Union supplied the Iraqi
Government with arms to use in their battle against the Kurdish
rebels, while the Shah supported the same rebels with US and
French weapons and allowed them refuge in Iran. Finally, in
March 1975, agreement was reached: it was announced that
the Shatt-al-Arab boundary was to be a median line along the
deepest part of the waterway.

By 1972 Iran was Russia's second largest commercial partner
in the Middle East, but Russia's friendship with India and Iraq
still fuelled the Shah's underlying fear of Soviet encirclement,
especially when groups like the Popular Front for the Liberation
of Oman appeared on the other side of the Gulf. In 1974 he
went to Russia on what *Tass* described as a 'friendly business
visit'. In June the Shah decided that he wanted a fourfold
increase in the price of the gas Iran was exporting to Russia,[24] a
round sum that would have seemed just in view of the fourfold
increase in the price of oil the previous October. But after ten
days behind closed doors in August, it was announced that the
Russians would pay only 85 per cent more for the gas.[25] Only
three months later, the Shah went to Moscow to 'talk trade' and
to press for his idea of the Middle East as a (militarily) nuclear
free zone – an idea that he has since said would have to be
abandoned if any other Middle Eastern nation began to show
signs of nuclear restlessness.

Meanwhile the massive build-up of conventional arms
continued, with the US and Britain, in particular, falling over
themselves to supply the Shah (now their biggest customer for
arms) with all his requirements for defending what he stressed
was the longest front line of freedom in the world – his 1,400
mile border with Russia. In November 1976 a huge arms-for-oil
barter was announced: £4,000 million-worth of Rapier intercept
missiles would be supplied by the British Aircraft Corporation

in return for crude oil delivered to Shell and sold for foreign currency. Britain was so keen to sell Chieftain tanks to Iran that the first forty-five delivered to her had been diverted from British units in Germany, who got second priority.[26] The quantity and quality of the orders rose until, in August 1976, it was estimated to be worth (for 1,500 tanks) in the range of £450,000. At the same time a gigantic order for over three billion dollars' worth of arms to be bought from the US over five years was announced.[27]

The Shah was showing more and more belief in his own military creed: that 'You cannot completely depend on alliances. First of all you have to depend on yourself',[28] and 'You see proof every day that an unprepared country is almost a dead duck'.[29] The type of potential enemy he had in mind was evident from the weapons he ordered: F.14 fighters, 'so sophisticated that even the US air force is having difficulty using them', fitted with a Phoenix missile that could challenge the Soviet MiG 25, and the Spruance-class destroyer, fitted with more sophisticated equipment than those belonging to the US Navy.[30]

'Fortunately,' he told Lord Chalfont, 'the Soviet Government say that their government relations with us is quite separate from the activities of the Communists. And [sigh] all right, we accept that. But then we deal with the Communists in one way and we deal with the Soviet as our good neighbours in another way.'[31]

On intermittently strained relations with Arab nations in the Gulf he said in 1974, 'That is very funny, because without Iran [to defend them] they would be dead. Our first choice is to cooperate with all Arab countries on an equal basis. Our second choice is to go it alone if necessary.' That could be said to be his attitude towards the world in general. To this end, out of the 1976–77 budget of 45 billion dollars, the Shah was spending 9.3 billion dollars on defence[32] – more than 20 per cent of his country's money, at a time when the euphoric expansion of the 1970s that followed the recession of the 1960s and received its biggest boost from the quadrupling of oil prices within two months in connection with the Yom Kippur War in October 1973 began to dip once more into deficit.

It had already begun to look as if, by the mid 1980s, Iran might

have more and better equipment than any other country except
the Soviet Union, the US and China.[33]

But the announcement of the huge 1976–77 purchases came
shortly after it was publicly revealed in Britain, and may have
long been known by SAVAK, that Russia's military expenditure
had been some 60 per cent higher than the West had previously
recognized. Russia's fast expanding navy was by far the biggest
in the eastern hemisphere, and her tactical air force combined
with that of her iron curtain satellites far exceeds the available
Nato air forces facing them across the Czechoslovakian and
Eastern German frontiers.[34]

Not surprisingly, the news of Iran's order of 3 billion dollars'
worth of arms (over five years) from the US in August 1976
drew a comment from *Pravda* in Moscow that 'American arms
sales to nations bordering the Gulf escalated the arms race in
that part of the world and threatened the security of the nations
in the region'.[35] The previous year, 1975, only the Soviet Union,
the United States, West Germany, France (who, like Iran,
leapfrogged Britain's spending on defence in 1975) and probably
China had spent more on arms than Iran. Iran's spending of
roughly a quarter of her budget on defence was double that
of most Middle Eastern countries (who spent an average of 12.4
of their Gross National Product on defence in 1974, against
Nato's average of 3.5).[36]

Even so the Shah's spending on defence was modest compared with what his father had spent – 43 per cent, in his first
year on the throne, and almost as great a proportion during his
entire reign.[37] Nor was he alone. In 1975 Saudi Arabia trebled
its defence budget, and in 1976–77 allocated 10 billion dollars
to defend its population of under four million, compared with
Iran's 35 million people; meanwhile Israel was spending about
a third of her GNP on defence.

Relations with these two countries provided the greatest clues
to the Shah's foreign policy during and after the Yom Kippur
War. With consummate skill (how many angels on the head of a
pin?) he managed to maintain a working relationship with both.
On 23 July 1960, he had announced the *de facto* recognition of
the state of Israel. Since 1953 his internal security system,
revamped as SAVAK in 1957, had received assistance from

On holiday by the
Caspian Sea, 1962

13 *Left:* The Shah at
target practice

14 *Right:* With the
Crown Prince

15 The Shah and the Empress Farah with their four children on holiday in St Moritz 1975

Israel's crack intelligence agency, the Mossad, as well as the CIA: it is said that the three networks still exchange information.[38] Israeli experts on irrigation and land reclamation transformed Iran's Qazvin Plain into a fertile oasis. But the main link is again oil: the Shah supplies Israel with 50 per cent of her oil. Yet in October 1973 when King Feisal of Saudi Arabia asked the Shah for help in the war against Israel, he immediately despatched six Iranian Air Force C-130 transports to ferry Saudi troops and equipment to the war against Israel.

Just as oil made for cooperation with Israel, it made for difficulties with Saudi Arabia. In 1971 Iran overtook Venezeula to become the third biggest producer of oil in the world, after the United States and Russia, but Saudi Arabia's proven *reserves* of oil are more than double those of Iran. Saudi Arabia with its huge surplus of dollars and small population, is still without the social, industrial and agricultural reforms for which the Shah urgently needs ready money. It is against the law in Saudi Arabia for anyone to drink, and for a woman to be unveiled or to drive a car; Saudi thieves are still sometimes punished in the traditional way by having a hand cut off for the third offence.

King Feisal was reluctant to add greatly to the already quad-rupled oil prices that had led to a drop in demand (average output in the Middle East fell by 10.8 per cent in 1975) and escalated world inflation. At Saudi Arabia's insistence, the price increase agreed by all OPEC members in December 1975 was only 10 per cent – half of what the Shah hoped for.

With Iran's hugely increased budget for 1975, the great plans for expansion and reform (projected spending under the 1973–78 five-year plan was doubled in 1974) and the needs of the oil industry itself – some thought that Iran would need £9,000 million invested in the oil industry by 1985,[37] which could eat up a whole year's oil sales – the Shah had been desperate to convince King Feisal and his Oil Minister, Sheikh Yamani, of Iran's case so that the other OPEC nations could be swung behind them.

Saudi Arabia's determination to take the lead in withstanding pressures for a huge increase came as a surprise to the most sophisticated observers. Interviewed by the US magazine *Business Week* in January 1975 Dr Henry Kissinger had said:

O

'The Saudis have performed an enormously skilful act of survival of leadership position in an increasingly radical Arab world. It is doing that by carefully balancing itself among the various factions and acting as a resultant of a relation of forces, and never getting far out ahead. Thereafter, I never for a moment believed, nor do I believe today, that the lead in cutting prices will be taken by Saudi Arabia.'[38] The Shah was taken as unaware by King Feisal's new resistance as Dr Kissinger. Having failed to persuade him and OPEC to hold out for a 20 per cent increase, the Shah had to think where else he could obtain revenues for his grand imperial designs. In January 1973 the new five-year plan had projected a growth rate of 14.3 per cent. By the end of 1973, after the Yom Kippur War, the actual growth rate was 50 per cent in 1974. The consequent ballooning of plans and expenditure, the huge new hopes of transforming Iran into an ultra-modern country, of doing in twenty-five years what the Japanese had done in 200, seemed miraculously within the Shah's grasp. Thwarted in his plans to exert sufficient leverage on OPEC to fund his revolution, he now turned his attentions to the oil companies in the hope of persuading them to lift more oil: but, just like the hated Dr Mossadeq twenty-three years previously he came up against a united Anglo-American front that proved impenetrable. In February 1976 Iran announced a reduction in the price of its oil: it was the first time that OPEC had failed to force consumers to accept unilaterally imposed price increases, and it was a major reversal, a public rebuff, for the Shah. Unlike Mossadeq, however, he had realized the falseness of his position swiftly and, realistic as ever, had capitulated to greater strength: this is the language he really understands.

I asked the Shah if he could imagine any situation in which his massive array of armaments, second only to Russia's build-up in this part of the world, might be put to aggressive use.

'Well, that depends what is aggressive – to attack another country, no,' he replied. 'But just imagine that something happened to Pakistan, a further disintegration of Pakistan, dismemberment of Pakistan, this we could not *stand*.' (Very quietly) 'Because the consequences would be, I mean, terrible. The whole aspect of things will change. It will bring down Some People to the Indian Ocean by way of land – we can't assist at that because we are going to die anyway later – so there are things which we *just could not* accept. But this is not an aggression if we try to keep the *status quo*. I don't consider that as an aggression. To change it would be aggression but not to keep it.'

I asked him about the great number of former CIA men still in Iran, many of whom are now training Iranians to use the complex Ibex intelligence system bought from the US. 'Well, they will go when our people are trained,' he replied, 'I mean every self-respecting country which is thinking of its own defence has got to have those means. It would be ridiculous when you can be independent not to be.'

Did he feel isolated as an Aryan state in this part of the world?

'Well, yes and no; no, because we, the Pakistanis, the Afghans and the Indians we are all Aryans and I hope that one day a true close friendship will be established between all these people. I work for that! . . . I work for bettering the relations between India and Pakistan and my own relations with India are excellent.

'My dream is the Indian Ocean – dreaming about an Indian Ocean Common Market or, sometimes one could even venture by saying commonwealth of nations, but this is maybe going a *little* too far. Oh, it will take a long time before we reach that because the peoples of the region are so different – different creeds, different religions, different beliefs.'[39]

How much more astute, incredibly well-informed, and just plain clever is the Shah's foreign policy than that of any of his predecessors. Every country is wooed; and not a few have also been insulted from time to time, including the 'almost masochistic' Israelis, and the 'permissive West'.

The Iranian gift for both flattery and invective is great. Arthur Arnold called Persia 'a country where it is a breach of good manners not to employ compliments, and of good sense to take them for more than mere words'.[40] The Shah has greatly polished the elementary, but apparently effective, tactics of Fath Ali Shah, who impressed James Morier by turning to one of his courtiers and saying of the French: 'They are *haivans*, beasts, wild men, savages. These are gentlemen.'[41]

Chapter 24

SAVAK

IF a combination of flattery and potential force is the anchor of the Shah's foreign policy, the same is true of his internal manipulation of the population. Always he believes in negotiating from strength.

Nowhere is Iran caught, splayed on the crossroads between East and West, in the spotlight composed of the lights of different régimes, more than in her Sazman-i-Amniyat va Kishvar: SAVAK, the State Security and Intelligence Organization, set up with American aid after the attempted coup and the Shah's successful counter-coup of 1953. With the help of the CIA and of Israel's intelligence agency, the Mossad, SAVAK has become one of the most efficient organs in a country where, outside this one organization, to give an order seldom means it will be carried out. 'They are extremely efficient,' icily notes one British specialist in Iranian affairs, 'and certainly as brutal as any secret police in the area.'[1]

As the Shah is at some pains to point out, every country has its history of brutality. In the Middle East it is still not condemned, and is even helped by Asian stoicism in the face of pain, greater acceptance of death, and the teaching of the Koran, which meant that a hundred years ago, as Arthur Arnold noted, it was not the state which was responsible for punishing murderers or would-be murderers: 'The theory and basis of punishment is, that the relations of the victim must take revenge upon the **actual** or would-be murderers.'[2]

This meant that traditionally in Iran there was a wide base for torture, and tribal law underlined this. The gradual transference of the powers of the court to the executive (and since 1945 largely to military tribunals) did not break down this background. The Qajar Shahs, of Turkish extraction, were no more brutal than, say, Shah Abbas, the Safavid, but they were more ingenious and vied with each other to invent new and more terrible modes of punishing anyone, from thieves to their highest ministers. Fath Ali, who sent some of his poems to the Prince Regent, was particularly ingenious even though his was noted as a reign of luxury not cruelty.

Modern technology and psychology have now been added to this tradition, and a huge army of informers – some suggest as many as one in eight of the Iranian population are part-time informers, though full-time officers are said by the Shah to be fewer than 3,000[3] – feed fact and rumour into what is virtually a vast intelligence computer.

SAVAK is now virtually another army behind the army. It is composed of three tiers. 'I am a great believer in a plurality of administrative channels and in having alternative channels always available,' the Shah says. 'I obtain information from many quarters.'[4] The main body is run by General Nematollah Nassiri, who, though he is some twelve years older than the Shah, was with him in the same squad at the Military Academy in the 1930s, became Commander of the Imperial Guard and delivered the *firman* dismissing Mossadeq from his post as Prime Minister. He was also police chief from 1963–65. He replaced General Pakravan, who the Shah decided at the end of his 'liberalizing' experiment in the 1960s was too soft.

Above this level comes the Imperial Inspectorate Organization, the IIO, which investigates those of higher rank – for instance, cabinet ministers and SAVAK itself. It reports direct to the Shah and comes under the aegis of General Hussein Fardoust, who as a boy was chosen as one of his friends to go with the Shah to Le Rosey in Switzerland, and thus ranks as a friend and colleague going back for nearly half a century, before the Shah knew General Nassiri and Mr Alam. Both Generals Nassiri and Fardoust are often invited to the palace to play cards with the Shah.

Above this is the third level, known as J2, the Intelligence Branch of the Imperial Armed Forces, also directed by a general with direct access to the Shah.[5] The Shah himself examines the record of any officer recommended for promotion above the rank of major.

In addition, a Special Supreme Council to eradicate corruption was formed in 1976. This is composed of the Prime Minister, the Interim Finance Minister, and Justice Minister, plus the head of the Imperial Inspectorate, and was ready to receive complaints concerning corruption from members of the public.

This huge network caught big and small fry. Offenders are usually tried before military tribunals, which were originally set up in 1972 to try two categories of prisoners – people involved in armed robbery and terrorism – but whose scope has since been widened to take in charges of corruption, high-pricing and almost any other offence at the discretion of SAVAK, and of course the Shah.

In 1974 three generals and two colonels were tried for embezzlement. The drive against corruption – for which the Shah himself seems to feel a personal, almost Western distaste – was intensified as Iran's plans were cut back with the drop in oil revenues, and early in 1976 five Tehran customs officials were sentenced on 124 counts of embezzlement and forgery involving almost one million dollars'-worth of rials; in February the former chief of the Navy, Ramzi Abbas Ata'i was sentenced to five years' imprisonment and fined the equivalent of 3.7 million dollars.[6] He, the deputy, nine other senior officers and two civilians had been tried before a military tribunal, which now deals with a variety of 'undesirables' as well as the 'traitors' (in terms of state security) for whom they were originally intended.

There were suggestions that many large foreign firms were involved in corruption in Iran. The Shah even ordered the Iranian delegate to the UN to table a resolution calling for member states to introduce legislation forbidding 'unethical' dealings and contracts.[7]

But a sour note crept into Iran's dulcet wooing of the West. It increased as the bonanza of 1973–75 gave way to a deficit due to the reduction in oil prices forced on the Shah. Suddenly, companies and countries that owed in some cases their survival and in other cases at least their comparative health to the Shah were accused. He bailed out the US Grumman armaments firm, ordered three Concordes when the future of this Anglo-French project depended on this Persian parachute, and signed industrial agreements worth initially 3,000 million dollars (expected to rise to 5,000 million dollars) with France in February 1974, worth 3,100 million dollars with Italy in June 1974, and worth 1,200 million dollars with Britain in January 1975 (as well as lending Britain large sums).

In Iran, emphasis is given to the anti-corruption aspects of SAVAK's work. Abroad, particularly in the West, the emphasis is on SAVAK's suppression of the opposition and particularly, on torture. Martin Ennals, the Secretary-General of Amnesty International, said: 'No country in the world has a worse record in human rights than Iran.'[8] What the Iranian Press had not been free to do, the foreign Press has tried, from a distance, to undertake. In particular, *Le Monde* and *The Sunday Times*, both stern critics of repressive régimes in many parts of the world, notably in the USSR, Latin America and Africa, have focused attention on this side of SAVAK's activities.

Two lawyers who went to Tehran from 28 January to 6 February 1972 as observers selected by the International Federation of Jurists and the International Association of Catholic Jurists sent a letter to *Le Monde* afterwards describing their experiences:

> . . . We were able to sit on four sittings of the military tribunal and were able to speak to two of the prisoners at the Evin prison. . . . [At first] we found access to the sittings had been refused us. It was only on a personal basis that we finally received authorization to attend certain parts of the trial.
>
> Twenty-three people were sentenced by the military tribunal between January 23 and February 2. Six of them had been condemned to death. Twenty new defendants were to be judged from February 6 onwards. They were accused of forming subversive groups, robbing banks and police stations, hijacking a plane. . . .
>
> While the authorities affirmed – and the newspapers printed – that these sittings were to be public, entry was in fact only permitted to holders of a special pass. The formalities for such a pass were such that the families of the accused found it practically impossible to get in.

In fact the accused did not have any of the fundamental guarantees of a serious defence.

According to the spokesman of the military tribunal, anyone arrested by SAVAK was taken before an examining magistrate within twenty-four hours in conformity with the Iranian law. But Nasser Sadegh and Ali Mihandoust, arrested in September and October 1971, only saw the Military Prosecutor for the first time in mid-January and did not see the examining magistrate until February 5, 1972, the day before we ourselves saw them.

A number of the accused had been tortured during the period of remand, the period of which had no limit to it. Sadegh told us how he had seen his friend Behruz Dehrani die under torture.

During the trial the accused were treated very well. They were not chained up, they were brought tea and cigarettes and if they wanted to they could talk about political beliefs without being interrupted.

On the same day Le Monde also published a letter from someone who had escaped from a Persian prison, Reza Rezai. It included the following extract:

> Since the urban guerrilla movement has grown up in Iran the intensity of tortures has been stepped up. Most of the brutality is inflicted on the guerrilla in the twenty-four hours after their arrest. . . . He then falls into a coma. . . . Then the SAVAK agents come to pick up the confessions which the prisoners have to sign which say they were not forced to sign by torture. These confessions go directly to the Prosecutor's file.

In April 1973 yet another plot against the Shah was uncovered. In October ten men and two women were arrested and accused of plotting to assassinate the Shah and kidnap the Empress Farah and the Crown Prince, who it was alleged were to be held for ransom: the release of political prisoners. In January the twelve were brought to trial. Six of them pleaded guilty and six not guilty. The army prosecutor asked for the death penalty; when the verdict was announced seven of the men had been sentenced to death, and five others, including the two women, sentenced to terms of imprisonment varying between three and five years.[10] (Imprisonment is a modern punishment for women: until this century, crime among women was so rare that no female institutions existed and the culprit was usually confined in the house of a *mullah*.) Two of those sentenced to death, young rebels labelled Marxists, were shot at dawn; the three others sentenced to death were pardoned.

Then in March 1975 came news that nine political prisoners, some of whom were nearing the end of ten-year prison sentences, had been 'shot while trying to escape'. They had been tried in 1969, when seven of them had been 'adopted' by Amnesty International. Now Amnesty asked some pertinent questions. Why should they try to escape when several of them were so close to the end of their prison terms in any case? And if they were shot while trying to escape, how did it happen that they were all shot *dead*? Agence France Presse reported bluntly: 'Nine prisoners said by the Iranian Government to have been shot while trying to escape were in fact tortured to death shortly before the expiry of their prison terms, according to a report by two Paris lawyers published today . . . their conclusions were based on conversations with people [in Iran] whose reliability is not in question.'[11]

In November 1974 four months before Iran's four parties were merged in a single party, 114 prominent opposition figures were brought from other jails to Evin prison near Tehran.[12]

In August 1975 British Labour MP John Atkinson and a lawyer, John Nash, went to Tehran as members of a parliamentary committee set up to investigate the plight of political prisoners. They claimed that defence lawyers for political suspects were specially chosen serving or retired officers, but some of these lawyers had themselves been put on trial for showing sympathy for their clients. 'We were told that in Tehran the President of a Military Court refused to give the death sentence. A little later, he was arrested,' they said. 'It is deeply regrettable that the regular recourse to the death penalty in Iran provokes so little indignation and even less international action, while such practices *in countries of less economic importance* [my italics] like Spain, arouse the emotion of world opinion. It remains to say that Iran is, in our eyes, endowed with one of the most disgraceful régimes on earth.'[13]

In March 1976 Agence France Presse reported from Tehran that two terrorists had been hanged on Sunday 7 March 1976, after being found guilty by a military tribunal of using force against a policeman and making and planting bombs at the

Aryamehr University in Tehran and the theological faculty at
Qum. The same tribunal sentenced five other members of the
same guerrilla group to death, but these had their sentences
commuted to life imprisonment by the Shah after having
'regretted their actions' the communiqué added.[14]

This brought to a total of more than 250 the official Iranian
figures for executions since 1972 (Amnesty gives a slightly higher
figure) plus some ninety deaths in 'shoot-outs' since 1972.

Others are in prison. How many? In 1971 Marvin Zonis
quoted a foreigner: 'By Middle East Standards, the 100 to
200 political prisoners now in jails is a relatively small total',
and added: 'It is by no means certain that the number is between
one hundred and two hundred, although it does appear that the
number is, in fact, substantially below the numbers prevailing
in other countries of the Middle East.'[5]

However, Mohammed Reza Shah Pahlavi himself evidently
sees his reign as more merciful than his father's. Questioned
about torture by Ian McIntyre of the BBC he said: 'First of all
they are too smart for this and furthermore when they start
interrogating someone they have already some evidence and
when confronted by that evidence they just collapse and tell
everything so they don't really have to have recourse to those
things any more, as maybe some organizations had to some
30 or 40 years ago.'[16]

When Lord Chalfont asked him about 'allegations of ill-
treatment and indeed torture of what are described as political
prisoners' by SAVAK he replied:

'What I can say is that we are now sophisticated enough to use
the same methods that you people are using for interrogating the
people that you have to.'

'Who are you referring to, Sir?' asked Lord Chalfont.

'Any of the sophisticated societies,' replied the Shah. 'They have
some very efficient system of interrogation, which is much more
psychological than physical. We do the same thing that you are
doing.'

'And do you regard that as justified?' asked Lord Chalfont.

'That depends on what cases. In case of betrayal of one's country,
I should say anything goes. . . . There is not a single man who has
been shot who has planned against myself. I have never pardoned

anyone who has plotted against the country in order to put it in the hands of a foreign power and I will never do it [while] I live.'[17]

Later that year I said to the Shah, 'You believe that a man should enjoy every liberty except the liberty to betray the country. You have shown several times that you're ready and willing to pardon those who've plotted against you.'
'Always.'
'But you cannot forgive those who've plotted against the state.'
(A sharp intake of breath:) 'No, I cannot, because I despise that – I really, I – I just cannot *stomach* a thing like that; and further more I have sworn to the constitution. One of the articles is to safeguard the security and the integrity of this country. Part of my duty.'
'You recently said that "anything goes" in interrogating these people. You prefer to use psychological means nowadays, but who decides who is guilty?'
'Ah the court. We have courts. But the evidence is produced like anywhere.'
'But you never yourself make up your mind or prejudge a case?'
'No no no.'
'And do you think you know all that goes on? Do you think you know all the methods that are used?'
'I cannot claim that I know everything – that's impossible. Because even let's say some complexed little crooked man could try to show his strength and personality over some poor creature, guilty or not guilty. This is always possible: in every country it's possible. No I can't say that I know every case. But the main thing is that *I* know – I am *sure* – that all these people certainly are Communists and Marxists. [Of] this I have no doubt.'
'Some trials are not fully reported, are they?'
'No. No some are in camera, and some others are public. And why they are in camera – just because of the ridiculous articles written by some foreign – either press, or some foreign lawyers, which have been sent by those special – specially Communist-penetrated organizations round the world who say [suddenly in a sneering tone] "Oh yes? You say these things?

We show you that this is none of your business; this is *our*
house."'

'But you hope that one day there will be no censorship of the
Press and that all trials will –'

'Well censorship, that depends what you mean by censorship.
Today also there is no censorship of the Press as long as it
regards criticizing what is wrong with our – with the daily
affairs of the country, all the shortcomings in this and that; but
if you say criticism of the Press should be that anyone could
denounce anybody he likes and drag him in the mud – and –
destroy him [very quietly] I don't know if I *like* that.

'Today time and again and invariably we have heard there
were lies printed in newspapers about the country, or ourselves
or the family; everybody from the Government of that country
where that paper was published, from lawyers, from everybody,
they all begged us "Please, don't pay any attention: it is not
worth it, because this is exactly what they want. They want to
be libelled and prosecuted in court because they will have more
publicity."'

A few days later an acquaintance eyed me for some time, then
burst out: 'I hear you asked His Majesty about torture!'

'Yes,' I said, and added hastily, 'Well, everybody does!'

'Oh yes of course everybody does!' he commented, a little
too quickly. An immense silence followed while we looked at
each other, expressionless. At last another volley shot out:
'What did he say?'

'He was very frank,' I said, my mind going blank; then,
recovering a little summarized my tape recording. 'He prefers to
use psychological methods, but he believes that all those who
are tortured are Marxists.' There was a still longer silence. Our
faces remained impassive; my eyes felt glued to the unblinking
eyes opposite me. It seemed that we were the two sides of a
spirit level which must not be allowed to shiver by one milli-
metre. Finally my questioner spoke, his eyes still clinging to
mine, his tone that of one very slowly saying a creed:

'That ... is ... what ... we ... believe,' he said.

Chapter 25

Rule by Decree

'FINALLY I became so exasperated that I decided we would have to dispense with democracy and operate by decree,' the Shah said ten years ago.[1]

He was looking back on his attempts to launch his White Revolution, and in particular to bring about the reform of land ownership which would break the power of his chief traditional opponents, the *mullahs* and the upper classes, and undercut the cause of his subversive Communist enemy, the Tudeh Party while at the same time increasing the wide base of his support among the peasants, and indirectly the middle classes.

Before resorting to *fiat* (decree) he said, in a true but simplified account of what had gone before, he had tried other methods of reform. First, example: he gave some of his own land away to the peasants, but the Thousand Families refused to follow suit. Then, law: he sent two land reform Bills to Parliament which (under Mossadeq) 'amended them to uselessness'. Finally he decided to impose his will by *fiat*.

His attitude to democracy had narrowed since the late 1950s. He became convinced that democracy, as the term is understood in the West, would serve neither his own interests nor those of his country.

After his return to power in 1953 his position and power were increasingly entrenched. Autonomous political parties were officially replaced by the Melliyun (Nationalist) and Mardom

(People's) parties, created by the Shah and led by two of his most trusted followers, Dr Eghbal and Mr Alam. Not surprisingly, 'foreign observers and local politicians were sceptical of the success of a two-party system introduced from above'.[2]

Then, late in 1963, while Mr Alam was still Prime Minister, a new party was created under Hassan Ali Mansur, who said that soon 'all the key posts in the Government will obviously go to Party members'. Within two months, 150 deputies had joined the rush to the new party. In March 1964 the Shah asked its leader, Mansur, to form a new government. This he did, and party members (it was known as the Iran Novin, or New Iran, Party) held all but two of the cabinet posts. Two months later, in May 1964, Mansur announced that the Shah would assume 'overall leadership' of the party.[3]

The uproar that ensued evoked the explanation from the Shah that the party simply had his 'support and interest'. It would be another eleven years before a single party was formed, uniting four existing parties in the new Rastakhiz Party or Iran Resurgence Party. It was the logical outcome and had been predicted in 1969 when one of its members, Mr Hamid Kafai, told a journalist: 'All three parties follow His Imperial Majesty since he took over the government. So it would be much better to have one single party.'[4]

In 1973 the Shah said, 'Look – to go through with reform one can't help but be authoritarian: especially when reform takes place in a country like Iran, where only 25 per cent of the inhabitants can read or write. Believe me, when you have three-quarters of a nation afflicted with illiteracy only the most strict authority can ensure reform; otherwise nothing would have been achieved. If I hadn't been strict I couldn't have carried through even agricultural reform and my whole programme would have been at a standstill.'[5]

In 1965 Amir Abbas Hoveyda of the Novin Party became Prime Minister. At the time of writing he still holds that office – by far the longest tenure of *any* Iranian Prime Minister, and impressive after an average time in office of nineteen months for previous Prime Ministers since the constitution was put into practice in 1907.[6]

But, as *The Times* noted in 1975 when describing the Iran Novin Party and the 'opposition' Mardom Party:

> The policies of the latter have never been radically different from those of the former, and since 1972 it has declined into almost total insignificance. In that year its secretary-general, Dr Ali-Naqi Kani, who had made the mistake of voicing genuine popular grievances and uttering actual criticism of the Prime Minister, was suddenly announced to have 'resigned' because of 'exhaustion and ill-health'. A wave of resignations from the Mardom party committees throughout the country followed, and in the local elections three months later the party hardly bothered to campaign. It won only 10.7 of the contested seats.

The Iranian Government took exception at the time to a report in *The Times* which said that this result indicated 'the collapse of the Shah's efforts to create a two-party system in Iran . . .'[7]

This opinion was quickly confirmed by a banner headline in Tehran: 'Shahanshah decrees single party for Iran'. Underneath, set on a black background, was printed 'Loyalty to the constitution, monarchy and revolution only criteria for membership'.[8]

The new party, which replaced parties previously created by the Shah, is known as the Iran Resurgence Party. Mr Hoveyda, Secretary-General of the Novin Party, now became Secretary-General of the new party and continued in office as Prime Minister.

Kayhan continued:

> The Shahanshah made it clear that there was no room for anyone to sit on the political fence any more. All Iranians must be politically involved. Everyone must make his position clear; there will be no political loners or militants. The monarch branded those militants who failed to subscribe to the trinity of principles as 'stateless' and said that their place was *either prison or abroad* [my italics]. Those militants who preferred to leave would be provided with all the facilities to do so, he added. However, those loyalists who openly and unreservedly subscribed to the Constitution, the Monarchy and the Revolution but preferred to remain inactive outside the political mainstream, would continue to enjoy their legal rights, the monarch pledged.

Seven months after the one-party system was introduced, I asked the Shah: 'For a long time you were in favour of the two-party system. You said that critics of the "loyal opposition" are valuable because they keep the majority alert. What made you change your mind?'

'Well, I will give you the reasons very clearly,' he replied. 'Because now instead of having one loyal opposition we have three or four, within the same party.'

'But that was so before – you pointed that out, that the two-party system didn't *just* mean two parties, it meant two main parties and then little segments.'

'Now: the other party, the opposition party, could not match during this period of creativeness and wonderful achievements when the standard of living of the people was increasing, growing in a very spectacular way – they had no chance against the established Government. Every time the government was going to the polls they were winning because the candidate presenting himself will say "well we have done this, we have done that, we have done this and that . . ."'

'A little example: in the two-party system there was an election in some place in the north and there was a very hard campaign – the Government candidate won. Two or three months later the *Majlis* was finished and we had what you call the one-party system. This time the previously *defeated* candidate won. This time 80 per cent of the whole deputies lost their seats; otherwise they would have all been returned. *Now* you have real democracy. Because now the party presents for each constituency three, four, five candidates: the people can choose.'

'What was wrong with the previous deputies?' I asked. 'Did you find that the rich, the Thousand Families, were still getting too great a share of the cake?'

'In the old system? No, not that – not that at all. But it is really free people. *We are not cheating in the elections any more.* Nobody *has* to cheat. Because with the three principles *really* accepted by all the people – the Imperial Order, the Constitution, and the Revolution of the Shah and the People – really our people accept that, we don't have to cheat now.'

'Who did cheat?'

'The parties.'

'All the time?'

'In the past, yes. Now we don't have to cheat.'

'It was taken for granted that everyone cheated?'

The Shah, 'Surely. Well, they were trying their best to get elected. We . . . Everybody has its Watergate.'

'The candidates must still try to cheat nowadays,' I suggested, 'each candidate wants to be elected.'

'No, they can't, because the machinery is set up – but also the party is supervised by all those inspectorate that we have. They *can't* cheat any more.'

'Couldn't that inspectorate have dealt with the previous cheating? Or didn't it want to? So it was to eradicate corruption?'

'Corruption, better representation of the people, and allowing many good elements that were in the opposition and who have never had a chance of doing anything positive in this country – only making a few speeches and maybe a few criticisms, that's all – now they are *actively* engaged in the – either government or in the apparatus of the state.'

'Three-quarters of the *Majlis* is now new blood?'

'Yes,' replied the Shah.

'And you feel this will make more progress?'

'No, not that. This is what is – more representative of the people. Otherwise why should you have elections at all?'[9]

It has not changed the balance of supreme power. The year before it was introduced, Prime Minister Hoveyda compared Iran under the Shah to France under de Gaulle and said: 'Parliament does not impede the executive so we have a more efficient system and there is a dialogue.'[10] That is how it appears to the loyal Iranians. To the West, where the Shah's radicalism still seems redolent in some ways to conservatism, it might be called more of a monologue.

But the one-party system is not entirely window-dressing. Robert Graham wrote in June 1976:

In both the anti-profiteering campaign and the drive against corruption the party has been used as a sort of vigilante organization, with students, for instance, sent out to check supermarket prices. The party itself has yet to find a real direction after fifteen months' existence. In the towns and among the educated classes it had run up against a barrier of cynical indifference, with only a few believing that it offers the chance of greater participation in real decisions. But in the countryside the party has had more impact, perhaps

P

largely because it has been seized as a means of making the Government pay more attention to rural needs and deliver on its promises of decentralization.[11]

Decentralization was an ideal of Zia ed-Din Tabatabai, not of Reza Shah: in this too the policies of the Pahlavi father and son have begun to diverge.

Chapter 26

Reformer – King of Kings

THOUGH Mohammed Reza Shah Pahlavi has grown more like his father in recent years in his authoritarianism, increasing isolation and, some say, his temper, there remains one tremendous difference between them. Reza Shah stayed essentially a soldier to the core. His son has a more complex nature and wants to benefit not only the country but the people.

'I could have been something quite different,' he told me. 'No, I think I would have been as well a soldier, professionally a soldier, or I could be a doctor – medicine. Either this or that. When I look inside myself I could be either – they are worlds apart, but I could be *this* or *that*, as well.'

'The two sides of your nature?'

'I think so, I think so . . . you know that in my reforms sometimes I go as far or even further than the Communists – but this is more human and more practical. But I always respect the freedom of the individual because I say that after all, what we do is for whom? – for the people. And people must be human creatures, not robots.'

The American financial adviser to Iran under Reza Shah recalled: 'I told the Shah that if the Army budget were increased we could do very little, if anything, for agriculture, education or public health. He said, "Very well then; we'll have to postpone those things".' His son is hurrying to catch up on them.

'I think the people of Iran have always expected to find their Shah a leader or father or teacher,' he says. 'I think it remains the same; and it's up to the Shah – today myself – to be or try to be what we should be to and for our people. I don't want to talk about other societies and peoples but for mine it is manifold: but the most important one is to catch up in technology and industry with the other countries of the world, because we don't want to be a second-rate nation and only a certain number of years is left. If we cannot do it in that period of time then it will be too late: we will never catch up.'[1]

Today Iran is the second strongest country in her part of the world, second only to Russia. The Shah dreams of Iran as a great civilization technically among the foremost in the world, and morally vastly superior to what he sees as the 'permissive West.'

It was not until 1967, when he had been on the throne for twenty-six years, that Mohammed Reza Shah Pahlavi crowned himself (after the manner of Napoleon and Reza Shah) with a crown weighing 10,400 carats.

In 1971 the 2,500th anniversary of the Persian Empire was magnificently celebrated at Persepolis. Many countries who did not send their highest-ranking representative in accepting the invitation have since sent some of their most senior ministers knocking at the Shah's door to ask for oil and loans.

But internally the Shah's problem remains colossal, on a scale so formidable that one is tempted to believe that only a mystical mind could envisage success against such gigantic odds. Well over half the people are still illiterate and many of the others are only marginally literate; only about a quarter of Iran's vast surface is irrigated, there are only some 10,000 doctors (half of them in Tehran) for a population of 33 million, major roads stop suddenly somewhere in the desert or the mountains, and even the Shah himself decrees the impossible: as he did at the end of 1974 when he announced free and compulsory elementary school education throughout the country when there were not even half the teachers necessary for this, and decided that each child should have daily a glass of free milk when Iran's dairy industry is much too small for this.[2]

But the Shah has his own way: he knows that to get anywhere in Iran you must think super-colossal. The village elder who, after watching a film for the first time, ordered a feast for the stars,[3] understands what the Shah says on television when a talk on his own rights or land reform would leave him bewildered.

Television is now nationwide in Iran. And the Shah says, 'My voice is heard everywhere, my face is seen everywhere; heard through the radio, seen through the TV. The contact is there.' Laudatory articles about the royal family appear in the Tehran newspapers at least every other day. They appear sycophantic to the majority of foreigners and educated Iranians, but are all part of the Shah's personal propaganda for his country's unity and development.

The Shah's brothers and sisters each has an important role to play – in the United Nations (Princess Ashraf is the Iranian delegate) or in charity or administering one of the vital new lifelines in the country.

'We have a Persian saying that the nightingale every year lays seven eggs,' Mr Alam told me, 'and just one becomes a Nightingale – and this is exactly the case with His Majesty Reza Shah's children. It's so clear.'

In October 1975 I asked the Shah whether he believed that he might consider Iran to be half way along the path towards the ideal state he envisages that it will become.

'You can say that,' he replied. 'I'm giving myself twelve and a half years' time, or thirteen at the most to achieve what I would consider such a solid foundation that nothing could rock it; that would be about achieving what you are today.'

This was just as the vast oil revenues bonanza that began at the end of 1973 and resulted in a doubling of much expenditure under the latest five-year plan (1973–78) was beginning to gush more slowly. Since then Iran has been forced to retrench.

Spearheading the welfare drive are the Literacy and Health Corps. The Literacy Corps is an alternative to conventional national service for some young men and women. Girls are sent to the more civilized schools and locations; men, often in twos, go to some of the extremely remote regions to give elementary lessons to the villagers and their children. 'The women are very good students,' I was told in one village; but attendance is irregular, particularly among the children who are often needed to help their parents on the land except when snow covers the ground.

There have been unexpected snags in agriculture. Land
Reform led to the formation of many small and inefficient farms:
80 per cent of the population cultivated holdings of less than
25 acres in 1974, and most were family farms of between five
and seven acres, supporting an average of nearly six people,
while methods of cultivation on the Iranian plateau had hardly
changed since Neolithic times.[4] Now many of these smaller
farms are being colonized or turned into agri-businesses: and
this poses new problems for those who do not want to leave
their small farm or village and move to a more efficient and
impersonal new farming centre. The townsman still earns more
than five times as much as his country cousin, and the gap
between rich and poor has traditionally been a source of discontent in the country. Television, showing the contrasts to all,
has put an end to the peasant's belief that a town is simply an
overgrown village.

Cheap industrial labour is a thing of the past in Iran. In
defiance of Government policy, wages rose by more than a
third in 1975 and nearly as much in 1976. But the Share Participation Scheme, whereby 49 per cent of shares in industry are
offered first to the company workers (with low interest loans to
help) and then, if they are not all taken up, to the general public,
means, as the Shah points out, that in the long term:

'If they do any monkey business it would be against themselves. In addition to this I want farmers to own shares in the
factories, I want white collars, every other section, segment, of
the population to own shares – why? They should not be
disinterested in what goes on in the industry of this country.
Maybe in many cases the weakness of the European societies
is that when farmers do something the others shrug their shoulders, when the workers are doing something the farmers shrug
their shoulders. *Here, No:* they will all have something at stake
in what the other fellow is doing.'[5]

Brilliant though it is, the scheme has produced troublesome
side-effects. When the Government announced that it was going
ahead with the scheme in July 1975, business investment began
to taper rapidly, and a year later confidence in business was still
affected.[6]

Yet to harp on the drawbacks, on the four-month queue that

sometimes stretches outside Iran's ports (new ones are being constructed with all possible speed), on the high prices of imported goods, on the huge urban sprawl in traffic-choked Tehran, is to ignore the fact that a two-generation miracle is taking place. In fifty years Iran has jumped from a feudal society to a state that in some spheres demonstrates machinery, techniques, and plans that are among the most modern in the world. Implementation remains the major hazard.

In her first year of marriage the twenty-two-year-old Empress Farah (who was seven months pregnant with the Crown Prince at the time) was visiting Abadan refineries in the Gulf, and asked to see the workers' living conditions. It was only eight months since her marriage had catapulted her from the school of architecture in Paris to her first and supreme job as Empress. What she saw of the workers' homes was evidently more than unexpected: she burst into tears. Thereupon an official who was accompanying her asked to be allowed to make a contribution for the benefit of the families concerned, and collected the names of those concerned, which he jotted down on a card: and then, 'as Farah Diba drove away, tore up the list and tossed it into the gutter'.[7]

Land reform has brought Shah and peasants closer together, increasing the support of the former and the income of the latter, and undercutting the power of the traditional landowning classes, the Thousand Families and *mullahs*; but there have been pockets of difficulties, particularly in remote areas. In 1974 a study of Luristan, in the west of Iran, showed that 'the land reform officials were often corrupt and allowed themselves to be bought by the highest bidder; and secondly arable land . . . was recuperated, as soon as the officials' backs were turned, by the former owners, whose *de facto* power in the village is stronger than any national legislature'.[8] No wonder the Shah told Gavin Young, 'It is one thing to issue an order and another to see it is carried out. . . . Remorseless following up is required.'[9]

As *The Times* once noted:

'Few Iranian monarchs have died natural deaths. [The Shah] was accepted only so long as he proved himself an efficient despot.'[10]

Whenever disaster struck a question was asked: '*Magar Shah mordast?*' (But is the Shah dead?) For it was on a Shah's death that things went wrong, that village life was disrupted, invaders destroyed the precious irrigation channels, the treasury was depleted. Therefore the Shah has also felt the need to provide a paternal umbrella for his people, to unite them in the belief that what he is doing is for their own good, to impose his good intentions on them.

In a society like that of Iran today, in a tumult of change, traditionally turbulent, still torn between sects, tribes and classes, the difficulty of combining the two roles, of being both benevolent and a despot, is indeed hard.

But the Shah recognizes that 'A country cannot be ruled by the force of the bayonet and secret police. For a few days, this may be possible. But not for all times. Only a majority can rule a society.'[11] Only, it seems, a majority led by a very strong ruler indeed.

I found the Shah agreeable and forthcoming: as he doubtless intended that I should. Since these qualities seem to be part of his basic nature while his ruthlessness has been deliberately cultivated, there are probably few people who do not find him personally likeable when he intends that they should. There are, however, few men with whom I should care less to be on very unfriendly terms. His nature would make him inwardly an implacable enemy, even though his usual pragmatism would control his outward actions.

Trained for his job since the age of six, and having come through the terror both of personal shyness and the dreadful insecurities of Iran during the war and in the Mossadeq era, he has now achieved a practised poise. This makes him more relaxed than either of the two politicians of whom I had previously written biographies, Robert Kennedy (whose taciturn and laconic style broke down only when I *un*-interviewed him – that is to say when *he* asked most of the questions and I merely replied or commented), or Edward Heath, whose great integrity and incisiveness were at first slightly masked by a constraint which only gradually disappeared over a period of months.

The Shah has been tempered in a hotter crucible than almost

any other head of state. Being almost born to the job has also given him an advantage over most others that he has been at pains to retain: a head start over the politicians from other countries whose destiny was only a question mark while they were at school.

At a personal level the Shah and Shahbanou can have few enemies. But this is the level which they have learned to regard as unimportant: progress can only be achieved by political means.

His agility saved the Shah's life during the first assassination attempt; his bodyguards saved his life during the second attempt; chance has saved his life by keeping him away from the scene of subsequent attempts. Now he relies on wisdom and caution. Because of the traffic jams in Tehran he travels to most engagements by one of two helicopters, both of which are constantly on duty and kept waiting. Neither pilot knows which of the two he will choose to step into until he actually does so.

He is becoming ever more remote from the people to whom his life has been dedicated: the structure of security, and of court life itself, mean that his contact with reality is often at best secondhand. He is also protected from *within* against doubts by his sense of mission.

Few men would seem able to solve a complex problem – few greater problems than emergent Iran *can* be imagined – more capably: but it is a tragedy that the freer speech of the 1950s and the liberalization of the 1960s brought troubles that encouraged a closing of the courtiers' ranks once more around their Shah, when he should be seen essentially as the People's Shah.

'Notwithstanding his momentous contributions to Iran, Reza Shah subordinated Parliament', the Shah wrote of his father fifteen years ago.[12] Today he himself has been tempted to take the same path in the hope of hastening progress towards the Great Civilization which he hopes to hand over, imperial and intact, to his son, Crown Prince Cyrus Reza, in less than a dozen years.

It is ironic that so many of Alexander Solzhenitsyn's words about oppressed peoples could be taken, out of context, for the Shah's. Solzhenitsyn, speaking of the fight against the 'savage structure, the pitiless aims of the Communist world', said of the West: 'The greatest danger of all is that you have lost the will to defend yourselves. And Great Britain – the kernel of the Western world as we have already called it – has experienced this sapping of its strength and will to a greater degree, perhaps, than any other country.'[13]

Yet the man on whom the US and Britain rely mainly to maintain the first line of defence against Communism himself tolerates some of the very activities that we find most deplorable in a Communist state: the deprivation of personal freedom and dignity, in the name of security. Yet, in practice, alternatives have been found wanting, and as the Shah points out all régimes resort to the same methods in times of emergency (Amnesty International reported that in 1975 more than 100 countries imprisoned people for their beliefs, denied them prompt or fair trial, or tortured or executed them); which only takes us full circle to the question of where one man's liberty begins and another's ends. And while philosophers and critics debate, politicians act.

Plans to expedite the issue of passports were recently drawn up. Previously, 'Under Article 17 of the regulations, the Passport office has been assigned to discourage the exit of certain Iranians *who have income tax dues* . . . (my italics).[14] Encouraging dissidents to leave the country could, if the Shah could overcome the memory of the inadequacy of exile in the case of General Bakhtiar, prove to be one way of dealing with the opposition that would prove ultimately more effective than present methods. These now leave Iran vulnerable to criticism from the West with whom it is so anxious, both in terms of Aryan race and in increasingly modern technology, to be associated. (At present wives still need written permission from their husbands before they can leave the country: this, too, is expected to be changed!)

Does the answer otherwise lie in the future, in the spread of education, of literacy, of participation, as the Shah and Empress believe? One would like to think so, though a more complex society to attempt to render cohesive it is hard to imagine. Without the attempt, however, there can be no progress at all at this level. The régime's fear of freedom of speech, together with the criticism of itself which that would necessarily entail, is its own greatest weakness, and therefore itself an impediment to the realization of the Shah's dream of the future Iran. Meanwhile at a practical level reform goes on, at the Shah's will. We in

Britain have recently had a chance to see closer to home another situation in which politics and sectarianism have become inextricably intertwined: Northern Ireland, where, as in Iran, social reform is opposed in the name of religion.

The great issue in Iran is: can reform ever be successfully *imposed*? So far the rate of success is almost incredible: but what of the casualties? It takes a man who can see himself as both soldier and doctor to advance in such conditions.

No man is faultless: yet we are apt to want to place our politicians upon pedestals. But using the argument that no man, and therefore no Shah, is without some fault (as the Shah has admitted of his father), I pressed Mr Alam, the Minister of Court, to tell me of a flaw, from *his* point of view, in his sovereign; it was an indelicate and most un-Persian thing to do.

'I cannot say that he is faultless,' Mr Alam at last replied. 'Everyone, as you say, has faults. But I may say something that – he might not like it, and perhaps it's bad for me to say it, or it might be interpreted as flattery, but what I can say (perhaps you will laugh at me too), his fault to my mind is that he is really too great for this people – his ideas are too great for we people to realize it.'

Anyone who knows a little of Persian political history and has visited modern Iran is likely to see the amount of truth, as well as the element of unconscious humour, in this classic Persian reply.

In his own land the Shah is known as the Shahanshah, the King of Kings: and it is well known that he is also the Shadow of God.

Select Bibliography

ABRAHAMIAN, Ervand, 'Kasravi: the integrative nationalist of Iran', *Middle Eastern Studies* 9, no. 3 (October 1973), pp. 261–95.
ARFA, General Hassan, *Under Five Shahs*, John Murray, London 1964.
ARNOLD, Arthur, *Through Persia by Caravan*, 2 volumes, London 1877.
AVERY, Peter, *Modern Iran*, Ernest Benn, Tonbridge, Kent 1965.
—— and SIMMONS, J. B., 'Persia on a cross of silver, 1880–1890', *Middle Eastern Studies* 10, no. 3 (October 1974), pp. 259–86.
BAKHASH, Shaul, 'The evolution of Qajar bureaucracy, 1779–1879', *Middle Eastern Studies* 7, no. 2 (May 1971), pp. 139–68.
BLACK-MICHAUD, Jacob, 'An ethnographic and ecological survey of Luristan, Western Persia: modernisation in a nomadic pastoral society', *Middle Eastern Studies* 10, no. 2 (May 1974), pp. 210–28.
CURZON, G. N., *Persia and the Persian Question*, 2 volumes, Longmans, London 1892.
ELWELL-SUTTON, L. P., *Modern Iran*, Routledge and Kegan Paul, London 1944.
FORD, Alan W., *The Anglo-Iranian Oil Dispute of 1951–1952*, University of California Press, Berkeley 1954.
LAMBTON, Ann, *Landlord and Peasant in Persia*, Oxford University Press, Oxford 1953.
—— *The Persian Land Reform 1962–1966*, Clarendon Press, Oxford 1969.
MALCOLM, Sir John, *The History of Persia*, 2 volumes, John Murray, London 1815.
MILLSPAUGH, Arthur, *Americans in Persia*, Brookings Institution, Washington D.C. 1946.
MORIER, James, *A Journey through Persia, Armenia and Asia Minor to Constantinople in the Years 1808 and 1809*, London 1812.
PAHLAVI, Mohammed Reza Shah, *Mission for My Country*, Hutchinson, London 1961.
SANGHVI, Ramesh, *Aryamehr, the Shah of Iran*, Transorient, London 1968.
SHUSTER, W. Morgan, *The Strangling of Persia*, T. Fisher Unwin, London 1912.
SKRINE, Sir Clarmont, *World War in Iran*, Constable, London 1962.
SORAYA, H.I.H. Princess, *My Autobiography*, Arthur Barker, London 1963.
TULLY, Andrew, *Central Intelligence Agency*, Arthur Barker, London 1962.
WILBER, Donald, *Iran Past and Present*, Princeton University Press, Princeton, New Jersey 1950.
ZONIS, Marvin, *The Political Elite of Iran*, Princeton University Press, Princeton, New Jersey 1971.

Notes

Notes

Notes

Chapter 1: MEETING THE SHAH

1. *Sunday Express*, 7 March 1965.
2. Leonard Binder, *Iran: Political Development in a Changing Society* (University of California Press, Berkeley 1962), p. 159.
3. HIM Mohammed Reza Shah Pahlavi, *Mission for My Country* (hereafter cited as *Mission*) (Hutchinson, London 1961), p. 323.
4. ibid., p. 322.
5. ibid., p. 318.
6. ibid., p. 320.
7. *Sunday Telegraph*, 24 February 1974.
8. Interview with Ian McIntyre, BBC Radio 4, 'Analysis', 28 November 1974.
9. Interview with the Shah in Tehran, October 1975.
10. *Mission*, p. 58.
11. *The Times*, 26 October 1967.
12. *Yorkshire Post*, 3 November 1959, quoting Marcelle Poirier from Paris.
13. Interview with the Shah, October 1975.

Chapter 2: CORRUPTION AND RESENTMENT

1. Shaul Bakhash, 'The evolution of Qajar bureaucracy, 1779–1879', *Middle Eastern Studies* 7, no. 2 (May 1971), p. 142.
2. P. W. Avery and J. B. Simmons, 'Persia on a cross of silver, 1880–1890' *Middle Eastern Studies* 10, no. 3 (October 1974), p. 259.
3. Arthur Arnold, *Through Persia by Caravan* (London 1877), vol. ii, p. 192.
4. Lord Curzon, *Persia and the Persian Question* (Longmans, London 1892), vol. i, pp. 462, 463.
5. Ann Lambton, *The Persian Land Reform 1962–1966* (Clarendon Press, Oxford 1969), p. 19.
6. Lovat Frazer, *India under Curzon* (London 1911), p. 112.
7. Interview with the Shah in Tehran, October 1975.
8. *Mission*, p. 36. In contrast, *Kayhan International*, 27 October 1975, stated that 'Reza Khan's father died when he was only a few *years* old': such contradictions are not uncommon.
9. Hassan Arfa, *Under Five Shahs* (John Murray, London 1964), p. 90.

Q

10. *Mission*, p. 36.
11. Arfa, op. cit., p. 115.
12. *Mission*, pp. 36–7.
13. Lambton, op. cit., p. 33.
14. *Mission*, p. 38.
15. Arfa, op. cit., p. 44.
16. *Mission*, p. 37.
17. Arfa, op. cit., p. 90.
18. ibid., p. 57.
19. ibid., p. 91.
20. ibid., p. 91.

Chapter 3: FROM COLONEL TO SHAH

1. Hassan Arfa, *Under Five Shahs* (John Murray, London 1964), p. 109.
2. Interview with the Shah in Tehran, October 1975.
3. Information supplied to the author by the Ministry of Court.
4. ibid.
5. *Kayhan International*, 27 October 1975.
6. Interview with the Shah, October 1975.
7. *Mission*, p. 40.
8. Arfa, op. cit., p. 113.
9. Interview with the Shah, October 1975.
10. *Mission*, p. 37.
11. Arthur Arnold, *Through Persia by Caravan* (London 1877), vol. 2, p. 34.
12. Arfa, op. cit., p. 126.
13. *Mission*, p. 49.
14. ibid., p. 49.
15. Interview with the Shah, October 1975.
16. Arnold, op. cit., vol. i, p. 15.
17. Interview with the Shah, October 1975.
18. Ann Lambton, *Landlord and Peasant in Persia* (Oxford University Press, Oxford 1953), p. 23.
19. *Kayhan International*, 27 October 1975.
20. Arfa, op. cit., p. 183.
21. *Mission*, p. 39.

Chapter 4: CROWN PRINCE

1. But an older Persian told me definitively, 'His father *was* believing in harem.'
2. Princess Shams, born in 1940, daughter of his first marriage to Princess Fawzia of Egypt.
3. Both the Shah and the Empress replied only about Princess Farahnaz, then aged twelve, when I asked them about their daughters. I came to the conclusion that they regarded Princess Leila, aged five, as a 'child', rather than specifically as a daughter. This would tie in with the Islamic outlook which allows children of both sexes to play together; girl children were not veiled until they were at least eight or nine.

4. Interview with the Shah in Tehran, October 1975.
5. ibid.
6. The Empress Farah and HIH Princess Soraya.
7. Ramesh Sanghvi, *Aryamehr, the Shah of Iran* (Transorient, London 1968), p. 31.
8. *Mission*, p. 49.
9. Marvin Zonis, *The Political Elite of Iran* (Princeton University Press, Princeton, New Jersey 1971), p. 19.
10. Empress Soraya, *My Autobiography* (Arthur Barker, London 1963), p. 68.
11. *Mission*, p. 45.
12. ibid., p. 49.
13. Hassan Arfa, *Under Five Shahs* (John Murray, London 1964), pp. 280, 281.
14. *Mission*, p. 49.
15. *Time Magazine*, 8 December 1958.
16. *Mission*, p. 47.
17. ibid., p. 49.
18. Ann Lambton, *The Persian Land Reform 1962–1966* (Clarendon Press, Oxford 1966), p. 34.
19. Arfa, op. cit., p. 111.
20. *Mission*, p. 42.
21. Information supplied to the author by the Ministry of Court.
22. Lambton, op. cit., p. 35.

Chapter 5: SEEDS OF INDEPENDENCE

1. *Mission*, p. 54.
2. Interview with the Shah in Tehran, October 1975.
3. ibid.
4. Mme Arfa died in Paris in 1959.
5. Hassan Arfa, *Under Five Shahs* (John Murray, London 1964), p. 226.

Chapter 6: EUROPEAN EDUCATION

1. Ramesh Sanghvi, *Aryamehr, the Shah of Iran* (Transorient, London 1968), p. 40.
2. Information supplied by M. C. Vuilleumier and Mlle Helen Schaub.
3. *Mission*, p. 62.
4. Interview with the Shah in Tehran, October 1975.
5. *Mission*, p. 61.

Chapter 7: A MARRIAGE IS ARRANGED

1. Princess Soraya, *My Autobiography* (Arthur Barker, London 1963), p. 34.
2. ibid., p. 69.
3. *Mission*, p. 65.
4. Interview with the Shah in Tehran, October 1975.
5. *Mission*, p. 218.
6. Cecil Beaton, *Near East* (Batsford, London 1949).
7. *Daily Sketch*, 3 September 1953.

8. Interview with the Shah, October 1975.
9. Ramesh Sanghvi, *Aryamehr, the Shah of Iran* (Transorient, London 1968), p. 73.
10. Interview with the Shah, October 1975.

Chapter 8: WORLD WAR AND SUCCESSION

1. *Mission*, p. 67.
2. ibid., p. 72.
3. Imperial War Museum film, *Britain and Soviet meet in Iran*, 1941.
4. Ramesh Sanghvi, *Aryamehr, the Shah of Iran* (Transorient, London 1968), p. 73.
5. Hassan Arfa, *Under Five Shahs* (John Murray, London 1964), pp. 302, 303.
6. Sir Clarmont Skrine, *World War in Iran* (Constable, London 1962) pp. 113–14.
7. R. Ghirshman, V. Minorsky, and R. Sanghvi, *Persia the Immortal Kingdom* (Transorient, London 1971), p. 192.
8. U.S. State Department Foreign Relations, 1942, vol. iv.
9. L. P. Elwell-Sutton, *Modern Iran* (Routledge and Kegan Paul, London 1944), pp. 187–8.
10. Arfa, op. cit., p. 306.
11. Skrine, op. cit., p. 169.
12. Peter Avery, *Modern Iran* (Ernest Benn, Tonbridge, Kent 1965), p. 364.
13. *Mission*, p. 76.
14. Skrine, op. cit., p. 174.
15. Arfa, op. cit., p. 307.
16. Avery, op. cit., p. 363.
17. Skrine, op. cit., p. 180.
18. Sanghvi, op. cit., p. 100.
19. *Mission*, p. 70.
20. Skrine, op. cit., p. 180.
21. ibid., pp. 179, 180.
22. *Mission*, p. 78.
23. Avery, op. cit., p. 367.
24. Arfa, op. cit., p. 324.
25. *Mission*, p. 79.
26. ibid., p. 80.
27. Arfa, op. cit., pp. 324–5.
28. Interview with the Shah in Tehran, October 1975.

Chapter 9: OIL AND POLITICS

1. Interview with the Shah in Tehran, October 1975.
2. Sir Clarmont Skrine, *World War in Iran* (Constable, London 1962), p. 170.
3. Arthur Millspaugh, *Americans in Persia* (Brookings Institution, Washington D.C. 1946), pp. 83, 87.
4. Skrine, op. cit., p. 210.
5. *Mission*, p. 87.
6. ibid., p. 87.
7. Alan W. Ford, *The Anglo-Iranian Oil Dispute of 1951–1952* (University of California Press, Berkeley 1954), p. 41.

8. Peter Avery, *Modern Iran* (Ernest Benn, Tonbridge, Kent 1965), p. 388.
9. Ford, op. cit., p. 43.
10. Avery, op. cit., p. 391.
11. *Mission*, p. 116.
12. Ford, op. cit., pp. 44–5.
13. Ramesh Sanghvi, *Aryamehr, the Shah of Iran* (Transorient, London 1962), p. 135.

Chapter 10: FIRST ASSASSINATION ATTEMPT

1. Princess Soraya, *My Autobiography* (Arthur Barker, London 1963), p. 44.
2. ibid., p. 70.
3. *Mission*, p. 57.
4. ibid., p. 57.
5. ibid., p. 57.
6. Ramesh Sanghvi, *Aryamehr, the Shah of Iran* (Transorient, London 1968), p. 163. The Fayadan-Islam was a small political group based on the *mullahs* and the Muslim religion.

Chapter 11: SECOND MARRIAGE: SORAYA ESFANDIARI

1. *Mission*, p. 220.
2. ibid., p. 220.
3. For this and subsequent quotations in this chapter see Princess Soraya, *My Autobiography* (Arthur Barker, London 1963), pp. 43, 12, 22, 71, 48, 69, 51, 77.

Chapter 12: CONFRONTATIONS

1. Peter Avery, *Modern Iran* (Ernest Benn, Tonbridge, Kent 1965), p. 411.
2. Alan W. Ford, *The Anglo-Iranian Oil Dispute of 1951–1952* (University of California Press, Berkeley 1954), p. 13.
3. ibid., p. 54.
4. Hassan Arfa, *Under Five Shahs* (John Murray, London 1964), p. 393.

Chapter 13: REALISM AND NATIONALIZATION

1. Ramesh Sanghvi, *Aryamehr, the Shah of Iran* (Transorient, London 1968), p. 156.
2. *The Economist*, vol. 161 (15 December 1951), pp. 1443–4.
3. *Mission*, p. 276.
4. ibid., pp. 90–1.
5. Sanghvi, op. cit., p. 156.
6. Alan W. Ford, *The Anglo-Iranian Oil Dispute of 1951–1952* (University of California Press, Berkeley 1954), p. 98.
7. ibid., p. 99.
8. ibid., p. 116.
9. ibid., p. 130.

10. Sanghvi, op. cit., p. 191.
11. ibid., p. 194.
12. *Mission*, p. 92.
13. Ford, op. cit., p. 154.
14. Hassan Arfa, *Under Five Shahs* (John Murray, London 1964), p. 399.
15. Ford, op. cit., pp. 155, 159.

Chapter 14: MOSSADEQ RULES

1. Peter Avery, *Modern Iran* (Ernest Benn, Tonbridge, Kent 1965), p. 430.
2. *Mission*, p. 222.
3. Princess Soraya, *My Autobiography* (Arthur Barker, London 1963), p. 109.
4. ibid., p. 107.
5. ibid., p. 82.
6. ibid., pp. 105–6.
7. Avery, op. cit., p. 434.
8. Hassan Arfa, *Under Five Shahs* (John Murray, London 1964), p. 403.

Chapter 15: EXILE

1. Princess Soraya, *My Autobiography* (Arthur Barker, London 1963), p. 91.
2. Ramesh Sanghvi, *Aryamehr, the Shah of Iran* (Transorient, London 1968), p. 210. For a detailed account of the role in fact played by the CIA, written by a former member, see Andrew Tully, *Central Intelligence Agency* (Arthur Barker, London 1962), pp. 91–101.
3. Princess Soraya, op. cit., p. 95.
4. Tully, op. cit., p. 95.
5. Peter Avery, *Modern Iran* (Ernest Benn, Tonbridge, Kent 1965), p. 439.
6. Tully, op. cit., p. 97. Princess Soraya gives a figure of $6 million in *My Autobiography*, p. 99.
7. Hassan Arfa, *Under Five Shahs* (John Murray, London 1964), p. 409.

Chapter 17: THE NEW RÉGIME

1. Ramesh Sanghvi, *Aryamehr, the Shah of Iran* (Transorient, London 1968), p. 241.
2. Peter Avery, *Modern Iran* (Ernest Benn, Tonbridge, Kent 1965), p. 462.
3. Ann Lambton, *The Persian Land Reform 1962–1966* (Clarendon Press, Oxford 1966), p. 50.
4. ibid., pp. 50–1.
5. ibid., p. 54.
6. Sanghvi, op. cit., pp. 243, 244.
7. Avery, op. cit., p. 458.
8. ibid., pp. 448–9.
9. *Jeune Afrique*, 6 July 1971.
10. Marvin Zonis, *The Political Elite of Iran* (Princeton University Press, Princeton, New Jersey 1971), p. 70.

Chapter 18: QUESTIONS OF SUCCESSION

1. Interview with the Shah in Tehran, October 1975.
2. Princess Soraya, *My Autobiography* (Arthur Barker, London 1963), p. 148.
3. Interview with Mr Alam, October 1975.
4. Princess Soraya, op. cit., p. 119.
5. Interview with Mr Alam in Tehran, October 1975.
6. Peter Avery, *Modern Iran* (Ernest Benn, Tonbridge, Kent 1965), p. 475.
7. Princess Soraya, op. cit., p. 133.
8. *Mission*, p. 106.
9. For a full examination of the Shah's system of coopting the opposition see Marvin Zonis, *The Political Elite of Iran* (Princeton University Press, Princeton, New Jersey 1971). In fact, one 1940s Tudeh member was made Minister of Justice in the early 1960s and one of Mossadeq's National Front activists was offered a job as a deputy minister but refused it and went to live abroad (see *Political Elite of Iran*, p. 25).
10. Avery, op. cit., p. 461.
11. *Christian Science Monitor*, 28 May 1963.

Chapter 19: THE WHITE REVOLUTION

1. Peter Avery, *Modern Iran* (Ernest Benn, Tonbridge, Kent 1965), p. 470.
2. Princess Soraya, *My Autobiography* (Arthur Barker, London 1963), p. 110.
3. Ramesh Sanghvi, *Aryamehr, the Shah of Iran* (Transorient, London 1968), p. 263.
4. Marvin Zonis, *The Political Elite of Iran* (Princeton University Press, Princeton, New Jersey 1971), pp. 47–8.
5. ibid., pp. 61–2.
6. *Time Magazine*, 19 May and 9 June 1961; *L'Express*, 5 August 1958.
7. *Newsweek*, 12 June 1961.
8. ibid.
9. ibid.
10. ibid.
11. *Kayhan International*, 24 May 1961.
12. Avery, op. cit., p. 496.
13. *Newsweek*, 16 April 1962.
14. *Echo of Iran*, Daily Bulletin 10, no. 199, 7 November 1962, 1.
15. Zonis, op. cit., pp. 72–3.
16. *Newsweek*, 5 February 1962.
17. Zonis, op. cit., p. 73.
18. ibid., p. 73.
19. ibid., p. 74.
20. *Time*, 1 November 1963.
21. Zonis, op. cit., pp. 45, 63n.
22. Interview with Mr Alam in Tehran, October 1975.
23. Zonis, op. cit., pp. 46, 44.
24. *Kayhan International*, 5 November 1964.
25. Zonis, op. cit., p. 75.

Chapter 20: PLOTS AND COUNTERPLOTS

1. Marvin Zonis, *The Political Elite of Iran* (Princeton University Press, Princeton, New Jersey 1971), p. 74.
2. ibid., p. 75.
3. From the official text as published in *Ettela'at* (Tehran), 24 January 1963.
4. *The Times*, 9 October 1963.
5. *The Times*, 28 January 1965, leader.
6. HIM Mohammed Reza Shah Pahlavi, *The White Revolution of Iran* (Tehran 1967), p. 38.
7. Zonis, op. cit., p. 115.
8. Ramesh Sanghvi, *Aryamehr, the Shah of Iran* (Transorient, London 1968), p. 286.
9. Zonis, op. cit., p. 52.
10. Interview with Mr Alam in Tehran, October 1975.
11. Zonis, op. cit., p. 52.
12. *The Times*, 16 September 1965, leader.

Chapter 21: THIRD MARRIAGE: FARAH DIBA

1. *Mission*, p. 226.
2. *Yorkshire Post*, 3 November 1959, quoting Marcelle Poirier from Paris.
3. Interview with the Shah in Tehran, October 1975.
4. *Mission*, p. 226.
5. Interview with the Empress Farah in Tehran, October 1975.
6. ibid., and *Mission*, p. 225.
7. *Newsweek*, 4 January 1960.
8. ibid.
9. ibid.
10. Hassan Arfa, *Under Five Shahs* (John Murray, London 1964), p. 427.
11. *Newsweek*, 4 January 1960.
12. *Newsweek*, 23 April 1962.
13. *Daily Herald*, 4 July 1958.
14. *Sunday Express*, 7 March 1965.
15. James Morier, *A Journey through Persia, Armenia and Asia Minor to Constantinople in the Years 1808 and 1809* (London 1812), p. 154.
16. ibid., p. 154.
17. F. Sahebjam, *Mohammed Reza Pahlavi, Shah d'Iran* (Berger-Levrault, Paris).
18. Interview with the Shah, October 1975.
19. Oriana Fallaci, *New Republic*, December 1973.
20. Interview with the Shah, October 1975.
21. ibid.

Chapter 22: THE LIFE OF AN EMPRESS

1. James Morier, *A Journey through Persia* . . . (London 1812), p. 39.
2. Crown Prince Reza (b. 1960), Princess Farahnaz (b. 1963), Prince Ali Reza (b. 1966 and named after the Shah's dead brother), and Princess Leila (b. 1970).

3. *Sunday Times Colour Magazine*, 17 November 1968.
4. *Daily Express*, 28 January 1974.
5. *Daily Mail*, 15 October 1960.
6. *Daily Express*, 28 January 1974.
7. Interview with the Empress Farah in Tehran, October 1975.
8. ibid.

Chapter 23: OIL, ARMS, AND FINANCE

1. Nasr ed-Din, letter to Akin ud-Dowleh, quoted by Shaul Bakhash, 'The evolution of Qajar bureaucracy, 1779–1879', *Middle Eastern Studies* 7, no. 2 (May 1971), p. 165.
2. *Sunday Times*, 7 November 1976.
3. *Europa (The Times)*, 6 March 1976.
4. Peter Avery, *Modern Iran* (Ernest Benn, Tonbridge, Kent 1965), p. 480.
5. *The Times*, 9 May 1959.
6. *The Economist*, 7 October 1972.
7. Chapman Pincher in the *Daily Express*, 15 June 1972.
8. *Daily Telegraph*, 12 October 1971, quoting *Le Monde*.
9. Arthur Arnold, *Through Persia by Caravan* (London 1877), vol. ii, p. 192.
10. *Mission*, p. 255.
11. *Middle Eastern Studies* 10, no. 2 (May 1974), p. 98.
12. *Sunday Times Colour Magazine*, 22 December 1974.
13. *The Times*, 22 May 1969.
14. *The Times*, 4 December 1964.
15. *Time Magazine*, 9 June 1975.
16. *Daily Telegraph Colour Magazine*, 2 February 1974.
17. *Tehran Journal*, 18 October 1975.
18. *The Economist*, 7 October 1972.
19. *Guardian*, 28 September 1971.
20. *Kayhan International*, 23 October 1975.
21. *Tehran Journal*, 9 October 1975.
22. *The Times*, 2 June 1975.
23. *The Economist*, 7 October 1972.
24. *The Times*, 24 June 1974.
25. *The Times*, 19 August 1974.
26. *Sunday Times Colour Magazine*, 22 December 1974.
27. *Financial Times*, 9 and 11 August 1976.
28. *Sunday Mirror*, 11 September 1966.
29. *Newsweek*, 14 October 1974.
30. Robert Graham in the *Financial Times*, 11 August 1976.
31. The Shah interviewed by Lord Chalfont, BBC Television, 17 June 1975.
32. *Financial Times*, 21 June and 11 August 1976.
33. *Guardian*, 23 July 1975.
34. *The Illustrated London News*, July 1976. Russia spends more than 11 per cent of her gross national product on defence, the United States 6·7 per cent, and Britain 5·7 per cent.
35. *Financial Times*, 8 August 1976.
36. Dr Christopher Bertram, *The Military Balance, 1975-6* (Institute of Strategic Studies, London 1975).

37. *Observer*, 22 February 1976.
38. Dr Henry Kissinger, quoted in 'A survey on oil and money in the Middle East', *The Banker*, March 1975.
39. Interview with the Shah in Tehran, October 1975.
40. Arnold, op. cit., vol. ii, p. 5.
41. James Morier, *A Journey through Persia* . . . (London 1812), p. 212.

Chapter 24: SAVAK

1. *Newsweek*, 14 October 1974.
2. Arthur Arnold, *Through Persia by Caravan* (London 1877), vol. ii, p. 34.
3. *Time*, 4 November 1974.
4. *Mission*, pp. 321, 322.
5. *Observer*, 23 October 1975.
6. *Financial Times*, 26 February 1976.
7. *Kayhan International*, 23 October 1975.
8. *Observer*, 26 May 1974.
9. *The Times*, 7 and 10 January 1974.
10. *Sunday Telegraph*, 24 February 1974.
11. *The Times*, 22 May 1975.
12. *The Times*, 26 April 1975.
13. *Le Monde*, 30 January 1976.
14. *Le Monde*, 9 March 1976.
15. Marvin Zonis, *The Political Elite of Iran* (Princeton University Press, Princeton, New Jersey 1971), p. 77.
16. BBC Radio 4, 'Analysis', 28 November 1974.
17. BBC Television, 17 June 1975.
18. Interview with the Shah in Tehran, October 1975.

Chapter 25: RULE BY DECREE

1. *Time*, 6 October 1967.
2. Marvin Zonis, *The Political Elite of Iran* (Princeton University Press, Princeton, New Jersey 1971).
3. *Kayhan International*, 31 May 1964.
4. *Evening Standard* (London), 22 May 1969.
5. Oriana Fallaci in *The New Republic*, December 1975.
6. Zonis, op. cit., p. 129.
7. *The Times*, 4 March 1975.
8. *Kayhan International*, 3 March 1975.
9. Interview with the Shah in Tehran, October 1975.
10. *Time*, 4 November 1974.
11. Robert Graham in *Financial Times Survey on Iran*, 21 June 1976.

Chapter 26: REFORMER – KING OF KINGS

1. Interview with the Shah in Tehran, October 1975.
2. *Time*, 4 November 1974.

3. *Time*, 6 October 1967.

4. *The New Republic*, 21 September 1974.

5. Interview with the Shah, October 1975.

6. *Financial Times Survey on Iran*, 21 June 1976.

7. *Time*, 12 September 1960.

8. Jacob Black-Michaud, 'An ethnographic and ecological study of Luristan, Western Persia', *Middle Eastern Studies* 10, no. 2 (May 1974), p. 226.

9. *Observer*, 16 November 1975.

10. *The Times*, Supplement on Iran, 26 October 1967.

11. Marvin Zonis, *The Political Elite of Iran* (Princeton University Press, Princeton, New Jersey 1971), p. 116.

12. *Mission*, p. 327.

13. A. Solzhenitsyn, talk on BBC Radio 4, 1 April 1976, reported in *The Times*, 2 April 1976.

14. *Tehran Journal*, 18 October 1975.

Index

Index

R

53; seriously ill with typhoid,
53–4; supernatural experiences,
54–5; education in Switzerland,
55–62, 64, 66, 86; return to Iran,
61–3; ambitions, 61–2; at
Military Academy, 64, 65, 209;
plans for his marriage, 67–8;
marriage to Princess Fawzia, 68;
birth of daughter, 69; and
Second World War, 71, 75, 78–9;
becomes Shah on his father's
abdication, 76, 77; and tripartite
pact with Britain and Russia, 78;
declares war on Germany, 80–1;
and Tehran Conference, 82, 83;
and Roosevelt, 82–3; and Stalin,
83; and his father's death, 85;
views on democracy, 86–7

divorce from Fawzia, 96, 103;
attempt to assassinate him (1949),
97–101; strengthens his
constitutional position, 100;
inauguration of Senate, 101;
marriage to Soraya Esfandiari,
103–10; life with Soraya, 109–10;
visit to USA, 113, 143; anti-
corruption campaign, 114;
announces reforms, 114; and
nationalization of oil, 116, 118;
and Mossadeq, 117, 120–39; and
Communism, 121; austerity in
palace life, 125; loss of executive
power, 125–6; recourse to
amusements and practical jokes,
125–6; gives up plan to leave
Iran, 128; attacked in Press,
129; Imperial Guard disbanded,
130; withdraws to north, 132;
flies to Baghdad, 133–4; in Rome,
134–7; his cause successful in
Tehran, 135–6; hears of his
victory, 137; returns to Tehran,
138

aims at absolute power, 138;
has no friends, 138–40;
encourages spying, 141, 155; on

the Iranian nation, 141; land
reforms, 142–4, 161, 227;
taxation proposals, 143; and
talks with Soviet Union, 145;
and Baghdad Pact, 145,

lack of heir, 151–2, 155, 156,
159–60; his brother's death,
153–4; in USA, 155; and
economic situation, 156, 157;
visits to Turkey, India and USSR,
157; secures more power, 158–9;
divorces Soraya, 160; and Dr
Eghbal, 161; visits Norway, 163;
cold reception on return, 163;
initiates land legislation, 164; his
six items of reform ('White
Revolution'), 167; and 1963
riots, 168–9; referendum on six
points, 171; rounds up National
Front leaders, 171; Marble
Palace plot, 172–3, 182; clemency
to plotters, 173, 182; further
attempts on his life (1967), 173–4

meets Farah Diba, 176–8;
engagement, 179; wedding, 180;
birth of son, 181, 192, 197; on
his marriage, 181–3, 185–6; birth
of daughter, 182; plans to hand
over power to Crown Prince,
184, 198, 229; on films, 185–6;
love of speed, 191–2; and his
children, 193

more aggressive policy, 197–9;
and Bahrein, 197; warning to
West and to Russia, 197–8;
defence of Persian Gulf, 199,
201; and Egypt, 200; and
Afghanistan, 200; and Pakistan,
200; proposal for pipeline to
Turkey disrupted by student
violence, 201; seizure of Persian
Gulf islands, 201; proposes
mutual security arrangement 201;
fear of Soviet encirclement, 202;
and price of gas for Russia, 202;
visit to Moscow, 202; and